D1261194

The Soul of Socrates

The Soul of Socrates

NALIN RANASINGHE

CORNELL UNIVERSITY PRESS

ITHACA AND LONDON

First published 2000 by Cornell University Press

Printed in the United States of America

Library of Congress Cataloging-in-Publication Data

Ranasinghe, Nalin, 1960–
    The soul of Socrates / Nalin Ranasinghe.
      p. cm.
    Includes bibliographical references and index.
    ISBN 0-8014-3746-6 (hardcover)
      1. Socrates. 2. Plato. Dialogues. I. Title

B317 .R36 2000
183'.2—dc21   00-021333

Cornell University Press strives to use environmentally responsible suppliers and materials to the fullest extent possible in the publishing of its books. Such materials include vegetable-based, low-VOC inks and acid-free papers that are recycled, totally chlorine-free, or partly composed of nonwood fibers. Books that bear the logo of the FSC (Forest Stewardship Council) use paper taken from forests that have been inspected and certified as meeting the highest standards for environmental and social responsibility. For further information, visit our website at www.cornellpress.cornell.edu.

Cloth printing   10 9 8 7 6 5 4 3 2 1

FSC FSC Trademark © 1996 Forest Stewardship Council A.C.
     SW-COC-098

43333586

This book is for my parents,

Felix and Angela Ranasinghe

Contents

Preface

Socrates was surely the most enigmatic of all men. Whereas even Jesus cried out to God that he felt betrayed and forsaken, Socrates never departed from his habit of ironic composure. Further, whereas Jesus claimed to fulfill the scriptures and reveal things hidden since the foundation of the world, Socrates loudly professed his ignorance and publicly conceded defeat in almost every argument he entered into. Despite these significant differences, these two unpublished artisans stand together as the two most influential figures in the history of our information-hungry global civilization. Their ideas so fully overcame the cultures that condemned them that Socrates and Jesus now epitomize (and obscure) the glories of Athens and Jerusalem—the cultural contexts whence they appeared. Paradoxically, the triumphs of the disciples of Socrates and Jesus have been so complete that we must strive mightily to reconstruct the cultural contexts in which their teachings were articulated. Just as the teachings of Christ withered away in Christendom—where everyone and no one was a Christian—the living presence of Socrates seems to have been lost in the verdant groves of academia. This work sets out to reconstruct the uncanny experience of meeting him.

Socrates is important to anyone pondering the basic questions of human existence. He led a life that seamlessly combined the seemingly incommensurable qualities of virtue and happiness. Furthermore, his speeches and deeds had a powerful effect on everyone who encountered him. Despite his often repeated claims of ignorance, Socrates spoke with an authority that compelled attention; it seemed as if he alone were alive while all others around him were dead.

Emphasizing the human reality of Socrates is crucial. If he were merely an unusually compelling figure of fiction, like Sherlock Holmes, we might suppose that Plato had constructed him as a kind of mascot for Academic philosophy or a ventriloquist's dummy. We might still enjoy the clever literary construction of the dialogues but pay scant attention to their existential implications. Our interest would be in the ventriloquist's cleverness, and we would not be even slightly interested in the matter used to fabricate it. The dummy is supposed to be real, even though of course we know that he is not. We willingly suspend our disbelief so that we may better enjoy the brilliance of the illusion. We enjoy the "cheek" of the dummy and laugh at his witticisms. We know, of course, that we are not supposed to take any of his utterances to heart. We would cheerfully disregard the urgent Platonic warnings, "You could learn a lot from a dummy!"

I am suggesting, of course, that many academics have approached Socrates in much that spirit. They are intrigued by the cleverness of Plato and enjoy the intricate dialectical but ultimately fallacious webs that Socrates weaves around his unwitting adversaries. They enjoy second-guessing his opponents and coming up with alternative argumentative strategies. They find even greater pleasure in uncovering the clever sophistries deployed by Plato against other sophists. "Ah, those artful Greeks" they say. "It's amazing that they accomplished so much with the little science that they possessed." They read Plato with a view to displaying their own cleverness and urbanity.

Many scholars, however, still take Plato the philosopher seriously and examine Socrates' moral precepts with the utmost sincerity. They genuinely believe in the possibility of virtue and defend Socrates against the charge of sophistry. Unfortunately, the approach of many analytical philosophers is overly serious: they refuse to pay serious attention to the dramatic context in which the dialogues take place or to acknowledge the peculiar nature of Platonic writing. They may interrogate the dialogues with the same rigor that they would lavish on a professional colleague, but by ripping an argument out of its literary context, these readers fail to see the dramatic unity of a dialogue. In other words, they cannot see the wood for the truth trees.

Still other Platonic scholars, recognizing the problems posed by such an approach, are keenly aware that a Platonic dialogue is as much a dramatic performance as a logical argument. They emphasize the difference between attentively listening to a text and merely subjecting it to reductive analysis. Accustomed to interpreting the trivia that litters up a literary work, they perversely go through the trash instead of attending to the clarified logical structure that their analytical colleagues have so kindly vacuumed. Yet, and quite paradoxically, many of their readings lead to a very skeptical opinion of Socrates. They suggest that his reality resides somewhat toward the bottom of an iron(ic) triangle formed with Xenophon's pious portrayal and Aristophanes' critical caricature at its base, and Plato's artistry at its apex. These dramatic readers pay close attention to the clever devices through which Plato pops up over the shoulder of Socrates, subtly interjecting his own observations to the knowing few. If Plato's prettified Socrates is used to edify the many and provide them with a salutary awareness of their ignorance, the close reader will draw attention to the irony with which Socrates' own utterances are rendered. They seem to suggest that whereas Aristotle criticized Plato openly, Plato is much more subdued in his critique of Socrates.

In short, while one school of readers believes that Plato's arguments cannot hold up to logical scrutiny, another school believes that his texts are written so as to reveal more to the careful and educated reader. Plato must be subtle because he is disclosing truths that would disillusion the common man.

I wish to make it very clear that I do not contest the validity of the procedures followed by those who practice Platonic irony at Socrates' expense. These readers are much more at ease dealing with the technical problems posed by the so-called later dialogues than I; it is from this vantage that they proceed to deconstruct Plato's earlier, more literary efforts. Although my own preferences veer in the opposite direction, I believe that Plato was very much aware that his elusive style of writing made such a choice of interpretations inevitable. I would only contend that it is equally possible to derive a more positive view of the human condition from the erotic vantage of the earlier dialogues. I am acutely conscious of my inability to prove the correctness of my interpretations over and against other styles of interpretation. I only hope to offer interesting and consistent readings that reveal the profound dramatic unity of the dialogues in question. This striving toward a thematic unity also requires that any effort to convey the meaning of a dialogue should itself follow a narrative style that is both more vulnerable and more demanding.

I am enormously indebted to the dramatic readers for the many long-concealed treasures they have brought to light. Nevertheless, I respectfully suggest that as much as the analytical readers ignore the dramatic

aspects of the dialogues, many dramatic readings have not paid sufficient attention to their erotic dimension. By eros, I do not mean sex; Socratic eros is not governed by the tyranny of physical lust. Although
this power is awakened in the soul by the beloved, eros is a transcendental force that attunes the loving soul to the cosmos.

When speaking of eros, I certainly do not mean that an invincible a
priori sense of metaphysical "presence" pervades every Platonic text—
far from it. Through his experience of Socrates, Plato understood eros to
be a state in which *poros* and *penia*, plenty and need, are in constant alternation. If we disregard this understanding of eros, reductive skepticism toward a dialogue is inevitable. I proceed on the assumption that
Plato does not intend us to fall into the dramatic abyss that opens between the promise of *poros* and the performance of *penia*. I argue, rather,
that it is precisely through alternating between these conditions that we
may begin to appreciate the topography of a dialogue. It was in a similar
vein that Kierkegaard claimed that the human condition consists of our
trying to express the eternal while remaining time-bound, individual,
and finite.[1] It will be through the infinite passion of our eros, rather than
the rigor and quantity of our labors, that self-knowledge (concerning our
tragicomic existence) comes.

Accordingly, it may not be possible for readers to gain an adequate
understanding of the teaching of Socrates by approaching Plato's works
as disembodied scholarly minds. My reading of Socrates presents him
as one who faced up resolutely to nihilistic challenges very similar to
those that confront us today. To do this, one cannot reduce Socrates to
a "talking head." It will not suffice to bear the death mask of Socrates
before us on a pike as we confront postmodernity. It is by coming to
terms with the human reality of Socrates that we may get a firm grip
on who we are and what we are defending. For reasons of both expedi-
ency and truth, Socrates must be presented to our fevered times as an
educator of eros. Neither anger nor nostalgic resentment can sustain
us against the advancing forces of cultural barbarism. If we wish to defend the Western Intellectual Tradition, we should truly believe in its
value, liberality, and vitality. If the Tradition is worth saving, it is
surely more than a graceful way of hiding life's emptiness from the
many.

We should beware of what Socrates called misology if we sagely assume that Plato had already given up on his own age, his own species,
and his own teacher. To do so is to presume that we can have learn
nothing about reality from Plato, since we know already that life is

meaningless, but merely how to conceal this awareness from the rab-
ble. By refusing to explore the texts with adequate eros and sufficient
patience, we assume in advance that Plato was as skeptical and pessimistic as our postmodern, radically deconstructed nonselves. My
reading examines the counterassumption that Plato was vehemently
opposed to nihilism, whether derived from the anarchic impulses of the
left or the authoritarian propensities of the right.

I believe that we can best revitalize the dialogues by paying closer attention to their erotic contexts. Accordingly, I undertake to liberate the
spirit of Socrates from their labyrinthine subtext. I approach the texts
very seriously while yet remaining attentive to the characteristic playfulness of Plato's "Grand Style."[2] Reading a Platonic text is like trying
to clear a minefield: beneath the smooth terrain lurk artfully concealed
devices that may detonate only after several unsuccessful sweepings.
Courage is essential to a successful reading of a dialogue. It is easy to
read a Platonic text as a skeptic; it is much harder to tease an argument
out and scrutinize it for its existential implications. In other words, one
must take a potentially explosive argument home and live with it. We
cannot be distant Platonic lovers of either Socrates or the text. We must
approach both of them with the virile passion of the black horse of the
Phaedrus yet retain all the wonder of the white horse. We must be as
powerful as stone-masons while remaining as gentle as midwives.

This book places much emphasis on the lived unity of the virtues. I
claim that Socrates does indeed serve as Plato's exemplar of the good life.
Far from being a vehicle of oligarchic disdain for Socrates' plebeian idio-
syncrasies, Platonic irony actually conceals Plato's own frustrations as he
strives to unearth Socrates' secret. Plato silently mouths the question that
Socrates asked when he heard the oracle's answer to Chaerephon: "What
does the god mean and why does he not use plain language? (*Apology* 21b).

Plato cannot express his conclusions in plain and direct words for
two very good reasons: first, because they are ultimately speculative;
second, because the reader must discover their validity within his or
her own soul. Plato is trying to speculate about Socrates' understanding
of a power that is a mystery to Socrates himself. Socrates is certainly
not Plato's creation; it is rather that Plato weaves an image of Socrates
as he continually mediates between the erotic richness of his recollections and the paucity of his actual knowledge.

The key to this mystery, wrapped in the enigmatic mask of Silenus, is
the self-knowledge of Socrates. I shall sketch a speculative reconstruction of the difficult path that Plato followed to discover how Socrates

understood himself. This, after all, was Socrates' great secret. How could this old, unhappily married, poor man, who had many important enemies, be the happiest man in Athens? How could the ugliest Athenian be the most erotic? These were the questions that Glaucon asked in book 2 of the *Republic*, and this book is an extended response to Glaucon. As I have suggested, the Platonic dialogue is not designed for direct Socratic self-revelation; indeed, it seems that Plato uses this medium as a means of invoking the ever elusive spirit of Socrates. On its surface, however, the dialogue serves mainly as an opaque surface upon which the souls of Socrates' interlocutors, ourselves included, may be revealed

In attempting to resurrect the daimon of Socrates, I have tried to recreate the Platonic emphasis on the ultimately erotic act of recollection. A Platonic dialogue is not a frozen artifact that must forever be "flawlessly flawful, icily perfect and splendidly null." Its very flaws point beyond itself; as its arguments self-destruct, they take readers beyond the sign and point toward the signified. Every seeming mistake in a Platonic text could turn out to be a magic chasm or cave concealing treasures of great but fragile beauty.

Plato relies enormously on literary and mythical imagery to hold his dialogues together. Every dialogue possesses a mythological subtext; an example is Jacob Klein's discovery of the tale of Theseus and the Minotaur in the *Phaedo*.[3] These mythical motifs that round off a dialogue occur too many times for their presence to be coincidental, and when addressed with sufficient care they display a remarkable consistency. They also prove themselves by resolving many of the nagging questions that remain after an exhaustive logical analysis.

In a crucial way, what I have recounted here can only be a myth. Yet it is my contention that I have used myth to resurrect meaning that is expressible only through myth; I have not recounted an ignoble fabrication about an older and nobler lie. A Platonic dialogue is a mytho-erotic act of recollection, written to encourage its readers to discover Socrates for themselves. Myth is the best way of conveying a meaning that pure logic finds ineffable.

A dialogue can do no more than remind the soul of its erotic potentialities. It is a uniquely human means of intersubjective communication. We do Plato a grave disservice if we make him into a divine figure, a benevolent inventor of salutary illusions and noble lies for the many. By ignoring his humanity, we discount the extent of his genius. It is only by recognizing Plato's own perplexity before Socrates that we may appreciate the extent of his achievement. To put it awkwardly, Plato thawed the frozen death mask of Silenus through the warmth of his passion. Plato's erotic humanism has much to offer a world that is precariously poised between the Scylla of fundamentalism and the Charybdis of rampant materialism. Although I have benefited enormously from the Platonic investigations of such giants as Stanley Rosen, Leo Strauss, and Jacob Klein, I find that as the philosopher was sent back to the cave, their works have driven me back to the texts. I gratefully acknowledge all the suggestive insights that have come my way over the years, but my concern is with Socrates alone; accordingly, this book does not contain many references to other scholarly works. Its unity derives from its single-minded focus on Socrates.

I call the exegetical method employed here the Antaeus principle. Antaeus was the son of the Earth who challenged Heracles to wrestle him. Each time Antaeus struck the ground, his strength doubled. Heracles finally had to hold Antaeus over his head until his earth-derived strength drained away.[4] True philosophy is like Antaeus in deriving its strength from a robust sense of reality. The moment it is uprooted from the desires and made abstract, it loses all its existential bite. (Plato—the winner of a wrestling title at the Isthmian Games—would surely appreciate the comparison.) This image has kept me faithful to the earthy presence of Socrates.

A student of philosophy could do much worse than continually evoke this uncanny presence. Socrates himself, in the *Greater Hippias* (304d) slyly complained of the obnoxious houseguest who never let him get away with an easy answer. Likewise, we must come home to this undomesticated Socrates at the end of the day. As urgent as it is to prettify the disheveled and ugly satyr for public consumption, he must never be anything other than himself in our hearts. Like Huck Finn, he must never be "sivilized."

Acknowledgments

An earlier version of the first chapter appeared in *Interpretation* in 1994.

I wish to express my sincere gratitude to several persons who made this book possible. Stanley Rosen revealed to me the erotic madness of Plato. Jude Fernando encouraged me to take my first steps in philosophy. Lakshman Corea convinced me that I had what it took. Leo Paul De Alvarez taught me how to read carefully and well. Many other fine friends provided me with vision and inspiration. David Baugh and I spent many wonderful evenings, discussing Plato. Dennis Sepper has always been a model of integrity. Robert Wood helped in many ways, great and small. Susan and Tom Kendall and Harry Butler were warm and sincere friends through trying times. Paolo Guietti taught me much about Christian eros. Harold Brogan has been the best of all possible friends. Joseph Lawrence has been a wonderful teacher and friend. Predrag Cicovacki has been steadfast and sincere. Roger Haydon of Cornell University Press kindly midwifed this project from untidy manuscript to contract. Heroic Lee Oser spent many long hours editing this manuscript. And last, but not least, Gudrun Krueger has served as an embodiment of the Good.

NALIN RANASINGHE

The Soul of Socrates

1 Glaucon's Republic

My reappraisal of the Platonic project commences with an original reading of the *Republic*. Many readers find themselves both dazzled by its brilliance and disgusted by the draconian state that it describes as "ideal."[1] How could the Socrates of the *Apology*, that martyred champion of intellectual freedom, espouse the totalitarian regime (complete with eugenics and newspeak) set out in the *Republic*? I try to answer this question in a manner that will do justice to the rich complexity of the *Republic*. Its true meaning must finally emerge, like a prisoner long held in a subterranean cave, before Plato can be taken seriously as a great liberal political philosopher. Only when the *Republic* is "recalled to life" and the old rumors of totalitarianism are put to rest will it be possible to behold the radiant soul of Socrates.

For better or worse, we tend to approach the *Republic* as Glaucon approached Socrates on that unforgettable night at the Piraeus. We somehow assume that Socrates is a reactionary sophist; we imagine that he will obligingly impart everything that Glaucon needs to know about politics. A bored undergraduate will consult his copy of *Cliffs Notes* in much the same spirit.

I suggest that far from being a summation of Plato's deepest thoughts on the art of ruling, the *Republic* is a labyrinthine process of pedagogy that tests the reader's reason and desires to the utmost. In other words, the form and content of a dialogue are not at variance. This means that reading the *Republic* is every bit as difficult as climbing out of the cave. I suggest that Plato did not choose indirection for the sake of elitism and obscurity. He wrote dialogues, rather than treatises, in response to the desire and incapacity of human beings to seek improvement through information transference and coerced order.

Of course, since Plato hardly expected that his writings would still be read more than twenty-three centuries after his death, we should gratefully accept historical data and literary trivia that may shed light on this distant time. We must remember that the original readers and auditors of the dialogue, as well as its writer, were more familiar with dramatic performances than with professionally constructed philosophical writings. We cannot expect Plato to conform to the conventions of a countergenre established after his death by a renegade student.

Fortunately, Plato sometimes provides cryptic suggestions about how to read his dialogues. Hints as to how the *Republic* should be approached are provided by the *Parmenides*. The narrator of the opening segment of that dialogue is a man called Cephalus, who travels to Athens to seek out Glaucon and Adeimantus. Since these characters play no further part in the dialogue, it seems reasonable to infer that these names build a bridge between the two dialogues. Another possible connection with the *Republic* occurs early in the *Parmenides* (128c–d), where Zeno describes his own style of writing. Zeno says that his paradoxes were written to defend Parmenides against those who made fun of him by claiming that his thesis led to absurdities. Zeno's book was a retort showing that their assumptions led to even more absurd consequences (128c–d). Zeno claims that he did not write dispassionately, as an older man would, but out of a youthful desire for controversy. We might infer that Platonic dialogues defend Socratic ignorance in the same way that Zeno's paradoxes protected Parmenides' poems. Like the shorter dialogues, the *Republic* does not set out to convey knowledge wholesale; instead, Plato's Socrates indirectly leads individual minds by drawing attention to shortcomings in the positions taken by his interlocutors.

Additional light on the context of the *Republic* comes by way of Xenophon. He describes Glaucon seeking political office even though he was less than twenty years old. None of his friends or relatives could stop him even though he would make himself a laughingstock by being dragged off the podium when he tried to address the assembly. The *Memorabilia* relates that only Socrates, who took an interest in Glaucon for the sake of Plato and Charmides, managed to check him. Socrates did this by questioning Glaucon. He helped Glaucon to see that his ignorance prevented him from making any contribution of value to the polis. This gives us some sense of how Glaucon was regarded in his own day and age; he was never a potential Alcibiades, Dion, or Alexander being groomed to establish and maintain a noble tyranny. We should also keep in mind the *Seventh Letter* and Plato's passionately expressed distaste for the methods of the restored oligarchs (*Seventh Letter* 324b–325a). The *Republic* is not an academic exercise blithely undertaken by one unaware of the practical consequences of political frustration and hatred.

Ultimately, all we learn from Xenophon and history can only redirect us to the text. Although a Platonic text is autonomous, like natural theology it is in theory both readable by reason alone and open to illumination through revelation. In this context, the recollections of Xenophon are all the more helpful because they restore to us what was presupposed as general knowledge in the audience for whom Plato wrote. We may ask whether Socrates intends (and succeeds in) dissuading Glaucon from entering politics. We may also ask why Plato seems to depict Socrates, the reputed corrupter of Critias and Charmides, in the act of corrupting their nephew and his brother, Glaucon. This question becomes even more significant in light of Xenophon's claim that Socrates undertook to educate Glaucon because of Plato and Charmides. Although Leo Strauss, who points out the importance of Xenophon's information, reads the *Republic* as "the most magnificent cure ever devised to every form of political ambition," Xenophon's Socrates may not be hostile toward all political ambition. Immediately after describing the conversation with Glaucon, Xenophon recounts Socrates' much earlier encounter with Glaucon's uncle, Charmides, during which he encourages Charmides, against his will, to enter politics. We might wonder, of course, whether Socrates has become wiser over the intervening years.[2]

Another relevant source is the *Charmides* itself. This dialogue seems to foreshadow the themes of the *Republic*, for reasons that go beyond the relationship between Critias, Charmides, and Glaucon. A lack of *sophrosune* (temperance or self-knowledge), the quality supposedly described in the *Charmides*, engenders the fevered political climate that is both described in the *Republic* and seen in the political careers of Charmides and Critias. Strikingly, the tyrannical Critias defines justice as the minding of one's own business (*Charmides* 162e); this is surely illustrative of the intemperate soul's inability to take its own knowledge to heart. Furthermore, before providing the charm to cure his headache, Socrates desires to see whether Charmides possesses sufficient temperance to use it (158c). In other words, knowledge is useless without temperance.

Glaucon's place in the *Republic* is crucial. If we remember that it is Glaucon whose political ambitions are being discouraged by Socrates, then the dialogue can be seen as a response to Glaucon's understanding of justice rather than a treatise on the nature of the Just. In other words, the *Republic* does not represent Socrates' account of the perfect form of Justice. Rather, Socrates serves as a midwife who delivers the unsatisfactory implications of the views that Glaucon holds but does not make public. We should examine very closely the demand that Glaucon makes of Socrates in book 2 before drawing any conclusions about the political ideas that Plato endorses in this work. In Aristophanes' language, the *Republic* is "Cloud-Cuckoo-Land" and Socrates is a philosophic midwife / cuckoo who runs away with and hatches another bird's "wind-egg" (*Theaetetus* 151e). We must not fault Socrates for refusing to provide an explicit account of justice at this time. The discussions of justice occur against the comic background of Glaucon's unwillingness to learn temperance.

It may even be that the very notion of justice is too stultifying or negative a term. It is too opposed to eros, and too tied in with the statesman's need for stable self-conserving systems, to offer much possibility for genuine equity. *Dike* (justice) and *Nike* (the spirit of victory) must always be opposed to each other. This could even be related to the all-too-human tendency to see injustice writ clearer than justice. Perhaps the very Socratic revolution consists in the replacement of political justice by human temperance, the substitution of friendship and goodness for the just order of a righteous ruler. The Athenian Stranger's observation in the *Laws* (628d), that a sick body, even after receiving a medical purgation, is inferior to one that has no need of such remedies at all is well worth pondering. In other words, just as the good is beyond being, friendship and temperance are better than justice and continence.

In short, the *Republic* may not be a Platonic attempt to construct and conserve a perfectly just regime through necessarily draconian measures. We must not strain forward, with bated breath and sharpened pencil, to await an account of the perfect political regime. Instead, we should lean back and consider the possibility that Socrates is revealing the impossibility of imposing virtue on other souls. Further, even if we grant the impossible and assume that Socrates possessed such knowledge, it should be evident that the youthful and intemperate Glaucon is the last person with whom he would share it.

Glaucon plans to rule over a city. Instead of deriving his political philosophy from a clear awareness of human nature, his intemperate soul

is blindly driven by a fierce ambition to exercise power. Should one re-
form first the city or the soul? Glaucon says the former, but Socrates
knows better. A true understanding of the polis must derive from an appreciation of the capacities and limitations of human nature. A mere
desire to rule others is indicative of a disordered soul that does not
know itself. An unexamined life, such as Glaucon's, cannot be the basis
for statesmanship. The subtext of the *Republic* reveals an argument
that Socrates conducts through and with Glaucon's ambitions, making
Glaucon aware of the absurdity of his political ambitions without publicly shaming him.

An argument is also subtly conducted against Aristophanes and the
various conservative accusers and critics of Socrates. Socrates reveals
the dangerous consequences of literally re-creating the comically invoked idyllic past, a golden age of perfect justice that has never existed
in fact. The opening of the *Republic*, with its treatment of the questions surrounding the repaying of debts, seems designed to call our attention to Aristophanes' charge in *The Clouds* that Socratic dialectic is
unjust because it teaches debtors to quibble about what is properly
owed instead of making prompt and literal performance of what is expected of them. It turns out that Glaucon would like to bring Aristophanes' comic vision into literal existence: this is part of Plato's indict-
ment of the mimetic tradition. We see Glaucon eagerly embracing
Socrates' parody of Aristophanes' satire. Our own age witnesses the
compounding of this absurdity when literal readers of the *Republic* go
on to accuse Plato and Socrates of totalitarian ambitions. We are truly
in a situation where men blindly interpret shadows at several removes
from the truth.

Glaucon in his state of ignorant ambition is identical to the man not
in possession of his wits who was refused restitution of what he entrusted for safekeeping (331c). In book 2 of the *Republic*, Glaucon arro-
gantly confides his tyrannical dreams to Socrates; he confidently ex-
pects that Socrates will not be able to win an argument against tyranny
conducted in the language of hedonism. But instead of the easy triumph
that he had been misled to expect, Glaucon is repaid with Socratic interest: he gains valuable insights into his unsettled condition and consequently chooses to renounce his tyrannical fantasies. Like the dog
that did not bark in the night, Glaucon is perhaps best remembered for
what he did not do: he did not follow the example of Critias and
Charmides and share in their notoriety. Like Odysseus in book 10 of
the *Republic* (620c–d), he apparently chooses a long, inglorious life of

obscurity and takes his leave, rejoicing in his good fortune. This chapter tries to follow the powerful but subtle chain of reasoning that sends him on this path. Far from being a blueprint for totalitarianism, made seductively available to would-be tyrants, the *Republic* is nothing more or less than an account of the unorthodox way through which Socrates rehabilitates Glaucon.

Glaucon's views on justice and injustice are filtered through book 1, which recounts a series of increasingly spirited exchanges about the nature of justice between Socrates and Cephalus, his son Polemarchus, and the sophist Thrasymachus. All three interlocutors anticipate Glaucon's position that the just life is unhappy because justice is essentially antierotic; the raging force of eros compromises and threatens any possibility of justice or social stability. When Cephalus tells Socrates that his advanced age has made him immune to desire and more susceptible to speeches, he quotes Sophocles as saying that he felt as if he had run away from a frenzied and savage master (329b–d): a tremendous amount of youthful energy is expended in alternately serving and fighting desire. We shall see how Socrates proposes to enlighten these desires.

Socrates suggests to Cephalus that it is his wealth and not his good character that enables him to face the disabilities of old age. It is because of his money that he can make reparation to gods and men for the sins of his lustful youth. His wealth serves to protect him from the worst of the fears afflicting old age. Because he inherited his money, he did not need to accumulate wealth out of necessity, a form of desire that makes justice in the sense of strict reparation impossible. If Cephalus is not as attached to his wealth as one who had to earn it, how much more under the grip of necessity would one be who had not earned enough? This is one of the recurrent themes of the *Republic*: Is justice *knowledge* of what is appropriate need, or is it *poetry*, with wealth suppressing the necessary desires of poverty to secure conditions of stability and order for itself? The complexity of this question is compounded by the strategic need for the second type of justice to disguise itself as the first.

Polemarchus, not Cephalus's only son but the sole legatee of his argument, is all too aware of the problems that beset the defense of inherited wealth amid conditions of political instability. If Cephalus represents the no longer tenable old order, then Polemarchus stands for the uncertain present and Thrasymachus for the threatening future. Cephalus views justice in terms of reparations to others, but Pole-

marchus desires coerced restitution of property from enemies. Polemarchus also cites a poet, Simonides, to buttress this position, claiming
that justice is giving to each exactly what is owed (331d). This definition repudiates the very origin of the Athenian polity when Solon abol-
ished debt slavery and canceled all other debts.[3] Socrates points out
that since giving what is owed implies knowledge of what is appropriate, simple reparation is not so easily made. Polemarchus evades discussion of this question (which entails knowledge of what is good and
evil) by saying that he understands justice as doing good to friends and
harm to enemies. Polemarchus views justice in subjective and partisan
terms: a man's friends are just, and his enemies are unjust. The love he
feels toward his friends leads him to find relish in giving his enemies
their just des(s)erts. Repayment has little to do with settling material
accounts; honor and dishonor are the currency of the realm of spiritedness. As a result, these spirited men find it hard to acknowledge the
most basic property rights of their enemies.

There is the further problem that spiritedly just men such as Polemarchus do not seem to have any positive or nondestructive traits or
skills. An adversarial relationship is implied by the long series of contrasts between crafts and justice: all the productive skills seem to be
connected to injustice—that is, not being part of the just faction—
rather than justice. A just man cannot be only useful as a guardian of
what has been entrusted to him when the origins of property reside in
acts of violent acquisition. He also needs productive enemies who can
be plundered or controlled with the assistance of other just friends.
Plato obviously meant his readers to note that the dramatic context of
the *Republic* provided poignant testimony to the transient nature of
such friendships. While the two young aristocrats, Glaucon and
Adeimantus, are at present on good terms with the wealthy, resident
alien family of Cephalus, in a few years Polemarchus will be killed and
his family robbed of its wealth. These acts will be committed by an
aristocratic faction led by the uncles of Glaucon and Adeimantus:
Critias and Charmides. Justice turns out to be the highly profitable (albeit dangerous) art of punishing injustice. Paradoxically, it appears that
justice can be practiced only amid conditions of chaos and instability.

Socrates soon convinces Polemarchus that greater benefit and harm
can be visited on friends and enemies, respectively, once one knows
who his friends and enemies really are, as well as what is truly beneficial. This is the positive value of justice, and its importance is considerable in an adversarial situation where internecine conflict is more the

rule than the exception. Polemarchus admits that since doing injustice to enemies only makes them worse, although it may seem to be advantageous to injure an enemy, it could never be just. Justice, by its very essence, cannot produce injustice.

Justice is like all the other arts in that it improves all those who come into contact with it, with respect to its subject matter. This view is flatly opposed to the adversarial procedure by which just men define their enemies as unjust to justify subsequent malevolent conduct toward them. In the language of the *Euthyphro*, the just is not just, just because it is called just by the just; it is called just by the just because it is just. Socrates' view of justice stresses the unity and common interests of a polis, while the other definition would emphasize, exacerbate, and exploit antagonisms between various economic and social strata.

Thrasymachus now violently introduces his thesis that justice is the advantage of the stronger. Justice, in the idealized sense that Socrates has described it, is illusory and dangerous. A polis that ignores the differences between the weak and the strong would engender social and moral chaos. True justice, as Thrasymachus depicts it, is a stabilizing force, overcoming the tragic delusions of idealistic ethics. It would regulate the health of the polis and purge citizens of surplus quantities of time and wealth that had destabilized the whole. Socratic rationalism leads the individual to make impossible moral demands of life; this is why Thrasymachus accuses Socrates of sniveling and needing a wet nurse. He would agree heartily with Nietzsche's claim that justice is in the service of life; justice has no right to make unrealistic demands of life because justice is a creation of life. The strong construct objective justice for men unable to seek their own advantage, so that these weaklings can live without moral vertigo. This is why the perfectly unjust ruler must appear to be perfectly just and even demand recompense for his seemingly just deeds. The weak merely seek order. They would be quite content to tacitly accept injustice (the advantage of the stronger) as the price of order, as long as this advantage is consistently enforced. Thrasymachus' theory is perfectly consistent with a cynical reading of the *Iliad*: the justice of Zeus means nothing more or less than the necessity for order. In other words, instead of saying, "Let there be light," Zeus says, "Let there be order, and may its origins be shrouded discreetly in darkness."

Socrates defeats Thrasymachus by forcing him to admit that justice is a science with an objective subject matter rather than the divine art of imposing order upon a godless chaos. Should he deny the reality of nature and the possibility of science, Thrasymachus would openly reveal himself as an atheist and nihilist. This is also why he cannot take the easy way out offered by Clitophon and claim that justice is what the stronger believes to be advantageous to him (340b).

In response to the sophist's earlier charge of sycophancy, Socrates could make Thrasymachus admit that he conducted his own professional activities according to the predatory model just described. Thrasymachus is unable to display his ideal of the perfectly unjust ruler openly; to do so would discredit him in the eyes of the many. His blasphemy would expose him to the possibility of exile or even execution. He would not even be able to present himself as a reliable tutor of the few, since he would be describing a state of affairs where all trust would be folly. His anger towards Socrates' idealism forces him to speak of unspeakable matters. Now, in midstream, he remembers how publicly untenable his positions are.

Glaucon is acute enough to see that Thrasymachus's weakness lies not in his argument but in his imprudence in giving open expression to an impolitic idea. The famous blush of Thrasymachus is a belated recognition of this need to preserve appearances. Socrates allows him the option of defeat, without forcing him to gain a pyrrhic victory at the expense of his career. Socrates has shown that he is the more prudent man in this battle between just and unjust speech. Glaucon now wishes to know why Socrates, who evidently knows the secrets of the sophists, prefers to be poor and politically unsuccessful. Just as Socrates asked Cephalus whether a life without desire was worth living, Glaucon now aims the same question at Socrates. What secret pleasures does he conceal behind his ironic facade?

Glaucon asks Socrates whether he would truly persuade or merely appear to have convinced them of the superiority of justice. This question shows that he is very much aware of the distinction between appearance and reality underlying Socrates' apparent refutation of Thrasymachus. Glaucon sets up a threefold classification of goods: those desired for their own sake, those desired for their consequences, and those desirable both for their own sake and for their consequences. Glaucon believes that justice is practiced only for its presumed consequences and not for its intrinsic qualities. He challenges Socrates to defend justice strictly on the basis of its inherent goodness, although Socrates has already told him that he understands justice to be preferred both for itself *and* for its results. Glaucon's challenge presupposes the impossibility of the good life. Not content with denying the good effects expected to accrue from a just life, he goes on to burden such a life with every misfortune and asks Socrates to compare it to an unjust life that has every material advantage. Adeimantus compounds the problem by excluding consideration of rewards and sanctions in the afterlife.

By framing the question in this extreme fashion, the sons of Ariston make it impossible for Socrates to defend the good life in any positive way. To win, Socrates must take the offensive and attack the counter-ideal of the unjust life. In the *Gorgias*, Socrates has already rather easily debunked crude hedonism, he now faces a far more formidable adversary. Glaucon describes a life conducted according to scientific injustice, which allows the unjust man to prosper long and gloriously. The perfectly unjust man would be a practitioner of the kind of master science that so fascinated Glaucon's uncle Critias in the *Charmides* (166c ff.). This master science would situate itself above good and evil; it would derive all morality from the law of nature that only the strongest and wrongest should rule. Such a master science thus replaces temperance because its self-knowledge amounts to a sovereign knowledge of its own creation and business. Glaucon seeks to escape the problems that confounded Callicles, who conceded that the unjust man was a sort of natural slave to desire (*Gorgias* 493d–494e). In effect, then, Glaucon aims at overcoming the disjunction faced by Achilles, who had to choose between a long, obscure life and a short, glorious career of injustice.[4] Although Socrates believes in a long and happy life led through the education of eros, he cannot defend this possibility before he has shown that injustice and lasting happiness are incompatible.

Glaucon reveals what his own inclinations are when he informs Socrates that he too would emulate Gyges were he possessed of the power to act unjustly with total impunity. "Give each [man] license to do whatever he wants, while we follow and watch where his desire will lead. . . . we will catch the just man red-handed going the same way as the unjust" (359c).

Glaucon's story of the ring of Gyges is almost certainly his own invention; it is very different from that recounted by Herodotus. The "Father of Lies" tells the story of a king who was so enamored of his wife that he contrived for his best friend to spy on her while she undressed. The queen, finding out about her husband's folly, summoned the friend and informed him that he had a choice: he could either die, or murder the king and rule in his stead. She explains that only one man could see the queen naked.[5] Glaucon's story of Gyges tells about a ring that conferred invisibility on an inquisitive shepherd. The connection between the tale told by Herodotus and the one invisibly substituted by Glaucon is subtle but pointed. The queen had her husband murdered because he could not keep a secret. The price demanded of the successful practitioner of injustice was that he share his secret with nobody. The tyrant must draw an impenetrable veil around his injustice.

Because he openly endorsed injustice, Thrasymachus was publicly shamed and discredited. The best tyrant will be invisible in his injustice; he will suppress his natural needs for recognition and friendship in order that he may secretly enjoy his possessions. Glaucon thus uses his version of the story of Gyges to inform Socrates, in a secretive but emphatic fashion, that he can keep a secret! Glaucon is willing to sell his soul in order that he may enjoy the boundless material spoils of tyranny. By the very making of this veiled boast, however, Glaucon gives himself away: no other man can know the tyrant's secret. The playful implication of this situation is that Socrates' life is in jeopardy! He has to persuade Glaucon to renounce his ambitions.

Both Socrates and Glaucon are aware that the discussion in book 1 has done none little or nothing to overcome Glaucon's hidden desire for tyranny. To achieve the desired catharsis, Socrates must descend into the underworld of Glaucon's desires and vanquish the desire for tyranny. In a sense, any intellectual attempt to display the superiority of the just life is doomed in advance. At best, the desire for tyranny will only rationalize endlessly to justify what it has already accepted prerationally. Socrates cannot win his battle for Glaucon's soul by demolishing one set of rationalizations; another sophist will soon replace these as long as Glaucon secretly continues to desire tyranny. It is not sufficient to address the symptoms of Glaucon's malaise; to cure him, the allure of tyranny must be discredited.

Socrates purges Glaucon of his unjust eros by offering him a city instead of a soul. Socrates refuses to depict a perfectly just life which encountered misfortune and misery as a consequence of its virtue. He will not play the pander and discredit his own view that virtue *is* desirable for its consequences. Instead, he offers what Glaucon truly desires. Displacing Thrasymachus, Socrates offers Glaucon the totally unjust life, perfectly disguised as the perfectly just life. He suggests to Glaucon and Adeimantus that it would be easier to observe justice in a city than in a soul. By watching the city grow, they would presumably be able to observe the genesis of justice and injustice. The origins of cities reside in the absence of human self-sufficiency. This is also a timely reminder to Glaucon that human life cannot be led apart from society; self-sufficiency is the delusion of a rich man with an exaggerated notion of his capability. The just life is justified through its political consequences.

The first city described by Socrates, although materially sufficient in all other respects, is not found by Adeimantus to be either just or unjust (372a). Although this city, more than any other, is characterized by men minding their own business it is significant that this definition is not introduced, even though such a depiction of justice would have been wholly consistent with the positions that both Cephalus and Polemarchus held. Justice can make a belated appearance only *after* the erotic Glaucon bursts in, like a wild beast, upon this bucolic society to demand *opson*—that is, meat (372c). Glaucon's description of this community as a city of swine suggests that he has his own ideas as to how the deficiency may be overcome (372d). Only after Glaucon's introduction of "relishes" is justice needed. The luxurious city also needs swineherds, for although the city of swine already has shepherds and cowherds, "this animal wasn't in our earlier city—there was no need—but in this one there will be need of it in addition" (373c).

By outstripping the bounds of necessity, the city soon needs an army to acquire and defend its luxuries. In keeping with the principle of specialization, it must entrust this responsibility to Guardians who combine in their natures the sheepdog's capacity for loving friends and hating enemies. Justice is introduced only after injustice and eros pervade the city. This is consistent with justice being a restraining influence on desire; in this city it is simply politically mandated restraint that makes weak men mind what the strong have determined as their own business. Justice is the advantage of the stronger imposed on the weak in order to maximize the superiority of the strong. In the crudest terms the Guardians become necessary after the strong have already grown accustomed to the taste of relishes; their purpose is to guard and preserve this culinary advantage from the enemies of those who creatively define justice.

The Guardians of this city must love friends and hate enemies. Socrates says that a Guardian will be like a dog in showing hostility toward a complete stranger "even though it never had any bad experience with him." Conversely, "when it sees someone it knows, it greets him warmly, even though it never had a good experience with him" (376a). Like Polemarchus, this dog is totally ignorant about its true friends and enemies. Such a Guardian is "truly philosophic": "It distinguishes friendly from hostile looks by nothing other than having learned the one and being ignorant of the other. And so, how can it be anything other than a lover of learning, since it defines what's its own and what's alien by knowledge and ignorance?" (376b). Unless the reader recognizes that this passage reeks of irony, he or she will miss the point.

The education of the Guardians consists entirely of Noble Lies. Because the purged city seeks to downplay the freedom of the individual in order to promote community values of endurance and stability, the educator of the Guardians will use religion accordingly: instead of describing a shadowy existence in Hades where all shades are gray, he will speak of significant otherworldly rewards and sanctions in the Blessed Isles and Tartarus respectively. Homer's accounts of Hades serve to remind men of the tragedy and uniqueness of worldly existence; in contrast, myths about reincarnation emphasize social continuity and remind the many that they cannot escape punishment for their actions. We shall see that another reason for expunging Homeric accounts of the underworld is that Socrates is describing a very similar subterranean community.

The educator of the Guardians will maintain every outward pretense of virtue. He will seek to eradicate any thought of untruth, and his greatest falsehood will be the denial of both the possibility of deception and the conceivability of "the thing which is not." This is why artistic virtuosity is regarded with fear and loathing: the tyrant must be the only muse in his city if its citizens are to be reduced to mere shadows of their human potentiality. Similarly, the ruler treats laughter with great hostility because of its connection to aesthetic distance and self-consciousness (388e–389a). In order for perfect mimetic obedience to be instilled in them, the citizens of this community must become as literal-minded as possible. The two-dimensional reality of the cave is foreshadowed here!

Socrates now proposes that the Guardians live under conditions of strict communism (416d–420a). This follows from their obligation to love friends and harm enemies: the just man pillages his enemies and gives everything to his friends. This Spartan regimen is found to be all the more appropriate because of the principle of specialization: any accumulation of possessions would make the Guardians that much less efficient at their specialized task. In response to an objection by Adeimantus, Socrates points out that the Guardians exist for the sake of the city and not vice versa (420b). What is important is the happiness of the city, not the individual happiness of its constituents or classes. Although the Guardians "must give up all other crafts to become craftsmen of the city's freedom" (395c), *they* do not receive any freedom. We are reminded of the discussion with Polemarchus in which it was agreed that the proper practice of a skill could not engender its very opposite. The response to this complaint is that all the crafts, not excluding medicine, exist for the sake of the city; they must produce or fabricate good citizens. Just as justice derives from the advantage of the stronger, all of the virtues are defined according to this highest end.

The manifestly austere and artificial regimen prescribed for the Guardians necessitates the creation of another class of Guardians whose task is to educate the first class and "guard over enemies from without and friends from within so that the ones will not wish to do harm and the others will be unable to" (414b). The former Guardians are to become Auxiliaries; only the guardians of the Auxiliaries will be Guardians proper. This refinement of the structure of the city follows from the necessity that the true Guardian should possess proper knowledge of his friends and enemies. The Auxiliaries function merely as dependent and ignorant bodyguards, creating a sort of "ring of Gyges" around the true Guardians to render their workings invisible to the many. This structure mirrors the gradual corruption of the idea of justice over the course of book 1. First, the Artisans see justice as speaking the truth and repaying what is owed. Second, the Auxiliaries help the friends of the city and hate its enemies. Finally, the true rulers, who become the most powerful in the city through duping the Auxiliaries, act according to Thrasymachus's definition and seek their own advantage while cloaked in the appearance of justice.

Once the hierarchy of the seemingly just city is completed, its Guardians may proceed to purge and pillage the Artisan class through the Auxiliaries. The function of the Auxiliaries is thus turned from protecting the city against its external enemies to policing its own citizens; the army is transformed into the mother of all secret police. The various restrictions on music and poetry, devised for the sake of the Auxiliaries, will affect the cultural life of the city significantly.

Socrates next describes economic measures to complete the transformation of the city of swine into a totalitarian state. The stability of the Artisan class is most threatened by wealth and poverty: the one engenders indolence; the other, wrongdoing (422a). Furthermore, through either ennui or necessity, both economic extremes introduce innovation to the city. We are not told where any economic surplus would be diverted, but since neither the Auxiliaries nor the Artisans are supposed to be wealthy, it could only end up with those who are both discreet and immune from the temptation of eros: the Guardians. The heavy-handed emphasis on the perfect unity of the city also means that the Guardians will micromanage the procreation, employment, and marriages of the citizens.

Let us pause to compare the life of the Guardian of the just city with the unjust life that Glaucon described. According to Glaucon, the unjust man "rules in the city because he seems to be just. Then he takes in marriage from whatever station he wants and gives in marriage whomever he wants; he contracts and has partnerships with whomever he wants and . . . gains because he has no qualms about doing injustice. So then, when he enters contests, both public and private, he wins and gets the better of his enemies. In getting the better, he is wealthy and does good to friends and harm to enemies"(362b).

When a Guardian's life is measured by these criteria, it is self-evident that he rules in the city because of his appearance of justice. As for marriage, because the Guardians have unlimited control over the lives of their subjects, this requirement is also satisfied to an extent unimagined by Glaucon. Because the Guardians have the power to elevate and demote persons from one class to another, the seemingly just man can select and exploit his friends with total impunity. Regarding contests, in book 4 Glaucon finds unnecessary the very question as to whether the seemingly just life is preferable, because its superiority is so evident (445a). And it is obvious that the Guardian is in a unique position to obtain great wealth and visit enormous benefit and damage on friends and enemies respectively.

Socrates has thus duly described a perfectly unjust life according to Glaucon's specifications. He must now go on to demonstrate the impracticality of this life and reveal to Glaucon the superiority of the truly just life. This process commences when Socrates suggests that the soul should be divided and ordered as the city was. As a result, justice recedes still further, collapsing within the soul of the Guardian himself. The Guardian, having become the knowledge and wisdom of the city, is compelled to train his own soul even more rigorously than he ordered the lives of the Artisans and Auxiliaries. He is forced to see how much effort is expended in keeping *Fortuna* compliant with his domination. So enormous an act of will is quite beyond the capacity of anyone who wishes to enjoy his relishes. Power loses some of its allure, and the just city begins to look a bit absurd.

We must remember that Glaucon is not a crude hedonist of the stamp of Callicles. Rather, he is ambitious enough to desire power, and sufficiently presumptuous to believe himself entitled to it by virtue of his high birth. Glaucon is a prime example of the banality of injustice: left to his own devices, he would do little more than maintain the status quo with some degree of ruthlessness and allow himself some profit for his pains; corrupted by Thrasymachus, he could prove to be quite dangerous.

Glaucon honestly believes that injustice is natural and that he, a member of the natural aristocracy, is born to rule. Too indolent to enjoy the exercise of power for its own sake, however, he is certainly not willing to practice injustice as a full-time occupation. Socrates will force him to see the unnatural absurdity of attempting to suppress desire in the name of justice. In short, although Glaucon has sought to suppress the desires of others in order to enjoy his supposed natural superiority, he will come to see that he has unwittingly fashioned a prison for himself. He has become the ruler of a grim, austere cave without friends or leisure. Glaucon may very well echo the words of Achilles and prefer the life of a landless serf to ruling over a principality of shadows.[6] It is highly significant that these words from Homer are to be stricken from the reformed canon (386c).

Because of the artificiality of his enterprise, the tyrannical Guardian increasingly depends more on himself and less on his supposed natural advantages. Ironically, the very totality of the domination he enjoys also means that he can never depend on a status quo to support him. The Guardian's security cannot be built on ground that he has previously devastated and impoverished. Looking into himself, in search of capacities to sustain these increasingly unnatural and poetic efforts, Glaucon cannot but reexamine his ambitions and desires. Only self-knowledge can lead him toward a less adversarial understanding of justice in both city and soul.

Socrates' thought experiment is intended to make Glaucon see the tragic consequences of seeking, secretly, to gratify his own desires at the expense of everyone else's. One must distinguish between bodily desires and the tragic potential of spiritedness. In pitting the mind against desire, one creates a situation in which the energies of spiritedness are blinded, angered, and directed to serve the ends of the body. The mind is compelled to devote all its power to repressing this blind force; the tyrannical Guardian can achieve nothing better than a stalemate because of the unnatural character of his objectives. If he can only accept that eros / spiritedness is not incorrigible and should not be lied to, he will be in a far better position to reorder the soul and achieve a truer state of happiness. Spiritedness becomes the natural ally of reason when it is granted, and reminded of, a proper role in the economy of the soul.

Whereas the needs of the desires are specific and limited, spiritedness desires to transcend these particularities altogether. Socrates now uses the story of Leontius and the dead bodies to prove to Glaucon that spiritedness can and does oppose the bodily desires in the name of something more honorable (439e–440a). Reason must navigate a course for spiritedness, just as spiritedness should supply reason with the strength and the integrity that it needs to attain its proper ends. Once reason and spiritedness are reconciled on these reasonable and honorable terms, it becomes possible to arrive at a more nearly adequate understanding of one's proper business.

A man's first and most proper business is the ordering and continual governance of his soul, and *sophrosune* must precede politics just as self-respect should precede civic friendship. This was the lesson that Socrates unsuccessfully attempted to administer to Glaucon's uncles in the *Charmides*. The *Republic* is an advance on the earlier dialogue because of its far greater reliance on action and poetic imagery. This approach is used in the remainder of the work to introduce Glaucon to philosophy and show him how much more he needs to learn about both city and soul. Glaucon has already received the information necessary to repudiate the unjust life; now Socrates will help him apply these insights to the city, so that Glaucon may reject oligarchic politics and choose justice of his own free and informed will.

As we enter book 5 the absurdity of returning to a natural state by means of high artifice is heightened by Plato's use of Aristophanic devices. Since we have completed the male drama, we must now go back and complete the female (451c). Comedy and ridicule, hitherto excluded from the city, now reenter and reveal precisely why they were excluded: the city itself has been a poetic creation. Socrates' arguments in favor of a community of women are lifted directly out of Aristophanes' late play *Ecclesiazusae*, where the heroine discusses at great length the advantages of communism.[7] Aristophanes' last utopia also provides for statutory couplings controlled by the leading stateswoman to her satisfaction. Instead of the three waves of ridicule, which drowned the just city, three aged hags—each older and uglier than the one preceding her—demand sexual congress with a reluctant young man. When he refuses the first woman on the grounds that she is old enough to be his mother, she is joined by the two others, who are presumably *too* old to have conceived him.[8] This early fourth-century play, which would presumably have been known by the readers of the *Republic*, reminds Glaucon that dirty old men would inevitably occupy the best positions in the sexual pecking order of the just city.

One of the most celebrated images in political science well illustrates the tyrant's predicament. Machiavelli said that *Fortuna* was a woman who was most attracted to brutal young men.[9] Socrates warns that *Fortuna* is a hideous crone whose insatiability would blunt the erotic urges of even the most shameless and power-hungry youth. Socrates' method of argumentation seems to be an anticipation and refutation of the Machiavellian temptation. He intends to deflate Glaucon's erotic designs on the body politic by showing him how unattractive, aging, and draining a task tyranny would be. The secret of the queen in the Herodotean story of Gyges was not her beauty but her ugliness! This is why no other man could see her naked.

Even after the first two waves of absurdity have come crashing down on his city, Glaucon still desires to bring it into existence. Brushing aside all other considerations, he earnestly asks whether and how this regime could be set up (471c–e). Socrates warns that he has created a city in speech to display the political consequences of justice and injustice; he does not intend to dwell on whether this city should come into being (472c). He then makes his famous statement that since political power and philosophy must be combined to cure the ills of cities and souls, any separation of the two should be made impossible. This remark makes Glaucon tear off his clothing of justice and demand that Socrates explain himself or suffer the consequences (474a). As far as Glaucon is concerned, philosophy is simply the goose that lays the golden eggs. Once he has obtained the blueprint for the perfect tyranny, he will not have any further use for Socrates or philosophy.

Conversely, Socrates is trying to teach Glaucon that philosophy is necessary for the well-being of the city; only the philosopher is able to reorient and reconcile the many desires and souls. The philosopher is not a demagogue or oligarch, studying desire with the sophist in order to manipulate the opinions of the many or the moneyed; he is "willing to taste every kind of learning with gusto, . . . approaches every kind of learning with delight and is insatiable" (475c). This means that a philosopher does not seek to destroy opinions and desires in the name of truth; his task is to educate them by revealing the truth animating their spiritedness. Truth is more than the advantage of the victor in a battle between blind and insecure factions. In that unhappy situation, while the citizens destroy their polis, it is only enemies of the polis and panders like Thrasy-

machus who profit. Glaucon must learn not to mistake a thoroughly coerced state of artificially uniform opinion for a healthy polis.

Before Glaucon becomes better aware of the truth about philosophy,
and the need to liberate both soul and city from the tyranny of opinion,
Socrates must respond to a challenge from Adeimantus. Glaucon's
brother asserts that persons who persist in philosophy beyond their
youth (shades of Callicles) often become either strange or vicious, and
even the best cases are completely useless to the city (487d). Socrates
responds with his celebrated image of the ship of state (488a–489c). The
true navigator's advice will not be heeded by its drunken crew. They
prefer drinking and feasting to the serious work of steering the ship to
its proper port. This nautical imagery also carries overtones of Athenian thalasocracy and readies us for the shipwreck that will shortly
ensue. Socrates warns us that the best natures are always led astray in
their youth, since the very talents of such souls, not properly attended
to, can breed disaster:

> What do you suppose such a young man will do in such circum-
> stances, especially if he chances to be from a big city, is rich and noble
> in it, and is, further, good looking and tall? Won't he be overflowing
> with unbounded hope, believing he will be competent to mind the
> business of both Greeks and barbarians, . . . exalt himself to the
> heights, mindlessly full of pretension and empty conceit? (494c–d)

This remark reminds us of Alcibiades, but Socrates is also thinking of
Glaucon and his uncle Charmides:

> If someone was gently to approach the young man in this condition
> and tell him the truth—that he has no intelligence in him although
> he needs it, and that it's not to be acquired except by slaving for its ac-
> quisition—do you think it will be easy for him to hear? (494d)

Socrates' strategy toward Glaucon is different from the direct and unsuccessful approach followed in the *Charmides*. Instead of denying the
young man what he desires, Socrates has presented him with sovereignty over a virtual state. This experience, will allow Glaucon to see
for himself that the life of the landless Socrates is preferable to that of a
prince over the dead souls of a tyranny. This is a choice that only Glaucon can make, and we have seen Socrates refine and educate his understanding of what it means. Adeimantus has complained that Socrates'

method was to continually shift the ground of the argument a little at a time so that "when the littles are collected at the end of the argument the slip turns out to be great and contrary to the first assertions" (487b). This is precisely what happens here. The philosopher is in love with the truth (485b). Such a man will not tolerate the elaborate edifice of lies that the just city consists of. Yet the philosopher is supposed to be the savior and king of this regime. This crowning absurdity is intended to shift Glaucon's attention from city to soul, so that he may finally see what ambition has made him blind to and renounce his fantasies.

By introducing the concept of the philosopher-king Socrates has subtly prepared the way for the replacement of monarchy by philosophy as the highest life. While a king rules over a city, enshrining his opinions and worshiping his desires, the philosopher tends the mystery of his soul and serves the good. Yet Glaucon is not prepared for anything like an adequate account of the philosophic life; his eyes are not ready for the erotic glories of the good, and neither are ours. Socrates has already warned Adeimantus that the proper preparation for philosophy entails many years of being tested by images of fears and pleasures. As a consequence, he is hardly in a position to offer Glaucon who has had only a few hours' exposure to these images, anything more than a very tentative representation of the process. "I only wish," says Socrates to Glaucon, "that I were able to pay and you were able to receive [the Good] itself and not just the interest. . . . be careful that I do not in some way unwillingly deceive you" (507a). This language also harks back to Aristophanes' charge mentioned earlier, about repaying debts.

The bewildering account given of the philosopher-in-training's preparation is not an actual account of philosophy itself. Socrates never describes how these studies extend beyond the lower half of the divided line; his intention is to impress Glaucon with the exceptional amount of learning that even this philosophical prolegomena entails. This was the strategy followed in Xenophon's version, where Glaucon was forced to concede that he lacked the logistical knowledge required to function as an effective ruler. Plato's Glaucon was told quite clearly, in response to his request for an account of the power of dialectic, that he would not be able to follow Socrates at this point, though this would not be through any lack of eagerness on the part of Socrates himself (533a). Such an education could be given only to someone already possessed of a great deal of practical experience and knowledge.

For the present, Glaucon is told that the Good is "what every soul pursues and for the sake of which it does everything. The soul divines that it is something but is at a loss about it and unable to get a sufficient grasp of just what it is" (505e). Strife between reason and desire can be resolved only through an awareness of the Good, since the disagreement is over what is most meaningful and pleasurable for man. Such a resolution of strife is tied to the celebrated Socratic dictum that man will do evil only out of ignorance; both reason and desire will make ignorant choices in isolation. The context of the *Republic* makes it even easier to see why knowledge of the Good cannot be extrinsically imposed: both reason and the desires must become aware of the efficacy and sovereignty of the Good.

Socrates uses naturalistic imagery to describe the Good. He contrasts the natural to the artificial to support his claim that the tyrant's promise to restore a state of nature begets a thoroughly unnatural and unjust state. As the sun is the principle of order and growth in nature (508b), the Good is the source and aspiration of all human actions and desires (517b). It follows clearly that desire should be educated. Accordingly, just as the light of the sun conveys the nurturing power of life to nature, so too should eros mediate between humans and the Good. Since the Good is the very origin and meaning of eros, it is the basis for the educated harmonization of the desires of every human soul. By contrast, the insatiable and solipsistic desires of the tyrant represent a perverse falling away from this goodness (508d). The nocturnal conversation at the Piraeus, in which the eros of everyone other than the tyrant has been stifled, mirrors a situation parallel to that of the cave, which excludes the light of the sun in favor of artificial light.

The model of the divided line is the broadest depiction of the terrain and scope of knowledge provided in the *Republic* (509d–511e). The relation of reality to illusion at the lower half of the line is paralleled by the relation of intellection has to thought in the upper half and by the original division between the visible and the ideal. Just as reality is the measure by which appearances should be assessed, we must similarly allow the ideas to shed light on empirical reality. This means that the city of swine, which became untenable through the proliferation of desire, can be ordered in a nonreductive way by the education of desire through the ideas. This procedure stands in stark contrast to that followed in the perfect regime of Glaucon, where deceit and illusions were the solution to the malaise of eros.

The full extent to which deception defines and pervades the seemingly just polis is revealed when Socrates describes the cave—a grotesque and completely inverted representation of the divided line.

Instead of the Good and the sun, we discover the fire and, with considerable effort, the wholly invisible tyrant. This is appropriate, since the very word Hades derives from *a-ides*, meaning "the unseen one" or, literally, "no-idea." Once the tyrant is seen, it must be concluded that he is the cause of all that is wrong and unjust in the cave. Just as the divided line accommodated both pure and applied thought, the cave has provision for the Tyrant and his Auxiliaries.

The pure thought of the philosopher has its practical issue in the working hypotheses that the healthy polis uses to educate and enlighten desire. This procedure is imitated by the Tyrant, who gives his Auxiliaries the modes and orders necessary to suppress totally the prisoners' desires as well as their own. Instead of artisans who trust in natural reality, we encounter prisoners who are totally unaware of themselves and the physical conditions they live in. Consequently, there is an inversion of the respective domains of illusion and nature, so that appearance passes for reality and vice versa. Although the cave image is a criticism of poets and democracy, the escaped prisoner's need to accustom himself to shadows and reflections *outside* the cave proves that he has been conditioned to view something even more delusory. We must remember that the proportion of appearance to reality recurs over at least three points along the divided line. The implication is that transcendent reality cannot be reduced to parochial terms; as we shall see, this is why Socratic philosophy rejects the comic solutions of Aristophanes.

The cave image strikingly depicts the contrast between education and coerced habit. The cardinal error (alas, a common one) is in assuming that the cave and the just regime of Glaucon are not identical but represent the respective extremes of reality and ideality. Socrates states that the educated Guardian must not lead the prisoners out of the cave; instead he must preside over what his educated vision finds to be a very unsatisfactory state of affairs (519d–520d). This is the clearest proof that Glaucon's city is not the just polis but a reductio ad absurdum of an inadequate and inequitable view of justice that serves the interests only of an invisible fourth party.

It is significant that the ring of Gyges, in Glaucon's story, was found in another *chasma* (cave *beneath the ground*) by his ancestor, a *theteuonta* (hired serf) of the king entrusted with the king's flocks (359d). Just like Achilles, Gyges' forebear had to choose between being a hired serf / glorified sheepdog / just guardian on the one hand and, on the other, an invisible king who truly exploited and ruled over his spiritually dead herd. The only time Plato refers to a *chasma* outside the *Republic* is in the *Phaedo* (111e), where he says that most human societies reside in the chasms of the earth; those who, like Socrates, have left their caves stand out like the living among the dead (*Meno* 100a). Uses of *chasma* elsewhere leave no doubt that the word has very hellish overtones. Hesiod, for instance, speaks of the great chasm of Tartarus as "a marvel that is awful even to the deathless gods."[10] It is from this hellish desire for tyranny that Socrates seeks to deliver the soul of Glaucon.

The real problem with coercion is its inability to bring true knowledge; this is because the whole soul, and not merely the mind, must be prepared to apprehend truth. The head of the prisoner in the cave cannot be turned in the proper direction unless his body is released from bondage. Neither can we transfer knowledge via coercion or habit:

> Education is not what the professions of certain men assert it to be. They presumably assert that they put into the soul knowledge that isn't in it . . . but the present argument . . . indicates that *this power is in the soul of each* and that the instrument with which one learns—just as the eye is not able to turn toward the light from the dark without the whole body—must be turned around from that which is coming into being together with the whole soul until it is able to endure looking at that which is. . . . there would therefore . . . be an art of this turning the soul around, not an art of producing sight in it. Rather, this art takes as given that sight is there, but not rightly turned nor looking at what one ought to look at. (518b–d).

Once education is understood in this manner—and *never* (except in perhaps in the *Gorgias*) does Socrates seem more serious—light is shed on the injustice and inadequacy of the "just city," revealing its draconian essence and supporting the claim that it is the Cave.

Even the philosopher-Guardian of this monstrous regime is coerced to remain in the cave. The man who has seen the glorious realities of life is now reduced to fashioning crude shadow representations of these ideas. The Auxiliaries will use them to stage shadow spectacles that seduce the prisoners' natural upwardly mobile desires. The idea of a lover of truth devoting his life to propagating falsity is not the least of the many absurdities testing the credulity of the literal reader of the *Republic*. The so-called just regime "produces such men in the city not in order to let them turn whichever way each wants, but in order that it may use them in *binding* the city together" (520a). Such a city, where all three classes forgo happiness to serve an abstract definition of happiness, conclusively demonstrates the absurdity of reductively defining justice as the suppression of eros. The practical question of who gains emerges here. Human nature would not allow such a city to come into being unless it was conceived by the desires of some invisible party. Logic demands that we deduce the existence of a wolf in shepherd's clothing who uses this definition of justice to seek his own advantage. "No, Virginia, he is a Tyrant."

Now that philosophy has been contrasted with telling effect to the delusory order of the cave, Socrates can tell of the disintegration of this supposedly just regime. His objective, all along, has been to show Glaucon how impossible the conservation of such a city is, even in the unlikely event that all the prior conditions for its genesis are met. It is thus necessary that his argument derive from the divided state of his young comrade's soul. Half of Glaucon, his oligarchic side, is attracted to the material allure of the unjust life; the other half, his spirited side, is attracted to power and the prospect of resolving the divisions that plagued Athens. Accordingly, Socrates uses both practical and moral arguments to show Glaucon that his desire for power is both impractical and immoral.

Socrates demonstrates how this division within Glaucon's soul will cause his city to degenerate with dramatic swiftness. Glaucon has already acknowledged that Socrates, through his discussion of philosophy, had indicated the existence of a still finer city and soul than those described to him (544a)—regime characterized by temperance rather than coerced continence. It now remains for Socrates to drive home his advantage and to help Glaucon recognize every propensity toward injustice in his soul.

In book 9, Socrates offers a model of a compound creature: a human exterior enclosing a many-headed beast, a lion, and a man (588c–589a). Glaucon can no longer believe that some are born wearing spurs while others are destined to bear saddles. Although explicit reference is made to Hesiod's account of the ages of man, the myth of the three metals seems to be derived from Hesiod's threefold classification of human types: those who think for themselves, those capable of being advised, and those incapable of being advised.[11] Socrates points out that all three elements are present in every human soul. In other words, Hesiod's classification cannot be the basis for a doctrine of human essences; it reflects the temporary balance of power prevailing in every soul.

This recognition further discredits the ingenuous statement that the failure of its eugenic class structure brought about the seemingly just regime's degeneration (346a–347a). It is hard to comprehend the jargon that Socrates uses to explain this process, and harder still to resist the inference that he does not intend to be taken seriously. It seems far more likely that this pseudomathematical Pythagorean gibberish is the language of the appearance of learning which is used by the Guardian class to conceal their true motives. The Guardians' model seems to be Aristophanes rather than Pythagoras. The truer reason for the degeneration of this polis lies in the failure of the rulers to resist the temptation to enslave the Artisans and to flaunt both power and wealth. It is evident to Adeimantus that Glaucon's soul is in a similar condition (548d); the young aristocrat is not inclined to sacrifice his relishes. It is inevitable that Glaucon's blinded *thumos* (spiritedness) and starved desires would turn against each other. After depicting Glaucon's soul as it is, Socrates then describes the evils that would result if Glaucon and his city were to progress without education.

Tyranny, desperate and shameless, here becomes the main subject of discussion. Socrates has already revealed that it is immoral and impractical, and Glaucon now learns that even the considerable and impressive material advantages accruing from such a life are inherently undesirable. He finds that tyranny results from reason's failure to bring the desires into a harmonious relation. This failure introduces insecurity, faction, selfishness, and a struggle between the wealthy and the many: "the city of the poor and the city of the rich, dwelling together in the same place, ever plotting against each other" (551d). Justice becomes the advantage of the stronger. These conditions of ignorance and despair set up a vicious dialectic between insecure anarchy and brutal authority which reaches a crescendo in the shameless violence of tyranny.

Socrates' discussion of the tyrant is consistent with his fundamental position that ignorance is the cause of evildoing. The desires of the tyrant are similar to those roused in a man lacking a healthy and moderate relation to himself: "When his reason is asleep . . . his beastly and wild part, gorged with food and drink, is skittish and, pushing sleep away, seeks to go and satisfy its dispositions. . . . It dares to do anything. . . . [It is] rid of all shame and prudence" (571b–c). This "terrible, savage, and lawless form of desire is in every man" (572b). Socrates has already avowed that every soul can be enlightened; however, if man abuses this daimonic capacity, the most unfortunate consequences could ensue. A soul becomes tyrannical when this part of man becomes "drunken, erotic, and melancholy" (573c). Glaucon now readily agrees with Socrates that one who sees through the facade of pomp set up by the Tyrant would find him to be slavishly dependent, exceptionally fearful, poverty-ridden, and insatiable. The Tyrant is not the omniscient and omnipotent Guardian he claims to be; he is, in Winston Churchill's memorable image, a fearful dictator perched precariously on a hungry tiger.[12] Even the gaudiest pleasures of his life are illusory because they give only temporary respite from his infinite neediness and make his desires more insatiable, even as they are appeased.

Book 10 brings this feast of poetry to an appropriate conclusion by considering the issues involved in the famous quarrel between poetry and philosophy. Although the *Republic* is notorious for its stated hostility toward poetry, Socrates' single-handed performance violates all the dramatic guidelines set forth in book 3—further evidence that the *Republic* is a satirical work.

The serious issue in book 10 concerns the proper relation of philosophy to poetry. In Chapter 5 I argue that they stand in the same proportion as reason and desire; poetry provides reason with the eros that philosophy needs to educate and inspire both cities and souls. Philosophy protects poetry from the tragedy of a profligate and disorderly eros that falls victim to tyranny. True poetry is "not only pleasant but beneficial to regimes and human life" (607d); by this, Plato does not mean sycophancy to the status quo, but poetry which reminds the soul of its true regime and loves. The *Republic* is an example of genuine philosophic poetry.

Plato's principal disagreement with the poets is over their belief that imitation and habituation are the principal tools of education. In the seemingly just regime we saw that painting was the paradigm for statecraft. In book 4, the fashioners of the city were painters who possessed the best knowledge of what was appropriate for the various parts of the city (420c–d). Then again, in book 6 we are told of painters who "take the city and the dispositions of human being, as though they were a tablet . . . which in the first place they would wipe clean" (501a). This is meant literally; at the end of book 7 we are told that the just regime could be founded only by exiling everyone over the age of ten and taking over their children (541a). This ex nihilo model of statecraft is totally inconsistent with the Platonic methods of erotic midwifery and recollected discovery. I have tried to show how the *Republic*, once it is approached as a satirical work, is consistent with such precepts.

Socrates prefers the quiet delights of discovery and midwifery to the profane pleasures of creation. He resembles an archaeologist as he lovingly recollects, recovers, and preserves human virtue. The image of the sea Glaucus is very suggestive here: "We no longer see his original nature because some of the original parts of his body have been broken off and the others have been crushed and maimed so much . . . that he resembles any beast rather than what he was by nature. We see the soul in such a condition because of countless evils" (611d). One could observe, sotto voce, that the *Republic* has suffered the same fate.

Glaucon must now restore to justice what Adeimantus and he unjustly borrowed from it: the good reputation it enjoys among gods and men (612d). This he does readily, choosing the just soul over the unjust city. Thus, instead of imitating that Corinthian Glaucus who was eaten by his own horses after he fed them human flesh, Glaucon emulates Glaucus the Lycian, who exchanged his gold guardian's armor for the bronze of a mere mortal.[13] Although Homer thought Glaucus deranged, we join Socrates in applauding this choice.

2   Protagoras and the Myths
of Sisyphus

The very readability of the *Protagorus* makes it only more difficult to discern the difficult line of thought that Plato follows.[1] Given the relative obscurity of the mythic subtext, Socrates' seemingly fractious dialectic appears in a very unfavorable light relative to the urbane pedagogy of Protagoras, the grand old man of the fifth-century enlightenment. Even though he is often disconcerted by Socrates' tiresome desire to score cheap debating points, it is Protagoras who tends to make a better impression on contemporary readers. This dialogue thus resembles the *Parmenides*, in which the wise old Eleatic effortlessly disposes of the upstart Socrates' facile and tendentious objections. Plato's unhappiness with Socratic sophistry is apparent; he seems to be exposing the shortcomings of his teacher while awaiting the messianic arrival of an Eleatic stranger or a Macedonian student.

Yet although with Plato's typical evenhandedness he builds up the strongest possible case for Protagoras, the mythological subtext of the dialogue both vindicates Socrates and reveals the completeness of his triumph over Protagoras. Although Plato's description of Protagoras is very attractive to many modern intellectuals, I suggest that Plato does not share this preference. From this vantage, the *Protagoras* is an exposé of the nihilistic soul and pessimistic beliefs of the pusillanimous "wise-guy." The theme of the unity of the virtues is not merely a curious Socratic doctrine, it is also the motif that holds the *Protagoras* together. Further, readers are required to practice courage in striving to hold the dialogue together; they cannot be content with regarding it as a source of interesting but ultimately disparate ideas. I have already employed this regulative idea in my reading of the *Republic*, with satisfactory results.

When Socrates, in the *Republic*, rejected Glaucon's naively cynical supposition that the just life was not justifiable in terms of pleasure, he did not provide an explicit demonstration of this point. Glaucon's understanding of pleasure was too immature for such an endeavor; it needed interlocutors of greater age and sophistication. The fullest treatment of the erotic happiness to be derived from philosophy appears in the *Symposium*, but the *Protagoras* continues the argument from where it left off in the *Republic*, providing a more positive account of the inherent and natural connection between virtue and happiness. The dramatically earlier context of the *Protagoras* also reveals the intellectual sources of Glaucon's view, which turn out to derive from the sophist's low assessment of human nature. In opposition to this view, Socrates will advance the position that the best life combines the five archetypal virtues of wisdom, temperance, courage, justice, and piety. He suggests, contra Glaucon, that the good life cannot be defined as a sterile state of obedient orthodoxy. Virtue is embodied in a heroic life; it rises above the mimetic mediocrity of the herd through independent thought and courageous deeds.

Our discussion of the *Protagoras* focuses on the special role played by courage in unifying the various human virtues. We shall also observe a fundamental divergence between Socrates and many other philosophers on the meaning of moral knowledge. The *Protagoras* suggests that man will experience the highest happiness when he acts in thoughtful and erotic accordance with the heroic virtues. This view differs from that held by those who aspire to the serenely unmoved inactivity of cosmological contemplation. According to them, pleasure and pain are no more than two impostors held at arm's length by the moral virtues of courage and temperance; the moral virtues, being concerned with the lower things, are auxiliary and do not participate in the highest intellectual virtue.[2] While this chapter will duly proceed to examine the intellectual roots of this position, Socrates' curious claim of virtue is the truest form of pleasure demands to be examined first.

This seemingly hedonistic position is best approached as a restatement of Socrates' seldom believed statement in book 2 of the *Republic* that true human virtue is desirable for both its intrinsic qualities and its extrinsic consequences. In the context of the *Republic*, Socrates had recourse to a reductio-ad-absurdum argument. He refused to satisfy Glaucon's demand for a demonstration of how a perfectly just life could be happy amid extreme conditions of pain, injustice, and obscurity.

Socrates could never construct such an argument because of his belief in the public potency and private efficacy of the practice of virtue. We may better understand that the celebrated Socratic precept that injustice does grave and lasting damage to the soul (*Gorgias* 524c–525a) when we realize that doing injustice affects the capacity of the soul to know genuine pleasure. Conversely, the practice of virtue concurrently prepares the soul to apprehend happiness. Socrates' ultimate position, as expressed in such dialogues as the *Symposium* and the *Phaedrus*, seems to be that the unification of the virtues leads to a qualitative leap from pleasure to happiness. Happiness in this light is an ecstatic and erotic condition that, unlike the pleasures, does not exclude self-knowledge. The *Protagoras* precedes the erotic ascent described in the *Symposium*. Socrates is in love with Alcibiades, but as he remarks to his unknown companion at the beginning of the dialogue, his encounter with Protagoras made him quite oblivious to the presence of Alcibiades (309a–b). Not the beauty of Protagoras but the divine presence of Hermes made him aware that Alcibiades was merely the sign of beauty and not the signified itself.

The body of this chapter is divided into three parts. The first explicates the dramatic background of the *Protagoras:* various significant historical and literary details that were obvious to Plato's original readers are entirely foreign to us but essential to my reading of the dialogue. The second part scrutinizes the "great speech" of Protagoras and brings to light certain concealed pessimistic and misanthropic presuppositions that constitute the dark underworld supporting the optimism of the Periclean Age. The third part moves from discussions of the writings of Simonides and Hesiod to contrast the respective views held by Socrates and Protagoras regarding the possibility and nature of a virtuous life. The status of courage and its relation to the intellectual virtues turn out to be the crucial point of divergence. Socrates' views on the unity of the virtues also partially account for the relative obscurity of the mythological underpinnings of this and many other dialogues. I further contend that two paradoxical Socratic doctrines, "only ignorance causes evil" and "virtue cannot be taught," become comprehensible in the light shed by the *Protagoras*.

I

The dramatic date of the *Protagoras* immediately precedes the Peloponnesian War and predates that of the *Republic* by about twenty years. Consequently, the tone of the dialogue is not as pessimistic as the tone of those that are set in later, more desperate times and reflect the ethos prevalent in the last years of the Peloponnesian War. Plato uses this dialogue to critique the so-called fifth-century enlightenment.[3]

It is fitting that Protagoras should serve as the mouthpiece through which many attitudes and assumptions of Pericles, whose close friend and adviser he was, are presented and refuted. The Periclean combination of optimistic rhetoric and opportunistic practice left Athens ill prepared for the great struggle with Sparta. Filled with exaggerated notions of their destiny to rule, many ambitious young Athenians felt that the virtues of boldness and improvisation would be sufficient to withstand the enormous resentment that their haughty imperialism had generated throughout Greece. The great speech of Protagoras echoes Pericles' funeral oration; both speeches support Thucydides' suggestion that the Athenians believed themselves to be beyond morality. *They* were the measure of virtue.

The dialogue is recounted by Socrates almost immediately after the conversation with Protagoras that it reports. No other dialogue is related as directly. We actually follow Socrates out of bed to his encounter with Protagoras. The effect is to suggest that the narrative is as realistic and uncontrived as anything that we could expect to get from Plato. Even though the unframed dialogue is evidently a poetic contrivance, no other *narrated* dialogue is related on the very day of the action that it describes. Indeed, many of these narratives begin with elaborate accounts of the roundabout fashion in which they were transmitted. In other words, readers are reminded that they are *not* encountering a Platonized Socrates made young, beautiful, and musical. The foresight and courage that Socrates manifests are emphatically his; they will be the basis for the respective doctrines of the forms and eros in dramatically later works.

Socrates is abruptly awakened by Hippocrates, a young man eager to be introduced to Protagoras as a suitable student. It soon turns out that Hippocrates cannot distinguish between becoming a sophist and merely buying what a sophist has to sell. This is significant, for lessons in sophistry were not to be purchased like a course in riding or wrestling; the student of a sophist also "participated" in the beliefs and practices of his teacher. That is, sophistry was not simply intellectual salesmanship; it was also a way of life. The itinerant sophists were wholesale distributors of what their students would soon disseminate throughout the body politic at the retail level.

While deferring the question concerning the sophist's wares, I propose that the real problem with sophistry resides not in the particular skills or knowledge dispensed by the individual "wise guy," but in the assumptions underlying its practice. In other words, we are being asked to identify the essence of sophistry, which seems to be distinct from the "swarm" of specialized sciences that derive from it. Protagoras identifies himself with this essence; he places himself above other sophists who dispense merely individual skills instead of sophistry itself. This distinction also explains the eagerness of Hippocrates to meet with Protagoras and him only. Although Athens is teeming with sophists, they are ignorant of the meaning of their activity. Protagoras the super-sophist suggests in his great speech that he is not merely more self-conscious than the others but also the only one capable of curing the problems caused by them.

Protagoras is staying at the house of Callias, a relative by marriage of Pericles and the richest citizen of Athens.[4] Socrates observed in the *Apology* (20a) that Callias spent more money on the sophists than the rest of Athens put together. It is also relevant to recall Socrates' statement in the *Meno* (91d) that Protagoras earned more money as a sophist than Phidias and ten other sculptors put together. Some idea of Callias's munificence toward the sophists may be gained from Socrates' wry observation that the room occupied by Prodicus had once been used as a strong room by Hipponicus, the father of Callias (315d). There are no longer any valuables left in the room—only sophists, who are doubtless responsible for this evacuation in more than one sense. Socrates also compares the house of Callias to Hades, and we should recall that Hades was the god of both death and riches. The connection with Pericles is also important: since Callias's mother was previously married to Pericles, it likens Athens to Persephone who, like the former spouse of Pericles, has been given over to the House of Hipponicus and Protagoras. Delicate suggestions regarding Pericles' shortcomings as a father (and statesman) are scattered throughout this dialogue. Callias is merely the son of Pericles' ex-wife, but the sons of Pericles (his half-brothers) are present as well, displayed by Socrates as proof that knowledge cannot be passed on from father to son. Protagoras, like Pericles, believes that a democratic polis must be headed by a prudent aristocrat who can generate the emotions of justice and shame (*dike* and *aidos*), which hold a political community together. Pericles is also the model Protagoras implicitly uses to describe and defend his understanding of political virtue. A good example of this implied parallel is Protagoras's contention that a man can be bold without being courageous, which corresponds to the charge that, despite his bullying style of diplomacy Pericles was ultimately timid in his military actions toward Sparta. The *Protagoras* can be read as an account of the uneasy conclusion of the Periclean Age: it represents the *consequences* of Pericles' commissions and omissions.[5]

When Socrates and Hippocrates arrive at the sophist's port of call, they find that many of the best and brightest young men of Athens and other parts of Greece have already been seduced by this new Orpheus and brought down to Hades. As we were reminded earlier, Protagoras has been in Athens for some time (310b). The *Protagoras* may be read *subtextually* as the story of Socrates' Odyssean descent into the realm of a Circe-like enchanter who used the promise of easy success in life to reduce many distinguished young Athenians to the moral stature of beasts. These future helmsmen of the ship of state, bewitched by Protagoras, are for the present delivered by Socrates, but their fate is already sealed. Like Persephone, the young men have eaten the food of Hades and cannot be fully rescued from the underworld.[6] Many of the figures Socrates and Hippocrates encounter in this land of the dead will earn a certain notoriety in the future. But with the exception of Alcibiades, not one of the young men here contributes to the discussion; it is as if they had all lost their wits through Protagoras's Circean musical speech and weaving motion (315b). Socrates, though not to blame for their corruption, is a convenient scapegoat.

Socrates and Hippocrates discover Protagoras flanked by two other sophists; by means of two short, sequentially reversed quotations from the *Odyssey*, Socrates suggests that he is in the company of two of the dead souls whom Odysseus met in Hades: Heracles and Tantalus.[7] On one side of Protagoras is the Heracles-like Hippias, who, despite his many technical skills, was shown in the *Greater Hippias* to be comically lacking in humility and self-awareness.[8] On the other side, we find the notorious logic-chopper Prodicus, whose booming voice cannot be heard (316a). Tantalus-like, he is trapped in his own torrent of words and cannot cross over to the world of deeds. In the language of deconstruction, one could say his words are related only to other words and have no connection to reality. Both shades have fallen away from Olympus. Heracles is but a wraith of his truer self that is feasting with the gods, while Tantalus, the only mortal entertained in Olympus, was banished because he chopped up his own children and fed them to the gods.[9] Individually and together then, both figures point toward extreme disjunctions between words and deeds.

The figure between these two personages in Odysseus's account is Sisyphus,[10] whose very name is derived from a redoubled form of *sophos*.[11] Although I expand on this point later, note here one marvelous instance of Platonic imagery and two rather telling consequences of this identification. There is first the delicious recognition that like the historical Protagoras, Sisyphus functions as a porter carrying a heavy load in Hades.[12] This image seems to corroborate the identification of Protagoras with Sisyphus. Additionally, by choosing the redoubtable figure of Sisyphus to represent Protagoras, Socrates is implying something about sophistical or shadow virtue. Also of more than passing interest is the old story that Sisyphus was the real father of Odysseus.[13] Protagoras's claim to be old enough to be the father of all those present (317c) should be taken with some seriousness in this context: Socrates-Odysseus must take some care to show that he is not a son of Protagoras-Sisyphus. Recall that in the *Apology*, Socrates named Odysseus and Sisyphus among the persons he would most like to interview in Hades (41c). The *Protagoras* offers a conversation, or duel, between these two wily men.

Socrates' mission in this underworld is quite clearly defined: he must show that philosophy and sophistry stem from different sources and try to deliver some of the young souls in Hades from the mouth of the sophist. His failure with many of the best young Athenians of this generation does not mean that human virtue is impossible. If anything, the *Protagoras* provides ample illustration of how courageously Socrates tried to show his fellow Athenians the value of the good life. Its early dramatic date suggests that the damage was already done when Socrates' public ministry began; we must not be too quick to blame him for their failure to learn virtue.

This point is driven home when Protagoras goes on to claim that Homer and some of the most eminent poets were the progenitors of the sophistical movement (316d–317a). In claiming to be their heir he is not merely flaunting his ascendancy over the declining house of Callias; he is proclaiming himself the successor to Pericles and the teacher of all of Hellas. Like his doorkeeper, Protagoras seems to hold that anyone who engages in discursive speech is a sophist. This claim is not as absurd as it seems: we must remember that the Athenians looked on Homer and the poets as we regard statesmen and founding fathers and could and would adapt a Homeric saying to suit any context and occasion. This skill, while bearing a great resemblance to Epimethean afterthought and sophistry, has little or no similarity to anything philosophical: reason is used to rationalize and justify what seems desirable to a given man; it is not the measure of what is rational and good for man—the so-

phistical interpreter is. Another subtextual theme is introduced when
Protagoras compliments Socrates on his *prometheia*, his literally
Promethean quality of forethought (316c). Protagoras soon proceeds to
interpret the story of Prometheus in a manner appropriate to the present context, as poets and tragedians have traditionally done. By
retelling this myth he demonstrates his claim that he is doing openly
and boldly what Homer and other wise men had been doing covertly.
As Protagoras implies, philosophy is the newcomer and interloper here;
the authority of traditional, pseudoprudential sophistry is unques-
tioned in *his* city. The wise guy is the measure. Protagoras, the foreigner, is courteously warning Socrates that they are on *his* home turf.

II

Socrates challenges Protagoras to explain how he can profess to teach
the political art in a democracy (319b), thereby setting a neat trap that
the sophist deftly evades. The dilemma is as follows: if virtue can be
taught, then the very basis of democracy is deficient, since it presumes
that one man's opinion is no better than another's. By positing this art
of political success, Protagoras cannot but offend the many since he is
calling their sovereignty into question by implying that democracy is
not the best form of governance. By teaching this art, however, he will
also give offense to the oligarchic elements, in two ways: by making
this art available to all who can afford it, and by implying his superiority to men (although no oligarch, Pericles is certainly a good example)
who cannot pass on their political skills to their sons or heirs.

Protagoras responds to this challenge with characteristic aplomb. He
asks Socrates whether he should answer in the form of a reasoned dis-
quisition or tell a story. Many of the company (literally, the *polloi*) ask
him to use whichever form he prefers (320c). Protagoras finds it more el-
egant to tell them a myth. This is consistent with his claim to represent
what is traditional and authoritative in the city. We must not suppose
that making man the measure allows moral and political anarchy to
reign. It is through pleasant and uncoerced persuasion that the opinions
of many are brought into harmony. Protagoras also must distinguish
himself from the various other sophists and the respective skills that
they teach. Currying sympathy with his audience of wealthy young
dropouts, he says that the other sophists maltreat their students by forcing them to resume study of the very arts that they had "rejected"

(318d).[14] Protagoras thus craftily places himself on the side of the wise men of the past and opposes these newfangled arts. Since these arts are the cause of the many problems that beset the polis, he will offer himself as the provider of the god-given cure. He thus defends tradition and attacks the rationalistic excesses of the sophists and Socrates.

Protagoras recounts the story of the creation with certain subtle changes. According to the traditional account, Prometheus made man out of clay.[15] Protagoras alters this story to claim that the gods formed all the animals, including man, from a mixture of earth and fire (320d). The task of Prometheus and his brother Epimetheus was to equip these animals with appropriate powers before they were brought out of the earth. According to Protagoras, Epimetheus endowed all the animal species on the basis of the principle of compensation: to ensure that none of the species would be wiped out, he tried to provide each one with some means of protection. When he came to man, the last animal, Epimetheus realized that he had no powers left to give him (321e).

What would man have been if Epimetheus had not failed him? It is clear that he would have been like all the other animals in having instincts (an Epimethean endowment) instead of Promethean forethought. Further, because Epimetheus was primarily concerned with the endurance of the species, one can deduce that individuality would not have existed; man would have been another herd animal with no need for individuating rationality. Only by the unequally shared Promethean arts were men individuated, so in this sense Prometheus *did* create man as we know him.

Prometheus stole fire and the arts from Olympus because he wished to protect man, the unfinished animal, from the consequences of his brother's folly. He was not pious enough to believe that Zeus would temper the wind for this shorn lamb. The significance of fire has to do with the destructive and form-changing forces unleashed by the Titan's theft. The suggestion is that the productive arts are, by their very essence, intimately connected to fire; as Protagoras states, *techne* cannot be wielded without it (321d). Fire also functions as a sacrificial agent; dealings with the gods assume significance only when individuated men fear death. Protagoras claims that it was by his possession of the divine powers of fire and *techne* that man believed in the gods and began to offer sacrifices to them (322c). Happy animals do not need religion. There is a fairly strong suggestion here that one should reverse this order of causation and see that it was through *techne* that man *needed* to conceive of gods. These anthropomorphic deities are closely connected to the violence unleashed by individualism and *techne*. The various arts would also seem to be related to the many evils that Prometheus (not Pandora, in Protagoras's story) brought to man. Man's unhappiness is thus directly derived from his Promethean endowments and aspirations.

Zeus is not blamed for man's sorrows in this seemingly very pious myth. Instead of saying that Zeus sent Pandora down in retribution for Prometheus's illicit generosity, Protagoras says that the sorrows afflicting man are caused by the arts, the practice of which makes it impossible for him to live at peace with nature (322b). Although the arts did make it possible for man to fend for himself, he could not make war against the beasts. The skill of warfare is thus separated from the arts by Protagoras, who claims that it is not an art but a part of politics (322b); in other words, it is not a technical but a rhetorical skill. He justifies this assertion by saying that men could not make war against the animals when they were divided among themselves (322c), for animals cooperate in herds. Like Circe, Protagoras is intent on overcoming this human alienation.

Protagoras is presenting his own version of the *Theogony*. He describes a chaotic age of Titanic *techne* and claims that it should be succeeded by Zeus-like statesmanship. He can even go further and claim that his art will usher in a divinely ordered age of Kronos which will reverse the chaos caused by the misguided individualism that Prometheus exemplifies. The benefits of the various arts can be enjoyed only when they are all brought under the control of the single master discipline that Protagoras professes to teach. Far from causing human sorrows, Zeus actually sends Hermes down to earth with instructions to preserve humanity by bestowing upon it the gifts of *aidos* and *dike*, which will make man more amenable to his destiny as a herd animal (322c). Men would no longer have individuality or freedom; their actions will be regulated to provide the nearest equivalent to instincts.

Paradoxically, the content of this gift of the gods would be the celebrated Protagorean teaching that *man* is the measure. Protagoras is saving man by leading him away from the dangerous forces of thought and inspiration. Instead of reason and revelation, post-sophisticated man is newly endowed with capacities for shame and respect. Of course, these qualities require the presence of a statesman who uses them to create a harmonious social order. Because the anarchic period of the many arts corresponds to a nasty and brutish state of nature, this condition seems to demand a Periclean master politician who can create the general will of the community. As arbitrary as this might seem from without, its internal cohesiveness will more than compensate for any deficiencies from an inaccessible standpoint of objective truth. The gospel / goodnews that Protagoras brings from Zeus is that mankind cannot gain any positive knowledge of the gods. Recall Protagoras's own words: "concerning the gods, I am unable to discover whether they exist or not, or what they are like in form; for there are many hindrances to knowledge, the obscurity of the subject and the brevity of human life."[16]

Unlike the various arts, each granted to only a few practitioners, Protagoras claims that the qualities of *aidos* and *dike* are distributed by Hermes to the entire human species (322d). We now understand Socrates' ironic suggestion, at the beginning of this dialogue, that Alcibiades' Hermes-like beauty was overshadowed by that of Protagoras (309c). The sophist urges Athens to reject the Pandora-like Promethean arts and instead embrace his gift from the gods. Protagoras states that *aidos* and *dike* are not innate but acquired by instruction. The greatest sin is the rejection of these god-given virtues; anyone who is incapable of them should be put to death as a plague to the city (322d). Here again, Socrates and the other sophists are warned by Protagoras that their speculations into the accepted *nomoi* (customs) of the city are impious. Protagoras self-consciously plays the role of Hermes in his myth; as a divine ambassador he warns against rejecting Zeus's gifts in favor of the disruptive Promethean teachings of Socrates and the sophists.[17]

Protagoras's oration concludes with a magnificent description of this cooperative venture of building the various virtues, a task he identifies as the activity all citizens must participate in to the best of their abilities (327d). He reproaches Socrates for failing to see that the whole political community is engaged in this task of teaching human virtue in one way or another (327e). Socrates demands that there be individual teachers of all virtue; he neglects to see the value of the many as he concentrates on demanding the ideal one. Protagoras describes himself with ponderous modesty as the one who excels in this art of assisting others to make some progress toward *dike* and *aidos* (328b). Through this great speech he promises the best and brightest young men of Athens that by following his instruction they may serve as worthy leaders of the School of Hellas.[18] In other words, they can learn to teach *dike* and *aidos* to the Athenians and their empire.

Protagoras's speech successfully combines the outward appearance of praise of democracy with a concealed reassurance that such a democracy must ultimately depend on a few wise guys: men who would im-

provisationally preserve the unity of the regime and develop all necessary virtues in the citizenry without being obligated to practice them
personally. The key to their virtue is not self-knowledge; it is rhetoric:
man can rectify mistakes through rhetoric instead of having to undertake the impossible task of self-improvement. According to this way of
thought, Epimetheus's real error was to allow Prometheus to intervene
instead of trusting in his powers of speech. In truth, of course, Prometheus's mistake was to give in to Epimetheus's persuasion and allow
his brother to equip man. Prometheus's competence is in deeds;
Epimetheus can only make speeches.

Although Protagoras identifies himself as Hermes and endows himself with Zeus-derived authority, we must remember that according to
Hesiod, it was Hermes who gave Pandora to Epimetheus. Epimetheus
accepted her despite Prometheus's warning that his brother should not
accept any gift of the gods. Hesiod says that before Pandora's descent,
and thanks largely to Prometheus, the human state was pleasant indeed: "The tribes of man had previously lived on the earth free and
apart from evils."[19]

Hermes was also commissioned by Zeus to teach Pandora "lies and
wheedling words and the treacherous ways of a thief."[20] Quite apart
from the many parallels with the practice of Hermes, Protagoras's de-
ceitful speech also indicates likenesses between Epimetheus and himself. Like a postmodern, he lives *off* reason and functions *after* thought,
since he suggests that he entered Athens to clean up the mess left by
reason and the various arts. Like the Epimetheus of his tale, he believes
that man would be happiest as a herd animal. It follows that it is the utmost folly for a man to live heroically in accordance with transcendental standards; Protagoras amiably suggests that human failings are only
to be expected. We have also seen that although the Hesiodic myth held
Epimetheus responsible for the dissemination of Pandora's dowry, Protagoras tries to shift the blame for this miscalculation to Prometheus. It
is far from inappropriate that, bearing these facts in mind, we should
regard Protagoras's gift of the gods with some suspicion. It does not take
Socrates long to reveal the very pessimistic views that the benevolent
Protagoras holds concerning human nature. We could say that Protagoras aims to bring about the end of history and the death of individuated
man—the end or *telos* of our species.

Although Protagoras seeks to transfer the responsibility for the unhappiness of man's condition from Zeus to Prometheus, the moral of
the Hesiodic story—the warning against tragic hubris and its desire for

enlightenment—continues to play the same role in its Protagorean retelling. If anything, his rendering is all the more vehement in its warning against enlightenment because Pandora and the enlightenment are identical. There is no need for Zeus to create woman; the seeds of Pandora are sown in the nature of man. Protagoras's fable is a warning against the dangers of education; it is pleasant to his listeners only because they are ill disposed toward what they understand to be a very laborious and tedious process.

Protagoras is openly expressing the very heart of the dispute between Socrates and himself: individual education and communal habituation are two essentially different and inimical processes. Protagoras's position is that it is *ultimately* a wise and sophisticated statesman such as Pericles who serves as the measure according to which the prudential standards, habits, and norms of a given community are constituted. To paraphrase Nietzsche, it is around such a man that a city is formed and created.[21] The power that undergirds this order is the wise cosmologist-statesman who defines, enforces, and conserves the habits of virtue appropriate to his regime. Protagoras proposes to endow the political community with what it should have had by nature; he offers to return man to a pre-fallen age that has never previously existed in history. He finds Socrates tragically hubristic in his public refusal to accept the sovereignty of the polis in matters of ethical definition.

Socrates responds to Protagoras's splendid oration with characteristic irony. He asks whether the human virtues are one or many (329c). He will use this line of questioning to try to make Protagoras reveal publicly that his good news of salvation is based on a pessimistic view of the capacities of human nature. Protagoras cannot afford to take up Socrates' challenge to affirm the unity of the human virtues because such an admission would entail accepting an absolute standard of human goodness and negate his relativistic model of local moralities functioning through the division and delegation of virtues.

In the ideal state that Protagoras has described, a statesman would use the greatest part of virtue, his Epimethean intellect, to form the various other human qualities into a harmonious whole. Protagoras believes that man is a political animal who is happiest when his virtues are supplemented and completed by those of others. It is precisely the disparity between the other virtues that compels wisdom to find its main business in giving them order and direction. Protagoras does not believe that the individual human being can be virtuous in an absolute sense. A man is virtuous according to the norms of his community; Protagoras cannot accept the idea that a community might exist to assist its citizens to attain virtue. Rather, virtues exist so that a species may be conserved.

Socrates soon makes Protagoras acknowledge that the various virtues cannot be both themselves and their contraries (331a), although such a position is the logical consequence of the situational relativism that Protagoras has just espoused. This leverage is all that Socrates needs to force him into conceding that all virtue is one. Protagoras now has to repudiate his earlier concessions and publicly aver that the goodness of a thing is determined entirely according to contextual exigencies and necessities. In other words, he is forced to act in a manner consistent with the position that he has just articulated. He hastily abandons his self-proclaimed pose as Hermes, the divine ambassador, and tacitly admits to being a practitioner of Epimethean improvisational afterthought.

Protagoras's refusal to cut short his answers as Socrates requested is in keeping with the adversarial model that he follows; the issue is not truth but victory or defeat. Admitting that he would have proved no better than anyone else at debate had he adopted the method chosen by his opponent (335a), Protagoras also concedes that it is rhetorical skill rather than wisdom that created the reputation he enjoys. Like the Anaxagorean *nous* (mind), his skill consists in creating the appearance of a cosmos out of chaos. He cannot accept the essences of virtues, because his claim to wisdom depends precisely on a denial of their integrity. He can be wise only in a world lacking inherent meaning. Unlike Socrates, he is wise because he knows that there is no truth.

Given the existence of such a world, it is obvious that *poiesis* (making) must take the place of philosophy if humanity is to survive. Man must create meaning to endure this inherently nihilistic world; simple knowledge of chaos can only nauseate him. Having voiced his concern for man's survival in his speech, Protagoras now challenges Socrates to best him on this, his own ground. The subject will continue to be virtue but will take the form of a contest in poetic interpretation—the traditional manner in which the disguised sophists of the past had handed down political wisdom.

The procedural bickerings that ensue at this point illustrate the significance of the disagreement. Socrates believes that short and direct answers can be rendered because truth is not a creation of rhetoric, as Protagoras, who insists on long roundabout orations, suggests.

III

The text that Protagoras selects is a poem by another itinerant, Simonides, whom he has previously designated as a sophist of the past. Protagoras directs Socrates' attention to Simonides' assertion that it is hard to become a good man. After making Socrates admit that the poem in question is a beautiful and well-written work to which he has devoted considerable study (339b), Protagoras attempts to spring a clever trap of his own. Because Simonides disagreed with Pittacus's famous adage that it was hard to be noble, Protagoras suggests that this poem is inconsistent and thus ill written. The sophist's intention is to force Socrates to recognize the inconsistency of the virtues in a humiliating fashion; by this device he hopes to illustrate the hubristic impudence of Promethean reason and having silenced Socrates, to explain the poem in his usual felicitous fashion. His exegesis would probably emphasize the danger of setting unrealistic standards for human conduct. By making common cause with the celebrated Simonides, Protagoras also strengthens his affiliation with the tradition of poetic statesmanship he has described. It is noteworthy that Simonides was reputedly the first poet to conduct his affairs on a strictly professional basis; he was also well known for his avarice and willingness to flatter tyrants and other rich and powerful men.[22]

Although Socrates claims to be taken aback by Protagoras's sally and the thunderous applause that greets it (339d), his first response shows that he has seen through the cheap distinction Protagoras made between being and becoming. Pittacus said that *being* virtuous was hard, and Socrates suggests that the contradiction in Simonides' poem could be overcome in accordance with Hesiod's view that although the path to virtue is difficult, once reached it is relatively easy to remain at the summit (340c). This, we may gather from the *Republic*, is Socrates' view; virtue is prized both for itself and for its consequences.

Protagoras heatedly contends that Socrates' suggestion contains an error greater than the problem it aspires to correct. All men agree, he says, that the possession of virtue is the hardest thing (340e). Just as Socrates stated his view on the matter of virtue while trying to figure out Simonides' position, Protagoras is now disclosing his own thinking on this subject. His willingness to reject the opinion of Hesiod, his self-proclaimed progenitor, in making this sweeping claim reveals the extent to which he adheres to the position of Simonides. Socrates indicates his awareness of this affinity when he jokingly suggests that *being* virtuous is a terrible (*deinon*) thing (341b). This interjection, often adduced as evidence of Socratic sophistry, suddenly becomes significant. Simonides and Protagoras hold that individual virtue is tragic and hubristic; it is a Promethean benefit that they are anxious to forgo.

Now that these preliminary observations have been registered, Socrates provides his own interpretation of what Simonides meant. Before analyzing his exegesis, however, we should consider the import of the earlier likeness between Protagoras and Sisyphus. As Socrates quoted it, Hesiod's exhortation in *Works and Days* was as follows: "The gods have put sweat on the path to virtue [but] when the summit is reached, hard though it was, then the task is light to keep it" (340d). The contrast to Sisyphus is striking when we consider the inability of that unfortunate to reach the summit over which he aspired to push the rock. Hesiod claimed that there were two ways of life: "One can get for oneself failure in pressing abundance; easily smooth and exceedingly short is the way to her dwelling. But the immortal gods require us to sweat in order to reach success [*arete*]: long and hard is the path to success; and it is rough at first, but when you have come to the top then you will find that the going is easy."[23]

As we observed, Protagoras stressed the ease of the path to success as part of his sales pitch. Socrates now forces him to disclose the converse of this state of affairs: his opinion that true human virtue is well-nigh impossible to maintain. Protagoras's views are very similar to those of Simonides, who said that "all good things come at last to the same horrible Charybdis."[24] In a sense, Protagoras turns out to be more pathetic than Sisyphus; too cowardly and pessimistic to undertake the terrible labors of education, he chooses to lead his students along the smooth and short path to failure. He does not believe in the possibility, subsequently realized by Socrates, of a long and noble life of striving. Promising his listeners a short and easy education, he ends up a Circean enchanter who turns men into beasts.

Socrates' analysis of Simonides' speech reveals his acute awareness of Protagoras' pessimistic views regarding the human capacity for virtue. Socrates first looks to drive a wedge between Protagoras and the many celebrated sages from whom the sophist has claimed descent. He describes an older tradition characterized by silently recollected Laconic wisdom rather than by poetic garrulity (342a–e). It is not inappropriate that Socrates should seem to champion the Spartans in a situation where Protagoras functions as the intellectual lion of Pericles' School of Athens. Socrates claims that the Spartans' virtues were not simply a matter of courage and military prowess; their conduct was based on certain fundamental values that are received and expressed as Laconic aphorisms. The implication is that these truths enabled the Spartans to display fearless composure and practice individual virtue—a conclusion also consistent with Socrates' previous emphasis on the unity of the virtues. These maxims remind the soul of its capacity for virtue, thus allowing courage to be expressed in simple but effective speeches and deeds. Men trained by the sophists in Epimethean glibness and opportunistic confidence would find this Laconic steadfastness to be quite terrible. This is what Socrates means when he describes the *terrible* javelin thrust with which the seemingly inarticulate Spartan reduces his overconfident adversary to childlike helplessness (342e).

We may also find in Socrates' speech, given just before the outbreak of the Archidamian War, a veiled warning, that Periclean rhetoric would not be sufficient to defeat Sparta. The reference to a javelin is especially significant, for Plutarch relates that Xanthippus, one of the sons of Pericles present here, gave wide currency to a day-long discussion between his father and Protagoras about a death accidentally caused by a javelin during a sporting event: was the thrower of the javelin, the sponsor of the games, or the javelin itself to blame?[25] This striking example of afterthought reveals the impotence of rhetoric in the face of deeds: Circe is helpless before the bared sword of Odysseus.[26]

Confronted with the potency of deeds, the rhetorician is unable to disentangle himself from his web of words without great difficulty and delay. His *internally* coherent referential system becomes incoherent in the world of deeds; once all is conventional, it becomes very difficult to deal with what is not amenable to rhetoric. We also recall Protagoras's earlier claim that the art of war was not a technical but a rhetorical skill (322b). Socrates' comparison of the House of Callias to the underworld acquires further credibility when we recall how keenly the inability to perform was felt by the heroes in Hades.

As Socrates points out at the end of his exegesis of Simonides' poem, his own view is that poetic interpretation is frivolous and inconsequential: "Conversation about poetry reminds me too much of the wine-parties of second rate and commonplace people. Such men, being too uneducated to entertain themselves, . . . pay well for the hire of an extraneous voice" (347c–d). Since "no one can interrogate poets about what they say . . . the topic is one on which no one can produce a conclusive argument." Socrates claims that the best people "avoid such discussions and entertain each other from their own resources, testing each other's mettle in what they have to say themselves" (347e–348a). Socrates has used Simonides' poem to describe the state of his interlocutor's soul. Protagoras used this very device, while recounting his creation myth, to accuse Socrates of being a dangerously hubristic sophist.

Having distinguished between traditional Laconic wisdom and cosmopolitan sophistry, Socrates may now proceed to turn the tables on Protagoras and explicitly accuse his opponent's role model, Simonides, of trying to overthrow traditional wisdom. According to Socrates, Simonides wrote his poem with the purely sophistical intent of damaging the fame of Pittacus and becoming the intellectual celebrity of his own day (343c). In opposition to Pittacus's saying that it is hard to be noble, Simonides does not content himself with saying that it is hard to be good. As Socrates reads him, Simonides implies that it is bad to strive to be good, since only those aspiring to goodness can become bad.

Simonides further says, "He cannot but be bad, whom once misfortune irredeemable casts down" (344c). Socrates develops this position to suggest that, according to Simonides, only the good man can *become* bad. Because the man under the grip of necessity has been bad all the time, "the bad man cannot become bad but is so of necessity" (344d). In effect, this means that although being bad is inevitable and excusable, *becoming* bad is culpable. But since becoming bad is inevitable, because it is impossible for any human to remain good, it follows that it is bad to strive to become good. This desire only causes man to sin many times.

Protagoras's great speech sheds light on this seemingly absurd position; recall his suggestion that human happiness can be secured only when all men become herd animals. A heroic individual's tragic strivings after unattainable virtue not only are bad for him but also destabilize the moral fabric of the community he dwells in. This is why Simonides says, "Never shall I vainly cast away in hopeless search my little share of life, searching a thing impossible to be, a man all blameless, among those who reap the fruit of the broad earth" (345c). He prefers a long existence spent reaping the profits of the earth to a short tragic life. Simonides and Protagoras advocate moving away from the impossible quest for a recollected and unified excellence to a pragmatic, less morally demanding measure of conduct which recognizes necessity and human frailty. They stand for enlightened cowardice.

After Socrates completes his explanation of the poem, he invites Protagoras to engage in a direct examination of ideas (347e). The latter consents very reluctantly; his lack of courage is made glaringly evident by the ensuing discussion, which comes back to the consideration of this very quality. When Socrates returns to the original question of whether the five virtues are one or distinct from one another, Protagoras modifies his original statement and concedes that four of these virtues—wisdom, justice, temperance, and piety—resemble one another closely, but that courage is very different (349d). In support of this view, he claims that there are many who lack the other virtues yet are preeminently courageous (349d). He would have courage regulated by the sophisticated intellects ruling the polis; the Guardians who govern the Auxiliaries.

This position is radically opposed to the unity of the virtues, and Socrates asks Protagoras whether he agrees that the courageous man is bold (348e). Protagoras accepts this view and the claim that virtue is *kalon*, the most noble and honorable of things, but distances himself from Socrates' next position: that the difference between courage and foolish boldness is knowledge (350c). He thus refuses to follow this reasoning to the conclusion that it is part of virtue to strive for what is *kalon*. Protagoras says that although all of the courageous are bold it does not follow that all of the bold are courageous (351a). He does not merely exclude the foolhardy from the ranks of the courageous; he claims that there are some possessed of both the intellectual virtues and boldness who are not courageous. The implication is that courage is a natural attribute that can be enhanced by nurturing (351b), but has no link to the intellectual virtues. Boldness, however, derives from skill or passion; it is manifested through rhetoric. Boldness is to courage what deeds are to speech.

As we observed earlier, Protagorean wisdom and statesmanship derive from the insight that the desire for individual excellence leads only to tragedy. The four virtues that Protagoras recognizes—wisdom, temperance, piety, and justice—are derived from the Zeus-inspired revelation that human virtue is impossible. Indeed, strictly speaking, the only universal virtues he acknowledges, *aidos* and *dike*, are clearly antithetical to courage if they are understood according to his dictates of passive conformity. Courage is not simply differentiated from the intellectual virtues; it is the greatest threat to their integrity, since wisdom and courage are seen as mutually exclusive qualities. Wisdom, according to Protagoras's position, generates a sort of intellectual boldness or daring that has nothing to do with the heroic virtue of physical courage. This boldness is exercised through rhetoric to prevent Promethean acts of courage and hubris, which the sophist sees as shortsighted acts of folly.

Of course, this distinction between boldness and courage could become a self-fulfilling prophecy. A reader of Thucydides could muse that whereas a Spartan is courageous without being bold, a sophistical Athenian is bold (in speech) without being courageous (in deeds). The bullying speeches of the bold are no match for the wary but resolute actions of the brave.

Protagoras's belief that human virtue is impossible can be traced even further back, to a lack of courage that makes it impossible for him to endure the difficult path to virtue that Hesiod spoke of. Once Protagoras concludes, however illicitly, that courage is immoral, it follows that expressions of courage or manly spiritedness (andreia) must be suppressed by both mind and polis. He would seek to reduce manly spiritedness to the level of the animal passions; it is not by accident that he is likened by analogy to Circe. His contention that courage is a physical attribute bearing no connection to intellectual audacity would seem to make the disjunction between mind and spiritedness unbridgeable. The purpose of the intellect is to bind Prometheus. Protagoras could never see courage as something necessarily accompanied by intellect in the Promethean sense of forethought. For him, intellect appears on the scene only as an afterthought. Its Epimethean role is to brood, like Minerva's owl, over the tragedy of andreia and demand an end to this vain striving.

In light of Socrates' contention that a moral failing is caused by ignorance, Protagoras's view could be understood as an intellectual deficiency. Courage is essential to knowing virtue because it sustains the soul's strivings toward the good. The issue has much to do with the nature of knowledge, and Socratic self-knowing is an erotic recollection that has little in common with the vulgar cynicism and insecurity that characterize Protagoras's view. In keeping with Socrates' belief in the unity of the virtues, courage must be seen as a kind of recollected imperative knowledge that is aware in advance of the value of what it strives for. Whereas such knowledge is formal and a priori, the intellect functions a posteriori on a parallel track as it traces the tragic history of spiritedness. These two sources must be synthesized if suffering is to produce knowledge.[27]

As Socrates' earlier analogy suggested, Protagoras is a new Sisyphus. His lack of courage may cause him to liken himself to an enlightened Sisyphus, but he is actually too deficient in courage to push his rock to the top of the hill. He would thus find comfort in the bold excuse that he is smarter than Sisyphus because he sees that his task is impossible.

The former porter has to concede that his seemingly more exalted new profession is not really very different from his previous occupation; Protagoras is a Sisyphus who has jettisoned his rocks. To put it crudely, this self-proclaimed "Father of all Sophists" is not just intellectually impotent; he is even unable to carry the burden of being a man. Socrates / Odysseus has clearly proved that Protagoras / Sisyphus could not have been his progenitor—a point subtly confirmed by Socrates' seemingly irrelevant observation that the doorkeeper to Protagoras's domain was also a eunuch (314d). Because of his incapacity for genuine eros, this Kafkaesque custodian anticipates Protagoras in taking Socrates' philosophic talk for sophistry.[28] Plato leaves little to chance!

Although eros is not discussed in the *Protagoras*, the dialogue does begin with a reference to Socrates' erotic pursuit of Alcibiades—clearly a sign of potency. The *Protagoras* points toward dramatically later explications of eros and its Hyper-Uranian origins in the *Phaedrus* and *Symposium*. In the present subterranean context it is inappropriate that such a discussion should take place.

Unlike Sisyphus, Socrates concurs with Hesiod's view that although the path uphill (out of the cave) is difficult, the life of attained virtue is pleasant. Thought requires difficult acts of courage, but courageous acts make it relatively easy for a man to recollect who he is (unlike those in Hades) and to sustain a state of unified virtue. In familiarly Platonic terms we could say that virtue becomes desirable for its own sake once the hero leaves the cave and gains that vantage where he attains some measure of self-knowledge, experiences the harmony of the virtues, and sees the direction to his strivings. (This ecstatic viewpoint is described in much greater detail in Diotima's speech in the *Symposium*, and the palinode in the *Phaedrus*.) We are not assured that human vulnerability is overcome by courageously unifying the virtues; however, this erotic vision briefly confirms the self-knowledge of the philosopher and fills him with hope, before it inspires him to return and grapple manfully with subterranean vicissitude.

Back in the dialogue, Socrates has reached the point where what lies ahead is relatively simple. He must force Protagoras to admit that intellectual virtue requires not simply boldness in thought or speech but moral courage. Once the intellectual and heroic virtues are reconciled and shown to be one, Protagoras's claim that individual virtue is impossible—the basis for his theory of education—collapses. His promise that virtue is easily imparted also stands refuted: the sophistical teaching that *andreia* is impossible can be transferred wholesale, but examination of the life and enigmatic conduct of Socrates suggests that an awareness of the unity of human virtue is earned, one soul at a time, through a life of courageous and thoughtful striving.

Socrates completes his refutation by asking Protagoras about his views on pleasure and pain. When Protagoras agrees that a man who passes his life in pain and vexation cannot be regarded as having lived well, Socrates goes on to connect these unpleasant consequences to an inability to act on one's knowledge of what is best (352d). Protagoras, having previously drawn so emphatic a disjunction between wisdom and courage, now concedes that it would be shameful for him to deny that wisdom and knowledge are the most powerful factors in all human deeds (352d). He is powerless to refute the view of the *polloi* as it is tellingly repeated by Socrates: "Many, while knowing what is best, refuse to perform it, though they have the power, and do other things" (352d). Protagoras must either accept that his conception of knowledge is practically impotent or deny the disjunction between knowledge and courage, on which his reputation for wisdom rests. Socrates then goes on to report the view of the many that being overwhelmed by pleasure or pain leads to the situation just described. This helps one to see how courage is related to the rest of virtue since without it the mind would be overwhelmed by the various desires. To defend the supremacy of the mind, Protagoras has to join Socrates and argue, against the many, that only ignorance can cause the mind to be overwhelmed by emotions that ultimately do more harm than good (357d).[29] It follows that a mind that cannot resist pleasure and pain is ignorant and deficient in virtue. Socrates points out that such an intellect is ill informed. The conduct of the wise man resembles that of the courageous man in that both follow what is good, though doing so may be initially difficult. By contrast, the ignorant and cowardly choose what is easy and deleterious.

Protagoras can no longer resist the admission that courage is knowledge of what should and should not be feared, but he refuses to concede explicitly that this is so (360d). His unwillingness to accept what is obviously true may be seen, with suggestive clarity, to be both ignorant and cowardly. Protagoras also refuses to answer Socrates' final question: Does he still hold to the view that a man can be deficient in the other virtues and yet be courageous (360e)? The point of this question lies in Protagoras's claim that the existence of such men is evidence of the incompatibility of courage and virtue. Instead, since Protagoras has now been shown to be unwise and cowardly, erotic Socratic courage has triumphed over impotent Protagorean boldness.

Although Protagoras has been defeated, Socrates does not provide any positive proof of the efficacy of the good life. It is worth noting that any attempt to formulate such a proof would refute the very position that Socrates has upheld here. This awareness cannot be conveyed (or ported) through purely intellectual means; it can be demonstrated only through courageous conduct. It follows that Socrates' actual courage rather than his often enigmatic utterances must guide us. Courage functions as the sheepdog of the virtues to the extent that it unifies and literally re-collects them. Protagoras's mistake was to postulate that virtue could be possessed in a purely intellectual way; virtue is incommunicable in this manner because it presupposes an unfolding life of heroic striving. Only knowledge understood in this fuller sense, married to courage, engenders virtue. All Socrates explicitly does in the *Protagoras* is reveal how much the formal notion of the unity of virtue implies about its content. Though Protagoras's position has been refuted, Socrates cannot play the role of a porter and physically transfer his own insights to his friends. Only cowardice and cynicism may be conveyed in this contagious manner. We must remember that Plato himself never claims to have been the recipient of any such direct revelations. It is thus entirely appropriate that Plato should rely on playfully concealed mythic allusions to convey the full import of his hero's teachings.

> There is a story . . . that virtue has her dwelling place above rock walls hard to climb . . . and she is not to be looked upon by the eyes of every mortal, only by one who with sweat, with clenched concentration and courage, climbs to the peak. (Simonides)[30]

3 Phaedo and the Socratic Mission

Although the *Protagoras* revealed the pessimism and cowardice underlying the seeming boldness of the sophist, it remained to be seen whether Socrates' own life could measure up to the high standards for human excellence that he affirmed in speech. Protagoras endorsed an Epimethean life of quick-witted improvisation, lived at the mercy of each passing fear and desire. His views made it impossible to speak of a soul in any meaningful sense. The Protagorean self has no depth or psychic substance; it is no more than a continual pursuit of pleasure and withdrawal from pain. This sort of wisdom makes one incapable of honestly participating in a political community. The sophisticated man will never be more than an itinerant opportunist.

Protagoras's reply to these aspersions would be that such a way of life is inevitable, given the absence of demonstrative certainty regarding the basic questions of human existence. Promethean forethought cannot occur in the absence of stable goals or standards. The creation of a false but reliable *mythos* is inevitable when one lacks the *logos*; the common man would prefer living in the cave to the meaningless meandering of the logically examined life.

I suggest that the *Phaedo* provides much evidence for understanding how Socrates overcame this abyss between uncertainty and truth.[1] Socratic irony derives from the double truth that he both knows and does not have: he is morally aware of what he is unable to prove demonstratively and possess objectively. The *Phaedo* shows how Socratic self-knowledge replaces the demand that truth be revealed with demonstrative certainty. Self-knowledge becomes possible in the light of unchanging standards according to which a soul can assess its conduct and goals.

Because Socrates was young and idealistic when he met Protagoras, the old sophist could very well have paraphrased the *Parmenides* and said that Socrates would think differently when he grew older. In reading the *Phaedo*, which recounts the last days of Socrates, we shall ask whether Socratic self-knowledge was sufficient to make our hero unafraid of his fast-approaching death. Then, in the final Platonic text that this book analyzes, the *Symposium*, we shall see whether Socrates was able to meet pleasure with the same aplomb that he displayed in the face of death. Although both the *Protagoras* and the *Symposium* deal with pleasure, these dialogues surely stand in awkward contrast to the puritanical otherworldliness of the *Phaedo*. It needs to be shown how Glaucon's challenge in book 2 of the *Republic*, that the virtuous life be justified in this-worldly terms, can be reconciled with the theme of life negation that dominates the *Phaedo*. If the *Phaedo* is read literally and then analyzed logically, it follows that Socrates has failed Glaucon's challenge. The reader is faced with the daunting task of reconciling these two dialogues.

A proper reading of the *Phaedo* will enable us to confront directly the issues of moral epistemology encountered in the *Protagoras*. His interlocutors demanded knowledge from Socrates just as Christ's disciples desired miracles. Neither group of adherents sought to emulate the way of life that made the prodigious feats of their masters possible. They were happy to elevate their teacher to the status of a divinity because this exempted them from the arduous demands made on their mere humanity. I argue that Socrates was—like Christ—a channel of recollection; no human actually possesses the divine images that so attracted Alcibiades to Socrates. Human beings, however, do possess the power to become aware of the transcendental influences that guided Socrates. The dialogues continually suggest that when a man is properly attuned to himself and understands that he is sustained by a transcendental order, his life becomes a wonder and an example.

Before turning to the *Phaedo*, let me make a general observation: Christianity could not have survived as a religion if it had not been for the disciples' dogged belief in their master's resurrection and continued presence for forty days. Likewise, Socrates' mission in Athens came to a successful conclusion in the thirty days that intervened between his trial and his execution. This lapse of time was probably welcomed by Socrates' enemies. They doubtless hoped that given a full month to review his situation, he would repent of the bellicose and arrogant course of defense he followed at his trial. They must have wished that both his friends and his family would succeed in persuading him to escape prison and go into exile, for such a course of action would have enormously discredited the philosophical career that Socrates had followed over his long life.

Unlike Christ's resurrection, which drew attention to the sacramental character of his death rather than to the virtues of his life, Socrates' conduct before his death served to highlight the precepts that had governed his life. He did not attempt, either implicitly or explicitly, to claim divinity; rather, his purpose was to urge his friends to follow the example he set by living and dying as a virtuous man. We must steadfastly resist the temptation to resurrect the physical Socrates. Not unlike John Brown's soul, it is Socrates' spirit that must be seen to march on. My reading suggests that we should be equally suspicious of any effort made to reincarnate dying Pythagorean doctrines in the figure of the dying Socrates.

I

We begin this analysis of the *Phaedo* by noting serious objections to the possibility of resurrecting the spirit of Socrates in our time. With the possible exception of the *Parmenides*, which sets out to describe an encounter that may never have taken place, the *Phaedo* is more distant from us than any other Socratic dialogue. Unlike the direct dialogues and those texts either narrated by Socrates or mediated through him, the *Phaedo* is recounted by a foreigner in a strange city that enjoys very little contact with Athens. Other than the *Laws*, it is also the only indubitably Platonic work set outside Attica. The true author of this dialogue, Plato, goes uncharacteristically out of his way to say that he was not present during the event described (59b). He is also clearly absent from the conversation between Phaedo and Echecrates that he uses to frame the narrative.

Unlike the *Crito*, in which Socrates' loyalty to Athens is pledged to a trusted old friend and fellow-citizen, the *Phaedo* is most easily read as a repudiation of politics and an affirmation of an almost solipsistic path of purification. This approach has not merely colored interpretations of the dialogue but also exerted a predominant influence on the history of Platonism itself.[2]

The *Phaedo* is further remarkable for the patently specious character of some of its proofs of the soul's immortality. We are bound to ask if such proofs should be taken at all seriously. Phaedo himself attests to the curious combination of laughter and tears that surrounded the deathbed of Socrates (59a). One task of the attentive reader is to separate the comic and tragic elements and decide which genre is to have priority. Ronna Burger suggests that the "Bull-like" expression of Socrates as he drinks the hemlock is a sign that he is seized by fear.[3] But although Phaedo and his spiritual peers are filled with fear as they watch Socrates die—behaving as if Socrates were the bull-like Minotaur and they his victims—it remains open to question whether Socrates is possessed by the same emotion.

This chapter strives to recover the concealed comic subtext of the *Phaedo* and display its consistency with the more erotic and political dialogues. My interpretation is appreciative of the fact that Plato seldom desired to provide proofs in any positive or strictly demonstrative sense. I focus instead on Plato's method of indirection, which operates through the suggestion of contradictions and inconsistencies between the speeches and deeds of the participants in a dialogue. Socrates' irony points beyond the contradictory proofs of the dialogue and toward the strange dramatic context in which he is embedded.

Given these methodological presuppositions, it would seem to be a matter of no small importance to raise the soul of the *Phaedo* from its unreliable material grave. By doing so, we may also recover a truer view of Socrates' own life and purposes. Clamoring for definitive knowledge or irrefutable proofs will only allow the fear of death to overwhelm our far more urgent need to remember how we should live. To die with the same grace and dignity as Socrates, we must live like him. We cannot encircle him, like scavengers, and demand cheap charms that would exempt us from bearing the heroic burdens of humanity. This was surely not the least of the lessons to be learned from the *Protagoras*; the theme returns with even greater existential bite in the *Phaedo*.

My reading of the *Phaedo* takes its orientation from the essential problems of interpretation and misreading that seem to surround this dialogue more than any other. These problems are crucial to the comprehension of any Platonic dialogue, because they draw attention to the ubiquitous question of why Plato chose to write in the dialogue form. In the preceding chapters I have offered suggestions as to why this form of writing was inevitable, given Plato's views on the nature of knowledge and the problem of its communication. The *Phaedo* treats these concerns in about as direct a manner as their subject matter allows. Both Socrates' views on the impossibility of direct communication and his warnings about the danger of "darkness at noon" are well worth heeding here.

By naming this dialogue the *Phaedo*, Plato clearly means to suggest that the identity of the narrator is of more than usual significance. Phaedo and Philebus are the only supernumerary characters for whom the dialogue in which they appear is named. The naming of the *Philebus* is relatively easy to understand because the theory of unconscious hedonism defended by Protarchus was originally expounded by Philebus. But Phaedo apparently does very little to deserve this distinction. Since Plato clearly means to suggest that Phaedo's role in the dialogue is worth drawing attention to, we are entitled to assume that his contribution is made in an editorial capacity. This assumption finds support in the fact that both Apollodorus, the narrator of the *Symposium*, and Euclides, the narrator of at least the *Theaetetus*, subsequently confirmed the details of their stories with Socrates.[4] Antiphon, the narrator of the bemusing *Parmenides*, is the only other source who does not check back with Socrates regarding the veracity of the conversation he reports. Phaedo is also the only *narrator* after whom a dialogue is named.[5] There must be a reason why the *Phaedo* is not more simply called "The Death of Socrates."

It is noteworthy that just as the *Republic* occupies the hours from sunset to sunrise, the *Phaedo* covers events that lasted from sunrise to sunset and therefore should result in a work of about the length of the *Republic*—yet the *Phaedo* is only about a fourth or a fifth as long. Even after due allowance is made for the various conversations that the narrator was not privy to, one must wonder about both the comprehensiveness of Phaedo's recollection and the extent of his comprehension. These reservations seem to support the view that this dialogue, unknown to its apparent narrator, treats the problems of reading and recollection as parallel aspects of the questions concerning the soul's potential for an afterlife. We are entitled to suppose that Phaedo has excluded matters that he did not consider germane to the discussion and has thus at least passively, and perhaps actively, emphasized the features that he considered important. For example, it is clear that the subject of the soul's immortality is of great importance to him. Plato's contemporaries would have known that Phaedo of Elis was taken prisoner during the Peloponnesian War and forced to serve as a male prostitute in Athens.[6] It seems that Phaedo had reason to despise the body.

One final note on the significance of the choice of narrator: when pronounced with the fashionable lisp—which would seem to be in keeping with his childish curls and unfortunate past career—the name *Phaidon* becomes *Phaethon*. This is the name of that unfortunate son of Helios who, in setting out to prove his parentage, attempted to drive his father's chariot across the heavens (from sunrise to sunset) with such disastrous consequences.[7] Among the profound consequences of this identification is the implication that Phaedo's claim to be the heir of Socrates could well prove to be as dangerous an undertaking. This surmise is consistent with Socrates' repeated references to the time until sunset, relating his impending death to the descent of the sun. We are again situated in a region of shadows, inadequate reproductions, and deceptive representations; like the prisoners in the cave, we should leave this suggestively described region in order to understand what Socrates is talking about.

The setting of the dialogue and the intellectual deficiencies of the narrator provide some indication as to how differently the figure of Socrates could be interpreted in a non-Athenian context. In a sense, then, Phaedo's rendering of the *Phaedo* provides further evidence to bolster Socrates' claim in the *Crito* that he could be neither properly received nor understood in a strange political regime (53a–e). It is certainly not the least part of Plato's genius that he manages to convey so much of the words and deeds of Socrates to our vastly different day and age. The *Crito* suggests that Socrates was sufficiently concerned about his posthumous reputation in Athens to portray his death as an ultimate act of civic loyalty. Traditional readings of the *Phaedo* have shown that his fear of being misunderstood was not groundless.

I believe that the various arguments about the afterlife follow a path parallel with Plato's desire that the erotic wisdom of Socrates should survive both the mortality of its principal and the inadequate remembrances of his less acute listeners. In a context where recollection serves as the strongest evidence of the possibility of the afterlife, it seems that the merely literal, and clearly incomplete, memories of Phaedo constitute a body imprisoning the *soul* of Socrates. It is this soul that Plato strives to re-create in his readers through an indirect maieutic process. Although we may scarcely hope to obtain any *direct* proof of this claim, Socrates' presence may be identified by its power to remind us of the transcendental ideas by which he oriented his life. This was the thread of Ariadne that Plato followed as he strove to understand this most enigmatic of teachers.

It is my hope that the Platonic Socrates reconstructed through these readings will be as faithful to Plato's Socrates as Plato's dialogues were to Socrates himself. In other words, Plato's achievement must consist not in his originality but in his ability to recollect both Socrates and the forms that Socrates helped him to discover. Similarly, Socrates' immortality must not depend on the literary genius of Plato. Although Plato is both a poet and a philosopher, his poetry must be seen to derive from his philosophy. The best proof of Socrates' immortality is his scarcely diminished power to remind us, after twenty-four centuries and through several intermediaries, of the truth, value, and beauty of the good life. In other words, this dialogue (and my effort to recover its genuine meaning) is about the *noncontiguous* causality through which Socrates continues to be alive to us.

II

The very first line of the dialogue, "Were you there with Socrates yourself, Phaedo?" (57a), points the reader toward the questions of absence and presence which pervade the *Phaedo*. Although Phaedo *was* present at Socrates' deathbed and Plato was not, Plato's artistry is such that the body of Phaedo's description is enslaved and made to serve a greater master. Athenaeus's Phaedo says that "he never said or heard what he was supposed to have said and heard in the dialogue named after him."[8] This, again, suggests that the form is of greater significance here than the matter of Phaedo's account. Plato's uncharacteristic disclaimer concerning his own absence seems to suggest that he does not offer this dialogue as a literal transcription of the last day of Socrates. His purpose, rather, is to give a parody of Phaedo's melodramatic account. Yet at a deeper level the dialogue is able to intimate what Socrates' dying beliefs were.

Echecrates' next words, "None of the people of Philus go to Athens much in these days, and it is a long time since we had a visitor from there who could give us any definite information" (57a–b), stress the foreignness of the events that Phaedo will describe. Here is yet another suggestion that Phaedo is at liberty to embellish his story and highlight those aspects of the tale that he finds most attractive.

The political experience and context of Socrates' teachings cannot be wrenched out of their Attic context. This position is supported by Jacob Klein's deduction that the Athenians present here are equated with the nine young boys Theseus took with him on his expedition to Crete, and the non-Athenians correspond to the five young girls.[9] Put very crudely, the suggestion is that non-Athenians, like women, are rather more prone to venerate the power of life and overlook that manly capacity for heroic existence that is realized only through philosophic midwifery. Socrates' two principal interlocutors in the *Phaedo*—like Phaedo himself—are foreigners and materialists. The dialogue soon implies that there are two different kinds of materialists: the skeptical Simmias represents the more thoroughgoing materialism; the less evident form of this persuasion is represented by the mystically oriented and life-negating Cebes. Although Cebes believes in the soul, he is not capable of understanding it in terms that are not materialistic. The Pythagoreans and other mystics affirmed the existence of a spiritual substance but generally understood its workings according to certain quantitative, physical, and material taboos. I argue that these prohibitions do not recognize the qualitative distinction between the ideal and the real domains. Efficient causality does not operate at the level of the Ideas.

My theory is that Plato uses the *Phaedo* to defend his recollection of the Socratic legacy against the false and inadequate renderings constructed by less erotic admirers and friends of Socrates. Phaedo himself was reputed to have written six early dialogues; he was also the founder of a neo-Socratic school of philosophy.[10] One not altogether reliable source talks of Plato's hostility towards Phaedo: according to Athenaeus, who is evidently not one of his greatest admirers, Plato was caught in the act of instituting against Phaedo the lawsuit in which Phaedo was charged with being a slave.[11] This external detail lends further plausibility to my claim that Phaedo was not chosen as the narrator of this dialogue on account of his philosophical acuteness.

Like any other Platonic composition, this dialogue should be read as a reductio ad absurdum of its chief interlocutor's philosophic pretensions—in this case, Phaedo's claim to be the beloved disciple of the Socratic tradition. Athenaeus speaks also of Plato's hostility toward all the other disciples of Socrates.[12] Even though Athenaeus wrote about five centuries after the death of Socrates, there may be some basis to these accusations. At the very least, one should not uncritically assume that Plato is well disposed toward Phaedo. Diogenes Laertius tells us that Antisthenes, Aeschines, Euclides, and Phaedo were, after Plato and Xenophon, reputed to be the four most distinguished Socratic philosophers.[13] I suggest that Plato's *Phaedo* is, in effect, a refutation of the portrait of Socrates rendered by a rival.

Phaedo explains that the lengthy delay between the trial and execution of Socrates had to do with an ancient Athenian tradition com-
memorating Theseus's slaying of the Minotaur. No public execution
could take place while a ship—according to the Athenians, the very
ship on which Theseus traveled to Crete—completed its *theorian* to
Delos in honor of Apollo (58b). The word *theorian*—like the ship,
which was called the *theoris*—carries much more meaning than its
standard translation as "mission" conveys. For one thing, though the
ship was regarded as the very vessel on which Theseus traveled to Crete
so many years earlier, the identity was purely formal. Plutarch reported
that all the original planks had been replaced with newer and stronger
timber.[14] As Ronna Burger has observed, the question of whether or not
this was the same ship on which Theseus traveled is very closely linked
to the approaching question of the soul's immortality vis-à-vis its constantly changing body.[15] Plato performs his reconstruction of the story
of Socrates' death in very much the same spirit. It is through the formal
rather than the material elements of the *Phaedo* that the spirit of
Socrates is to be preserved.

Plato's choice of the word *theorian* also suggests a structural parallel
between the mission of Theseus to deliver Athens from the tyranny of
Minos and the Minotaur, and the account that Plato will give of
Socrates' deathbed. The *Phaedo* recounts Socrates' speculative or theo-
retical efforts to rescue the souls of his young companions from the
tyranny of the body and suggests that the body imprisons the soul in a
subterranean labyrinth. Moreover, just as Theseus's mission delivered
the Athenians from the consequences of their envious killing of Andro-
geus, Plato's task is to purify Athens from the harm caused by its foolish execution of Socrates.[16] Not the least damage will be caused by
those who unintentionally render inaccurate accounts of Socrates.
Plato's mission will be complete only when the true spirit of Socrates is
properly recollected and restored to Athens. I find good reasons for suggesting that Socrates was neither a hater of the Athenian polis nor a
misanthropic mystic.

This attempt to enter the labyrinthine subtext of the *Phaedo* and to
reconstruct the battle with the Minotaur tries to reveal the manner in
which Socrates offers an account of the value of human life. We shall
see that such an account overcomes the power of both the Minotaur
and his labyrinth. In effect, Socrates—another spiritually androgynous
figure, as my reading of the *Symposium* will show—overcomes the
state of affairs that made sacrifices to the Minotaur necessary.

For the sake of contexts, we should note that it was during the archonship of another Phaedo, just after the battle of Marathon, that the oracle at Delphi commanded the Athenians to restore the remains of Theseus to a sacred place in their citadel. That Phaedo failed to carry out the directive; it was Cimon who succeeded in bringing back a suitable set of relics to Athens.[17] The playful implication is that this Phaedo absconded with the literary remains of Socrates or at least failed to restore them to their proper political context. Further, an Athenian would remember Theseus primarily as the founder of his polity, not merely as the slayer of the Minotaur. In a sense, then, the mission undertaken by Socrates and Plato is not simply a matter of purging the soul from the evils of the body. Like Theseus's mission, which seemed merely to undertake the appeasement of the Minotaur but actually destroyed its tyrannical rule and substituted a more just regime, Socrates' *theorian* is to deliver the body from fear of the passions by enlightening its desires.

The last and most comprehensive sense in which the *Phaedo* recounts the story of a mission has to do with Plato's portrayal of the way Socrates, in his final days, went about the task of providing a less ironic and more substantial defense of his philosophical methods and procedures.

These matters are not unconnected to Socrates' newfound interest in writing. When he uses a simile after the manner of Aesop, Cebes is reminded to pass on a question from Evenus regarding Socrates' sudden interest in composing poems. Socrates confesses that at many times in his life he had been visited by a dream urging him to work at cultivating the Muses. He had viewed this dream as encouragement for his practice of philosophy, the highest art, but it now occurs to him that the dream was urging him to practice music in a popular (demotic) sense (60e–61b). In other words, he was asked by the gods to make his art more intelligible to the many. Since Socrates, as we have seen, was personally satisfied with his philosophic life, perhaps it is Plato who follows the dream's instructions by providing posterity with a more satisfactory depiction of the living Socrates. The latter part of the *Phaedo* indicates the significance of music in this exceptional context in considering the image of the lyre—treatment supplemented by an account of the flute in the *Symposium*.

Socrates' choice of Aesop as the model for his almost-posthumous literary career was dictated by his view that poetry is imaginative rather than descriptive with respect to its subject matter. Since Socrates could not compose original poetry, he had to content himself with writing a hymn to Apollo and setting the easily accessible fables of Aesop in verse. Plato's dialogues seem to constitute a more adequate response to the divine obligation that was seemingly left unsatisfied by the historical Socrates. [18] A purely factual account of a philosophical conversation is ill suited to the poetic task of bringing out the pregnant significance of that particular event. In the famous words of Plato's *Second Epistle*, Socrates had to become beautiful / noble and young: *kalou kai neou* (314c). The problem of course is that the beautiful myths and rhapsodic accounts of Plato are, for all of their beauty, often expressed in an ironic context. Plato seems to suggest that pleasure and pain are intimately intertwined in the process of becoming acquainted with the *corpus* of his master.

The introduction of the figure of Aesop in this context (although the Platonic dialogues more often use Homer as the most accessible source of themes for philosophical poetry) suggests many parallels. Like Aesop, whose fables were based entirely on similes from the animal world, the Socrates described by Xenophon is not much of a mystic or mythmaker. He was more comfortable with images and examples derived from tradesmen and the marketplace. Unlike the cosmologists who were best known for their impracticality, but like Heracles' adversary Antaeus, Socrates was most formidable when his rough, unshod feet were planted squarely on the ground of everyday existence.[19] The soles of Socrates were faithful to the earth.

To come to grips with Plato's poetics we need to understand that his beautiful myths *do not lead us into a new realm of forms far away from the world of the polis and the agora*. Rather, they demand that we take our stand, alongside Socrates, on this very ground and allow the authority of the ideas to change our view of the world. It is not sufficient for Theseus to slay the Minotaur in Crete; he must complete his mission by bringing his young followers back to the city. And although the *Phaedo* may well reflect Socrates' recognition of his need for reincarnation, it is vital that we assess Plato's contribution to this expedition.

Plato's task of rescuing the spirit of Socrates from the imperfect interpretations of friend and enemy alike parallels the liberation that the corporeal Socrates is soon to undergo. The *Phaedo* is not simply about the problem of reading; it is also concerned with the temptation to indulge in mystical materialism. These matters are not unrelated; by becoming overly involved with the question of the soul's necessary (that

is, material) immortality, one can lose all sense of Socrates' own emphasis on the crucial significance of the virtuous life. The proofs of immortality, so earnestly derived from this highly ironic text, are surely
not the least burden that Socrates' spirit would be liberated from.
Plato's poetic recollections of his teacher are not intended to reconstitute literally or restore physically a *corpus* of pure Socratic wisdom.
The parallels with Christianity are obvious. By remaining fixated on
the physical death and possible resurrection of Socrates, the bad reader
ignores the significance of the moral archetypes that Socrates lived in
accordance with, and died defending. Hegel criticized the Crusaders'
obsession with the empty tomb of Christ for much the same reason.[20]

In light of both Plato's assertion of his preeminence among rivals and
his higher aims, it is appropriate to recall Socrates' observation that
when a person dies, "although it is natural for the visible and physical
part of him . . . to decay and fall to pieces and be dissipated, none of this
happens to it immediately. Indeed, when the body is dried and em-
balmed . . . it remains intact for an incredible time, and even if the rest
of the body decays, some parts of it . . . are practically everlasting"
(80c). For naive readers the improperly interpreted text of the *Phaedo*
will continue to suffer a similar fate. Plato uses the living spirit of
Socrates to remind us, indirectly, of the abiding presence of the transcendental powers. The promise is that these powers will guide a properly lived human life toward true happiness.

Because of its direction toward the soul of one particular interlocutor,
however, the erotic particularity of Socratic pedagogy could easily be
mistaken for mere irony by one ill prepared to recognize his maieutic
objectives and procedures. Not the least part of Plato's accomplishment
consists in the transcending of this irony by cloaking it in terms accessible to a careful reader.

III

When we first encounter Socrates in the *Phaedo*, he is taking leave of
his wife and infant son who have been with him since well before day-
break, which was the accustomed hour for his friends to visit him at the
prisonhouse. Since Phaedo says that on the day of Socrates' execution
they came even earlier than was their habit, it follows that Xanthippe
must have spent at least a part of the night with Socrates. This is Xanthippe's only appearance in the Platonic corpus; even in the *Protagoras*,

the only occasion on which the reader of a Platonic dialogue is allowed to visit Socrates at his home, she is not mentioned. Although Socrates was clearly indifferent to matters pertaining to the family, we are not entitled to conclude that he was totally separate from things of the body. Neither should we forget that he had apparently fathered two of his three children quite recently (34d). Like Moses, he seems to have left this world in full possession of his virility.[21] This inference would also seem to refute Xenophon's suggestion that Socrates concluded his life because of increasing physical debility.[22] His youngest child is tangible evidence that Socrates did not regard the body as the source of all impurity. Although his *indifference* to physical matters, evidenced in such dialogues as the *Symposium*, suggests that while Socrates did not worship the body, he was not a believer in the materialistic taboos of the Pythagoreans either. Instead of filling his last hours with some Orphic ritual or vigil, he spends some of these precious moments alone with his wife. Compassion and concern for his friends and family seem to have outweighed whatever concerns he may have had for his own future.

Socrates says that he is leaving life in obedience to the orders of the Athenians (61c). We may conclude that, although his *theorian* or mission, like that of Theseus in Crete, seems to be a task of quasi-religious appeasement, it actually aims at realizing more profound and less evident political ends. We are prompted to question the apparently religious tenor of his argument that suicide is prohibited because men are the property of the gods, and that it is the gods who would not like them to destroy themselves without divine permission (62b–c). In the *Crito*, Socrates revealed the political basis of his piety: he has not fled the city—a move the stricture against suicide would appear to dictate—because he honors the personified laws of Athens. Socrates said. These far from nebulous entities have nourished and sustained him all his life. If he were the property of gods whose sway exceeded the narrow domain of Attica, he would surely, as a good possession, be bound to take himself outside the dangerous confines of the city. Socrates' refusal, on the grounds of piety, to leave Athens surely indicates that he was not entirely ironic in claiming that his piety is directed toward these deified laws of Athens.

Socrates' civic piety is such that, at the conclusion of the *Crito* (54c) he magnanimously puts into the mouth of the personified laws of his polis words that exonerate it of all culpability: "You will leave this place, when you do, as the victim of wrong done not by us, the laws, but by your fellow men." In other words, the fault lies not in the laws themselves but in the inadequately educated citizens and ill-informed jurors entrusted by the laws with civic obligations. This being the case, Socrates' position is that he is quite content to die, as he has lived, in accordance with the laws of Athens. He is anxious to display, to the end, the consistency between the speech and deeds of a philosopher.

By choosing not to flee Athens, Socrates suggests that the philosophical life is rooted in a polis. Had Odysseus been interested simply in observing many cities and many souls, the desire to return to his native Ithaca would not have animated the *Odyssey*. Likewise, had Socrates been interested simply in theory observation and conversation, the prospect of exile in some other part of Greece would not have been so unattractive. (It is also noteworthy that the teacher of the doctrine of the soul's transmigration, Pythagoras, was himself a transplant and exile from his native land.)[23]

The unprejudiced reader cannot leave the *Crito* without a powerful sense of Socrates' passionate love for Athens. This love must also be understood as an unwillingness to defer, for any future incarnation or location, a task that has been assigned to one particular life, body, and polis. As our examination of the *Protagoras* has established, it is essential that a philosopher should demonstrate his willingness to take his stand, to live and die for his principles. Unfortunately, the tendency has been to read the *Crito* as an essentially ironic work yet to approach the *Phaedo* quite literally. Even the readings of the *Phaedo* that do take an ironic view of the proofs offered of the afterlife ignore the far greater ironies concerning the identity of the narrator and the relation between soul and body.

The peculiar contexts of the *Phaedo* warrant a different approach to the problem of suicide. Many of those present in the dialogue are youths and foreigners who grew up in the dark days at the end of the Peloponnesian War and, consequently, have little or no acquaintance with what it meant to be a citizen of a great polis. They have chosen philosophy not as an excellent way of living but as a way of escaping the daily privations of fleshly existence. Whereas the foreign Socratics toil in the defeated dreariness of postwar Athens, however, Plato recollects the glories of truly human existence that Socrates has enacted in Athens. The mission can be truly fulfilled only when the *theoris* returns to Athens.

As in other Platonic dialogues, the narrator's failure to understand this point of view reflects many of the perplexities and inadequacies of his own soul. The views expressed in the *Phaedo* must not be supposed without further deliberation to be identical with the attitudes of Socrates or Plato. The reader's soul is similar to that of Socrates' interlocutors in being complex and bewildered; it must be contrasted to the composed simplicity that the existential unification of the virtues has produced in Socrates' own soul.

After paying homage to Athens, Socrates turns to the prohibition against suicide. We must strive to understand why Socrates defends this doctrine so earnestly after he has just said that it is natural for philosophers to welcome death. As he points out, it does not seem reasonable to suppose that there are no situations where, for some people, death is better than life: "It probably seems strange to you that that it should not be right for those to whom death would be an advantage to benefit themselves, but that they should have to await the services of someone else" (62b). Cebes' agreement in his native dialect with this proposition suggests that the view is one he has entertained before, in his own thoughts as well as in the company of Simmias. As he stated earlier, Philolaus the Pythagorean, whose company both Cebes and Simmias kept, offered the same prohibition when he was in their company but never explained it satisfactorily. Socrates' urgent desire to warn against suicide would not make sense if death involved merely going before sympathetic judges.

This attitude should also juxtaposed with Xenophon's view that Socrates' death was a judicial suicide.[24] If Socrates expected judges who would view his virtual suicide with sympathy, it is hard to see why these same judges would be ill disposed toward suicides acting under far more urgent and compelling conditions. The issue is not the sanctity of human life per se but rather the significance and purpose of human existence at the distinct but interrelated levels of both city and soul. One cannot reject the possibility that spiritual purification may well occur through the fulfillment of obligations toward the political community.

Socrates is quietly confident in his own preparation for a higher level of existence. The spiritual preparation of his audience, however, is such that they must be exhorted by all possible means to aspire toward a similar level. An existence involving the spirited unification of all the moral virtues is quite distinct from the quasi-materialistic procedures of Pythagorean purification. Socrates must draw this distinction and allow for a transition from the one to the other. With this end in mind he must prevent his disconsolate young companions from taking the path of misology, despair, darkness at noon, and spiritual suicide—ill effects that would certainly result from too sudden an exposure to certain truths about human existence.

Socrates must convince his companions of the immortality of the soul as well as the inadvisability of testing this doctrine before they are adequately prepared for an afterlife. His teaching must sustain their exercise of virtue in the time between the demise of their living paradigm of the efficacy of virtue and the emergence of the beneficial results that only their own practice of virtue can engender. In other words, he feels that they should believe in the soul's capacity for immortality in order to embark on a course of spiritual training and pedagogic activity that may make them worthy of a future existence. The inability of Socrates' interlocutors to respond to true reasoning and their susceptibility to rhetoric demonstrates the inadequacy of their present spiritual state.

Socrates tells Cebes that if he shows *prothumia*, active spiritedness or zealous desire, he may receive a better answer someday (91c). In other words, it is not appropriate for anyone in Cebes' pusillanimous frame of mind to be told that he could face oblivion if he were to persist in his present disposition. Socrates is a midwife of souls, not an abortionist of human potential for virtue. We have seen that Cebes is already familiar with the view that existence is itself quite undesirable. By stressing reincarnation and otherworldliness, one minimizes the value of an individual human life in its relation to the greater scheme of things. The nihilistic prospect of Nirvana becomes quite attractive when one becomes nauseated by the prospect of undergoing countless incarnations; the soul becomes a crushing weight that stifles human eros. This is why the Pythagoreans had to condemn suicide so harshly.

Philolaus's prohibitions against suicide fail to convince because of his inability to explain the value of life itself. Moreover, the arguments that Cebes and Simmias advance against the soul's immortality make a good deal more sense once we see that they are not altogether anxious to be persuaded that the soul is immortal. It follows that they must be heartened by other means, and it is to this end that philosophic music must be employed. In a similar vein, we can see why readers of the *Phaedo* who come to the dialogue in search of proofs of the soul's immortality should not be discouraged. Plato's procedure is both to assure them of this prospect and to urge them toward a level of life that will best prepare them for the afterlife. The *causal connection* between philosophic virtue and the possibility of an afterlife is, for very good reasons, not stressed here. It is more to Socrates' purpose to prescribe a regimen of spiritual preparation that will turn out, surprisingly but pleasantly, to have much more to do with life, and *living*, than with death.

Socrates defends his nonchalant attitude toward his own approaching death by stating that he is leaving the service of good masters to enter the company of supremely good divine masters and of men better than those presently in this world (63b–c). Bearing in mind Socrates' implied identification of the laws of Athens as his guardian deities on earth, one can deduce that he believes he will now pass beyond these created deities to better, Hyper-Uranian gods. He does not expect to encounter other ordinary men in this realm. The veiled implication is that his own, philosophic, life is the only way of gaining immortality. Although Socrates then goes on to state that there is something in store for all those who die, the view that only the best men survive in the afterlife seems intended to convey some uncertainty as to whether *all* human souls are immortal. It is a view quite different from his publicly stated expectation in the *Apology* (40e) to meet and converse with all who have lived.

Socrates' speeches in the *Phaedo* may be seen as an apology for his previous failure to practice demotic music; hence, the reasons he will advance here are rhetorical rather than philosophical. As in any of the dialogues, Socrates exposes the souls of his interlocutors. The *Phaedo* thus consists of a reductio ad absurdum of the philosophy of Phaedo, Cebes, and other haters of life. It exposes the ultimate untenability of any argument for the soul's immortality that derives from a materialistic and pessimistic view of incarnate existence.

More than any other dialogue, the *Phaedo* is a comedy disguised as a tragedy; it may even be seen as the satyr play that concludes Plato's dramatic trilogy (*Euthyphro, Apology, Crito*) recounting the last days of Socrates. It is the capacity for philosophic irony that separates the two kinds of readers who come to the *Phaedo*. Those with less philosophical discernment will view it as a tragic account of how nobly Socrates spent his last hours; they will be led to believe more firmly in the prospect of an afterlife and order their lives in a way that will have healthy *this-worldly* consequences. The second kind of reader will see through the sentimental surface and better understand the scope and limits of prephilosophic rhetoric; only such a reader will understand how a philosopher's love of life can ensure that he will not fear death.

Before Socrates begins his explanation of why it is natural for him to be untroubled and confident in the face of death, he is interrupted by

Crito's warning that the hemlock may have to be administered more than once if Socrates becomes overheated through conversation. Socrates calmly replies that he is willing to take the hemlock twice or even three times (63d–e). Quite apart from the suggestion that talking confers a sort of invulnerability, this refusal to make any change in his accustomed behavior reveals the utmost consistency between the thoughts and deeds of Socrates. Even at the very threshold of death he remains steadfast in his self-possession. Just as in the *Apology* he refused to change his accustomed way of living, even at the risk of his life, Socrates finds his best assurance of immortality in continuing the very activity that has preserved his self-knowledge and made him Socrates.

He next proceeds to draw the distinction between a philosophical life and all other forms of existence, which is supposed to account for his cheerful attitude toward the fate that awaits him. He depicts a philosophical life as one spent studying dying and death. He goes on to claim that it would be absurd for one who had spent his life preparing for this occasion to be deterred from the actual event (67e). Further, if a philosopher spends his life surrounded by the spectacle of spiritual death, he will surely welcome an opportunity to show how life should be lived. It is no coincidence that many of Plato's most explicitly moral dialogues, the *Republic*, the *Protagoras*, the *Gorgias*, and the *Phaedo*, all possess underworldly subtexts.

Simmias observes that the many believe the philosopher to be verging on death already and deserving to die, this being quite consistent with Cebes' previous muttered comment in his native dialect about the virtue of suicide. Socrates responds, tellingly, that the many do not understand the sense in which what they say is true. Although many claim to be philosophers, few understand the true meaning of philosophy: "Many bear the thyrsus but few are devotees" (69d). If the true philosopher loves life because it enables him to live happily and deserve an even higher form of happiness, then Socrates' loyalty and devotion to the personified laws of Athens can be better understood: he is grateful to them precisely because they have provided him with the opportunity of both living a full and happy life *and* dying nobly.

Socrates' objective in the discussion that follows is to show how philosophy must distinguish itself from the traditional processes associated with spiritual purification. Those processes turn out to be too bound up with superstition, materialism, deterministic necessity, and life denial to provide a habitation for the unique needs and capacities of the soul. The subtext of the *Phaedo* deals with the failure of the despisers of life to provide an account of reality compatible with the soul's mission or *theorian* in life. The various fallacious proofs of the soul's immortality that Socrates advances in this context have the implicit effect of proving that man's natural concerns about his soul's continued existence cannot be satisfied by cosmological means. The numerous taboos of the Pythagoreans and cosmologists function in a negative and reactive way: materialistic fetishes cannot liberate the soul from the tyranny of the body.

It can now be seen that Socrates' condemnation of the body and his desire to liberate the soul from its carnal needs are not blanket condemnations of human life itself. Those who regard mortal existence as a sentence of imprisonment should always bear in mind that Socrates saw the goal of punishment as education rather than retribution.[25] Only to those who forget the true meaning and significance of life does it become a term of irrational imprisonment, a punishment only to those who torment themselves by refusing to live properly and well. Socrates never ceased to proclaim that the gods were good and wise masters. The belief that life has a human meaning is what ultimately dictates the Socratic turn from cosmology toward the moral and political concerns of philosophy. Cosmology, to the extent that it regards a man as just another body in motion, subscribes to a mechanistic outlook. In other words, the sort of physical asceticism that Phaedo and the Pythagoreans find so attractive is no more than a sort of inverted materialism. Their perspective fails utterly because it lacks any principle of spirituality of its own. Virtue understood in this fashion is no more than a state of privation that rejects what it concedes as constituting the basis of all reality.

Socrates now claims that the various human virtues make sense only when regarded from the vantage of philosophy. This is consistent with our previous recognition, through the *Protagoras*, of the unity of all human virtue. It also coincides with the position that the purpose of human existence has everything to with the opportunity to unify the virtues in the soul. This idea of the good life is what Socrates opposes to the tyranny of the body. He points out that only the philosopher truly practices the virtues of courage and temperance (68d–69b); the non-philosopher owes his seeming temperance to a preference for other sources of intemperance, and his courage to a fear of greater evils. It follows, then, that only one possessed of an appreciation of the value and meaning of human existence is in a position to practice virtue for its own sake. Although the *Protagoras* seems to endorse a sort of hedonistic calculus, such language is appropriate to its subterranean context.

The erotic temperance or self-understanding occasioned by his upward motion on Diotima's ladder still lay ahead of Socrates, but his basic belief that happiness is a positive state, and not a momentary respite from false pleasure and real pain, did not alter.

At this point Cebes says that Socrates' discussion of the soul leaves the average person with grave misgivings about its capacity for independent existence (70a). It is essential that the reader recognize how well founded these doubts are. Given what Socrates has just told him, Cebes has probably concluded that the *average* human soul is not destined for an afterlife. We have seen something of Cebes' character in his preceding remarks. The question of the legitimacy of suicide concerns him, and many of his queries seem to derive from a world-weariness that would only be encouraged if Socrates were to tell him that most souls will not survive death. Unlike Simmias, who is the more practical of the two (it was Simmias who brought money to try to buy Socrates' freedom), Cebes does not find it difficult to believe in spiritual entities, but he is troubled by the irrationality and blind fecundity that the cosmos seems to display. Recall that it was Simmias who was upset by Socrates' seeming eagerness to die; by way of contrast, Cebes was more disturbed by Socrates' prohibition of suicide. Simmias is the interlocutor more likely to be satisfied by the support given through "the best or most dependable theory which human intelligence can supply . . . assuming we do not have divine revelation" (85d); Cebes is more concerned about the fate of the individual soul. His moments of doubt and assurance alternate like the phases of life and death described in Socrates' first proof. It is essential that Cebes be taught something about the value of the opportunities afforded by incarnate life.

IV

Socrates' first attempt at responding to Cebes' concerns regarding the soul's capacity for an afterlife is couched in plainly cosmological terms. He suggests that the living come from the dead and vice versa in such a way that neither death nor life can ever be viewed as a permanent state of being. In support of this position he voices Cebes' worst fears when he suggests that everything that admits of generation, including animals and plants, comes into being through its opposite state. This theory was first postulated by Anaximander, who said that all things were composed out of the same indefinite *apeiron*, or originary substance;

generation and corruption occurred as the four elements made reparations to one another for their transgressions.[26]

Socrates' first proof is very unsatisfactory. It makes the fallacious assumption that changes in accidental attributes and relative states can
be likened to the substantial change in an individual from being to nonbeing. We must also examine the significance of an *apeiron* that allows
all things to pass over into, and become, all other things. There is no
guarantee that the thing generated out of the *apeiron* is the same as another that passed into it; the only abiding identity is that of the chaotic
substrate itself. But reincarnation is meaningless if some degree of personal identity and memory is not recollected and retained. Such questions of identity continue to beset us throughout the *Phaedo*. I suggest
that the conclusion Socrates would like to derive from this cosmology
of extremes is that personal immortality cannot be established or
proved by making man a part of nature's processes.

We can also try to examine the applicability of this theory to the principles of living that Socrates has just discussed. An exaggerated emphasis
on the evils of human existence could lead a neo-Pythagorean or callow
young pseudo-Socratic to construct a dualistic model of being. Such a
model would define virtue as the ability to resist and deny this life in the
hope of being rewarded by elevation to the higher state of being. The negative and passive content of this way of living naturally makes the idea of
a necessary dialectic of opposites the only way by which any transformation of states could be achieved. The obvious problem with combining
these two dualistic theories, moral and cosmological, resides in the inability of a descriptive account of necessary cyclical generation to accom-
modate an ethical prescription of life renunciation. There is no way to
halt this eternal cycle of regeneration or to privilege soul over body. If the
living can emerge only out of the dead, one must conclude that a soul
cannot stay in the other world indefinitely but will necessarily be drawn
back into the world it so blithely renounced. A truly dualistic account of
reality could certainly not allow contraries to generate each other in this
manner. If the two principles are bound together, the dualism would only
be apparent; reality itself would be monistic and irrational.

Cebes now claims that the theory of recollection provides further evidence in favor of this cosmological proof of the soul's immortality. The
immediate advantage to this theory of recollection is that, if valid, it
would seem to prove that an individual's psychic identity is retained
throughout the process of reincarnation. In practical terms, such a
theory of a priori knowledge could also be used to defend a position of

disengagement from being-in-the-world. It could be argued that the knowledge sought by the soul is inherent in itself. In the language of the *Phaedrus* (253c–e), unlike the insatiably erotic Black Horse of the soul, which lustfully seeks to obtain possession of all sorts of profane knowledge, the neo-Pythagorean's acts of knowledge are like the White Horse of the soul, which speechlessly recollects all manner of eternal truth through the chaste act of contemplation.

The chief weakness of this position resides in its inability to explain why a soul should be reborn if in a previous life it has already gained what was necessary to enter the domain of eternal truth. The terrors of a meaningless cycle of rebirth would seem to overwhelm and exceed the value of any assurance gained as to the continuance of the soul. It is hard to see how the soul could purify itself better while in the profane incarnate state. It would be absurd for bodily taboos and purgative procedures to be the means by which the soul is exalted. This reasoning is followed in Socrates' response to Simmias's argument that the tensions of the body define the soul. Some account of the significance of the possibilities for learning and action afforded by *this* life must be provided if the nauseating prospect of the eternal return of the same is to be avoided. An adequate account of the soul's otherworldly prospects must avoid both reductive materialism and the horrors of eternal regeneration. Man's insecurities about life and death may be relieved only if *both* the rationality of the whole and the integrity of the individual are preserved.

In the theory of recollection as it is set forth here, we should observe that the content of recollected knowledge is purely formal and never of particulars. In other words, recollection never consists of specific memories of specific objects in a previous life but only of moral and conceptual absolutes that are commonly accessible to all men. The proofs that one's awareness of these absolute conceptual measures could only have been obtained prenatally are specious; they fail to account for the possibility that recollected memories are not those of a previous existence but may have to do with what is potentially accessible to all human souls through the erotic power of the ideas themselves. To borrow one of Socrates' favorite arguments, one who had ever truly possessed this knowledge at any time would not have so much difficulty in expressing its content after his memory has awakened.

The real problem with recollection has to do with the soul's inability to remain attuned to the level of these ideas for any extended period. The process of recollecting what we are supposed to possess already is in many ways more arduous than that of acquiring empirical facts ex nihilo. In other words, it is far more reasonable to suppose that the soul experiences the erotic authority of these ideas in the present. This means that the so-called theory of recollection has nothing to do with memories of any past incarnation stored in the soul. It pertains chiefly to any human soul's capacity to reconstruct inductively the idea toward which all particular instances point and to gain some access to an eternally present realm of transcendental truth. In short, although one knows that real particulars fall short of the absolute, one does not possess any *positive* knowledge of what is signified but merely acknowledges that these ideas demand attention and duly recognize their capacity to order and transform the experience of reality.

I argue that the process of recollection has nothing to do with the remembrance of prelapsarian glories. According to the *Protagoras*, the soul's task is actively to re-collect and re-unify its various moral, erotic, and intellectual capacities in a good life. This kind of recollection takes place through the transcendental ideas that go about the Socratic task of ceaselessly reminding the soul of its identity and duties in *this* life. It is essential to remember that the content of recollection is not a kind of information that could somehow be collected and accumulated in the soul itself. A soul recollects in the truest sense of the term when it participates in an idea and acts on awareness of it. This is the ultimate measure of human virtue. Virtue can never be reduced to passive knowledge, like data to be absorbed and stored for examination purposes. For Socrates, virtue is not an unthinking, easily instilled habit; this is why erotic knowledge cannot be inherited, unthinkingly, from a past life.

Socrates now acknowledges that he has not established the more difficult part of the second argument. Even if one grants that a human soul once dwelt in marble halls of eternal ideas, it does not follow that this prior experience is proof of its immortality. Indeed, the very fall into the body suggests that the soul's relation to these higher truths was less than adequate. The rather feeble objection that unless the living come out of the dead, all the living would end up dead fails to address many crucial concerns having to do with the identity of the soul, and both how and why it comes into existence. Unless these problems are answered, one might just as well claim that a human soul is not simply immortal but also uncreated and eternal.

Up to this point, Socrates has used some altogether dubious proofs of the immortality of every soul to educate his listeners' appreciation of the issues involved. He has yet to explicate any plausible grounds for his belief in the continued existence of the virtuous soul after death. He must also provide us with an account of an afterlife that is more satisfying than the nauseating process of continual reincarnation. Like Theseus, he must find a way to escape the labyrinth of eternal recurrence after he confronts and defeats the Bullheaded fear that the soul will not survive death. Bear in mind that in the *Gorgias*, Socrates follows Homer in placing Minos as the judge of the eternally doomed shades in Hades (523e). The struggle to liberate Athens from the rule of Minos is connected to the mission of escaping from the doomed labyrinth of the body. Minos must be deposed and the true Athens must be reestablished at the end of this mission. The dominion of the underworld must be broken.

The argument at the other horn of this dilemma is rather more difficult to trace. The reader must pay the closest attention to the torturous twists and turn of Phaedo-Ariadne's tale if it is to be recovered and recollected. Phaedo, the narrator, is quite oblivious to the significance of the route taken by Socrates; however, Plato (the Daedalus of this labyrinthine tale) has designed his dialogue so that there is always sufficient psychagogic justification for every step that Socrates has his followers take. Whereas the surface teachings of the *Phaedo* probably bear a close resemblance to the philosophic doctrines taught by the narrator of the dialogue, the subtext is designed to undercut these very teachings, to provide the astute reader with Plato's own interpretation of Socrates' views on the significance of virtue and the afterlife. *This* rereading must be embarked upon if we are to make any headway toward understanding Plato's own grasp of the events he recounts. As observed earlier, the ultimately comic nature of the *Phaedo* can be overlooked only at the reader's peril.

Socrates' ironic claim that a combining of the arguments from the passing into each other of extremes and from recollection would allow a satisfactory proof of the soul's immortality draws attention to the earlier point that these arguments are incompatible. The one argument is for material and cosmic immortality; the other has to do with the identity of the individual. Further, the first argument postulates an ultimately monistic cosmos where no identity is constant; the other opposes the realms of eternal truths and transient chaos in such a way that they could hardly generate and interpenetrate each other. Plato thus pointedly suggests that so disparate and composite an argument cannot survive detailed analysis. This structural motif also prepares us for Socrates' third and best argument in favor of the soul's survival: that a simple and self-consistent spiritual entity which participates in the eternal order is not subject to the material prospect of disintegration. The *Symposium* will go on to suggest that the soul's purpose consists precisely in mediating between the two domains.

The bizarre combination of the respective arguments from recollection and extremes, of human and destructively bestial elements, resembles the nature of the Minotaur. Socrates, to the extent that his mission parallels that of Theseus, seeks to deliver his followers from being consumed by this creature in the senseless labyrinth of reincarnation. It is the combination of the fear of eternal recurrence and the fear of nonbeing that makes death so fearsome. Death would not be so fearsome if it led simply either to nothingness or to reincarnation with intact memories of one's former tenure of life. Most fearful is the Kafkaesque prospect of being reborn eternally and enduring gruesome punishments for crimes that one does not recollect or understand. Homer's account in the *Odyssey* shows that the Greeks were quite aware of such a prospect. One of the most fearful features of Hades is precisely in that the tortured shades in Tartarus have no recollection of the crimes that they are being punished for. The very word "Hades" is derived from a negation of the Greek word meaning look and idea. In other words, to be in Hades means to lack self-knowledge and to be morally invisible or unaware of oneself. This is a theme that Socrates likes to harp on.

The severance of the connection between recollection and identity is not the least potent argument that could be opposed to the doctrine of reincarnation. Although Minos demanded that Athens offer up its human victims in reparation for the loss of his son, no amount of human sacrifice could ever replace a unique individual who had been lost forever. The Minotaur might even be said to represent the inevitably grotesque consequences of emulating Minos's queen in trying to commingle with the brutal powers of nature.[27] Nothing spiritual can issue from the coupling of base desire and baser physicality. The irrationality of the labyrinth makes the force of death represented by the Minotaur inevitable and almost desirable. If men conclude that life makes little rational sense, it is only natural that they should wallow in materialism and ignore their spiritual capacities. When Socrates suggested that Simmias and Cebes were fearful that the soul would blow away and dissipate when it left the body, Simmias laughingly urged Socrates to convince them of the soul's immortality on this supposition (77d–e). Simmias went on to claim that rather than the prospect of the soul's extinction it was the bogey man representing death that he truly feared; in other words, he feared the process of dying more than the non-event of annihilation.

It is essential for any serious reader of these dialogues to bear in mind that Plato never pretends to offer anything in the nature of dogmatic knowledge concerning the soul's otherworldly fate. As tempting as it might be to regard Socrates as a precursor of Dante, the assumption that Socrates or Plato could reveal transcendent truth must fly in the face of a most basic tenet of Socratic pedagogy. Never having been made privy to any positive revelation himself, Plato never claims to do anything more than attempt to share the experience of Socratic negative pedagogy with his more attentive readers. At the most, his speculations are confined to explorations into the grounds for the possibility of this daimonic experience. As beautiful as Plato's myths are, they should never be treated as journalistic disclosures of transcendent truth. For the most part, a Platonic myth provides suggestive insights concerning the spiritual state of the soul to whom it is addressed.

If we forget that Plato was no more than an extraordinarily gifted member of our species, one who attempted to share what he learned about being human from another remarkable man, we renounce the best interpretive device at our disposal. The assumption of a shared humanity between these fifth-century Athenians and ourselves is what makes these dialogues readable today. The recognition of universal constants that are necessarily experienced by all of mankind makes Plato's style of indirect communication possible and constitutes the very cornerstone of his philosophy; it functions as both the matter and the content of his enterprise.

Turning now to examine Socrates' third argument in detail, we must observe that only this model of the soul as a transcendentally attuned harmony can account for interaction between the ideal and material realms of existence that the soul has access to. Striving to emulate the order of the ideal realm moves beyond the purely reactive and negative ethics that the second argument was confined to. The first argument from extremes was even less satisfactory, since it was unable to explain how the soul could be individuated from the workings of the monistic cosmos that contained it. As a consequence of this third argument and its moral implications, however, the whole notion of the soul's essential immortality has been greatly compromised. The human soul exists between the eternal and material realms; its subsequent fate has everything to do with how it prefers to orient its strivings. Man must either succumb to his carnal proclivities or fulfill his spiritual capacity to participate in those things that are invisible, divine, immortal, and wise. The curious combination of transcendental and carnal elements that constitute man must become more than a potential for madness and spiritual melancholy.

The starkness of the choice is reflected in Socrates' account of the fate that awaits the human soul after its death. There is no middle ground between the beatitude that rewards a truly philosophical life and the animal state of existence that awaits all other souls. Even the best unphilosophical souls "who have practiced popular and social goodness, 'temperance' and 'justice' so-called, developed from habit and training but devoid of philosophy and intelligence" (82b), will find their reward to consist in being reborn as tame social creatures such as wasps, ants, or bees. Socrates' belated admission of the possibility that these people might be reborn as decent men is highly ironic: it suggests that there is very little difference between the respective lives of the social animal and the man who follows laws and convention by unthinking habit. In effect, people who live such a life have already become social animals. The *aidos* and *dike* so generously offered by Protagoras yield only self-forgetfulness. Socrates insists that the purpose of punishment is education rather than retribution, but incarceration in an animal body serves neither educative nor retributive ends; it simply reflects the necessary consequences of the failure of a soul to maintain its humanity. The difference between the social animals of the *Phaedo* and the protagonist of Kafka's "Metamorphosis" is slight.

In other words, the unthinking soul merely receives a body appropriate to its spiritually bankrupt condition. The unexamined life is not merely not worth living; it is not living at all! It is this "craving for corporeality" which causes these souls to be "attached to the same sort of character which they developed during their life" (81e). If no personal recollection of identity is possible, Socrates can be seen to foreshadow Leibniz's view that having previously been the King of China matters little if one has no access to specific memories. In practical terms, it is as if the king dies and another man is born, with no further causal connection between the two events.[28]

It is essential to observe the psychagogic implications of Socrates' speculations on this subject. As we observed earlier, Cebes sees little value to life and is well disposed toward both suicide and the morally equivalent attitude of life negation. Because he confuses philosophy with hostility toward human life itself, Cebes must learn that the true philosopher's rejection of the body is not an act of sullen defiance; rather, it follows from his preference for a more satisfactory way of living. Viewed from this higher perspective, the fate of being reborn as an unreflectively industrious bee, a perverse donkey, or a violent wolf are morally equivalent: they all represent failures to realize man's potential for reflective virtue. Further, since the souls of these creatures are now appropriate to their bodies, they are no longer capable of following the rational path of philosophy. As we have noted, Cebes is afraid of the torturous processes of reincarnation; Socrates' fabulous description is a warning that the failure to follow an actively virtuous life will deliver his soul up to these blindly irrational forces. Socrates despises the body only insofar as it is transformed into a labyrinth imprisoning uneducated desires; this theme is consistently harped on in both the *Republic* and the *Phaedo*. He is opposed to *both* abstract intellectualism and unbridled hedonism.

Socrates now tells Simmias and Cebes, who claim to be reluctant to embarrass him by voicing their objections to his argument at the present time, not to be afraid that their continued questioning will distress him. Speaking as a well-harmonized lyre, he likens himself to a swan, which sings more loudly and sweetly than ever when it foresees its death. (I shall comment further on the most suggestive implications of this image: meanwhile, it is noteworthy that Socrates is continuing to obey the injunction, which he mentioned earlier, to cultivate the Muses.) We may understand this inspired utterance as a revelation of Socrates' innermost conviction that his soul has properly prepared itself for an afterlife, but both Simmias and Cebes express grave doubts concerning this expectation.

Simmias views the individual soul as a haphazardly rigged product of the various extremes rather than one of these eternally alternating dyads. His materialistic view of the soul thus constitutes a rejection of Socrates' first argument for its immortality. He does not, however, respond directly to the account of human existence that Socrates has just provided, and this reticence is surely significant. Simmias says that since certainty is impossible in the matters they are considering, it is most prudent to seek out the "best and least refutable theory" and use it as a raft to negotiate the dangerous seas of life. His imagery directs our attention to the figure of Odysseus, that most celebrated of raft travelers. But unlike Odysseus, who preserved his life by discarding his raft and holding on to something flimsy but immortal,[29] the prudent Simmias prefers to stay with his fast-disintegrating raft / body.

Simmias suggests that although Socrates has poetically fashioned a beautiful song about the soul's immortality, the soul—like the lyre / body through which the song was rendered— is constructed entirely of mortal materials and therefore ceases to be when the combination disintegrates. Socrates had earlier suggested to Cebes that they find a good singer of charms to replace him (77e). Simmias's criticism implies that Socrates' arguments are no better than the charming songs of a Siren or the dissembling yarns of Odysseus. He finds greater comfort in believing in the soul's necessary mortality, although as he has himself recognized, this assumption is itself entirely unproven and speculative. We can only conclude that Simmias prefers to ignore the dangerous spiritual obligations stemming from the soul's capacity for otherworldly existence.

Cebes' objections to Socrates' argument are subtler, though they proceed from a similar fear. He does not allow his belief in the soul's otherworldly origins to detract from his attitude that incarnate existence is not beneficial to the soul. Simmias compared Socrates to a singer of songs; Cebes evokes the image of an aged weaver who has reached the end of his rope. Although his creations are less durable than their maker, this fact does nothing to gainsay the fact of the weaver's own mortality. Depicting the soul as something that constantly changes through its transmigratory career, Cebes claims that we can know neither what is fatal to the soul itself nor whether it will survive any one of the many metamorphoses it undergoes. We cannot assume that the soul "suffers no ill-effects in its various rebirths and so does not, at one of its deaths, perish altogether" (88a–b).

According to Cebes, "no one but a fool is entitled to face death with confidence unless he can prove that the soul is absolutely immortal and indestructible. Otherwise, everyone must always feel apprehension" (88b). His argument leaves unexpressed the other extreme position that Simmias has just stated; that the prospect of death could also be faced with relative equanimity if one were presented with proof of the soul's complete mortality and vulnerability to destruction. It is the lack of definite knowledge of the soul's fate that makes death so daunting.

There are solid grounds for suspecting that Cebes' chief fear is that the soul will only partially survive its translation to another life state. Socrates recognizes this concern when he paraphrases Cebes' view to mean that despite the soul's past glories, its bodily incarnation is the beginning of the end. The human state is no better than that of a shade in Homeric Hades, for the soul's "very entrance into the human body was, like a disease, the beginning of its destruction; it lives this life in

increased weariness and finally perishes in what we call death" (95d).
Cebes confirms this diagnosis when he explicitly states that it is unnecessary to add or subtract anything from Socrates' summation of his
position. Cebes wishes this nauseating process to come to a speedy end:
hence his attitude of world-weariness, and his seemingly disparate interests in purification and suicide.

The arguments of Simmias and Cebes are complementary; when put
together they reveal the bankruptcy of the Pythagorean emphasis on
purification and life negation. If Simmias's position promises the destruction of every creature through the Scylla of disintegration, Cebes
entraps all living beings in a Charybdian whirlpool of eternal recurrence. Neither has any clear idea of the soul's essential qualities or the
value of human incarnate existence. Both reject all of Socrates' proofs of
the soul's immortality as unfounded myths. Indeed, their respective
images of singer of tales and aged weaver suggest that they see his accounts of the afterlife as no more reliable than Homer's. It is thus imperative that Socrates use the short time remaining to reiterate his theories about the moral mission of the soul and to explain why these
ideas are better founded than those previously set forth. Before he does
so, however, Plato draws our attention to the dialogue's dramatic fore-
ground: Phaedo's narration of this discussion to Echecrates.

V

We cannot afford to forget that Echecrates is largely oblivious to the
labyrinthine subtext of this argument. Consequently, he is bitterly dis-
appointed (as was Phaedo) by Socrates' inability to refute Simmias and
Cebes. The unusual prominence of rhetoric and indirection in the
Phaedo has to do with the undesirability of giving public currency to
Plato's appraisal of Socrates' views on the afterlife. Although a close
reading of the Phaedo points beyond its sentimental surface, readers
and spectators of the intellectual caliber of Phaedo and Echecrates will
always make up the large majority of those who read Platonic dialogues—as Echecrates' interruption of Phaedo's narration reminds us.

A large part of Socrates' mission has to do with using rhetoric to protect such souls from the pessimism pervading their cave or labyrinth.
Although these readers are not capable of fully understanding his philosophical pedagogy, Socrates (and Plato) must make every effort to defeat
materialistic pessimism in their eyes and urge them toward the thought-

ful practice of virtue. The relation of charming stories about the soul's immortality can never be an end in itself, but understood as a preemptive defense against the *rhetoric* of nihilism and pessimism, it prepares the soul for its encounter with true philosophy.

After Echecrates has voiced his disappointment that Socrates' apparently convincing arguments have been completely discredited by Simmias and Cebes, Phaedo reassures him that Socrates well understood the effect of these objections on his audience and duly proceeded to heal their dejected spirits. Socrates tells Phaedo that they should both shave their heads if they let his argument die. When Phaedo protests that even Heracles could not take on two at the same time, Socrates responds by promising to be his Iolaus. Socrates is determined that Phaedo, and other followers of his limited intellectual capacity, not surrender their desire to believe in the soul's immortality. Further, just as even Heracles, in this exceptional instance, had to call on his friend for assistance, the allusion reminds us that Socrates must depend on myths for the afterlife of his mission. Plato must do what was beyond Phaedo's (or Socrates') power.

The particular myth that Socrates refers to pertains to Heracles' and Iolaus's battle with the Hydra. This beast possessed an immortal head several mortal ones each of which, if destroyed, was replaced twofold.[30] Moreover, the Hydra's boon companion, a Crab, came out of its swamp to bite Heracles' foot.[31] The Hydra and Crab represent the respective fears of Cebes and Simmias: Cebes is terrified by the Hydra-like fertility of nature; Simmias's objections derive from a basic materialism that is symbolized by the grasping claws of the Crab. Just as the Crab attacked Heracles' feet, Socrates own feet—which were temporarily without sensation at the beginning of the *Phaedo*—will be the first area of his body to feel the effects of the hemlock.

The battle against the Hydra and Crab typifies the desperate struggle that Socrates is fighting against misology and misanthropy. On the one hand, the fears of Cebes and Simmias make them determined to reduce everything that Socrates has said about the soul to mere rhetoric. Like drowning men, they seem determined to drag Socrates down with them. Their charges are very difficult to refute while Phaedo and his kind are manifestly in need of sufficient rhetorical encouragement to sustain their quest toward philosophic virtue.

A parallel could be derived from Socrates' claim in the *Apology* that he was pursued by two adversaries: political injustice and physical debility (39a–b). Socrates can postpone his swiftly approaching death only through seemingly unjust speeches (in the eyes of Cebes and Simmias) for those like Phaedo. By attempting to respond adequately to the objections of Cebes and Simmias, however, he runs the risk of discouraging his less acute admirers in a context where the possibility of their continued education is very much in doubt. He must therefore combine the two processes: he must *charmingly* provide a profound explanation of the difference between maieutic discourse and the sophistical myths he was accused of dispensing.

As in Heracles' battle with the Hydra, it is not sufficient for Socrates to respond to the skeptical counterarguments of Cebes and Simmias with logic-chopping devices. These methods derive from the inherently skeptical paradigms of efficient causality and logical proof. As long as such men remain in Penelope's posture and content themselves with weaving and unraveling proofs like the souls in Hades, this battle will continue endlessly at very great cost. A qualitatively superior model of causality is necessary to get them out of these straits; they are in waters that teem with sources of self-forgetfulness, solipsism, pessimism, and insecurity.

When Socrates warns Phaedo against the dangers of misology, he is looking over Phaedo's head toward more discerning readers. We are cautioned that the unreliability of certain arguments (his own not excepted) should not lead us to reject truth itself and believe that we are superior to all other thinkers. Misanthropy arises from a too trusting acceptance of others without the recognition that most humans fall far short of perfection. Likewise, misology arises when we demand perfect communication through flawless reasoning. We fail to understand that humans are not capable of proceeding in this fashion. Due accommodation has to be made both for the relative inequalities of different human intellects and for the essential qualitative disproportion between the transcendental and physical realms. As Socrates says, it is the utmost folly when a man "undertakes to consort with men when he has no knowledge of human nature" (89e). Instead of falling victim to skepticism, "we should recognize that we are not yet in sound condition and strive manfully and eagerly to become healthy" (90e). Intellectual invalids are not in any position to pass judgment on the value of human reason. It is far better for them to try to arrive at some appreciation of their own condition.

It is from such a perspective that a reader of the *Phaedo* should try to understand Socrates' reasoning. Instead of presuming that Socrates is trying to present an abstract logical proof, one that superior intellects will triumphantly refute, we should recognize that he is adjusting his arguments to address the psychic deficiencies of his interlocutors. Turning back to the mission of Theseus, we must observe that Socrates is anxious that some of his friends not emulate Aegeus, the father of Theseus, who committed suicide under the mistaken belief that his son had failed in his mission against the Minotaur. Theseus was supposed to change the sail of his *theoris* as a sign of success but neglected to do so; his father's demise was thus attributable to a failure to overcome pessimism by taking anticipatory measures against its influence.[32]

Socrates now proceeds to respond to the arguments of Cebes and Simmias by asking the latter whether he accepted the previous argument that knowledge was really recollection of what the soul had learned from some previous life. When Simmias agrees enthusiastically, Socrates asks how this theory is compatible with Simmias's earlier view that the soul is no more than an epiphenomenal attunement of its body. The obvious way out of this dilemma is inherent in the very notion of attunement itself. A state of *harmonia* does not arise out of the instrument. It has to arise through harmonizing the instrument to some objective measure *beyond* itself.

Ronna Burger offers a helpful distinction between the "greatest music" and "demotic music."[33] The soul can either seek to learn the greatest music or imitate the standards of the demos.[34] The body is like a musical instrument through which the soul learns music; the analogy suggests that both the song-in-itself and the soul that has attuned itself to eternal *harmonia* persist after the lyre perishes and the performance is over. Socrates' dream is ironically suggestive in this regard: his soul has learned music, but his body has not yet learned how to make sounds that will also be pleasing to the demos.

Once Simmias has to explain how this process of attunement takes place, his argument obviously loses its power since the soul is the attuning agent rather than the tuned body. He cannot explain how a haphazard assembly of material components can give birth to human consciousness. As the fourth argument points out, life comes from beyond the material contiguity of bodies. To put it another way, the ability to follow a recipe does not imply that the cook possesses knowledge of nutrition, the human body, or chemistry.

It is also fascinating to note that another primary meaning of *harmonia* has to do with the act of caulking the various joints of a ship.[35] Quite apart from the significance of this allusion to the forthcoming discussion of Anaxagorean causality, Plato also provides the careful reader with a playful avowal of his own fidelity to the spirit of the *theorian* of Theseus and Socrates. This continued interest in the mission of Theseus is of the utmost significance to what follows.

Returning to the subject of *harmonia*, we see that Simmias's acceptance of the theory of preexistence is based on the soul's awareness of standards that are not of this world. We have already examined some of the fallacious assumptions undergirding the view that such knowledge is recollected from a prior existence. This argument ignores Socrates' discovery that we cannot give an objective account of this knowledge even after its supposed remembrance. As pointed out earlier, it is far better to recognize ignorance and acknowledge that humans merely apprehend the authority of these ideas. As Kant would have it, this knowledge or awareness has to do with practical reason rather than pure reason. Indeed, one could claim with much justice that Socrates, rather than Kant, was the first to discover the antinomies that result from the attempt to reduce these transcendental intuitions to the status of provable human knowledge. These ideas are *logically* rather than *temporally* prior to human experience. Men are thus 'reminded' of *the* universal and imperative quality of the Ideas rather than of *their* prior lives.[36]

Once one recognizes (or remembers) that the soul's awareness of transcendental absolutes is at stake, it becomes clear that this view of the soul is perfectly consistent with and greatly supportive of Socrates' third argument for its immortality. It is through a cultivation of the Muses in its attunement to the eternal verities that the soul raises itself out of the physical realm of decay to participate in the divine order. It is as if the soul must also become a *harmonia* in the third sense of this highly significant word, meaning "concord," "agreement," or "settled government."[37] It follows that by constantly attuning its own regime with that of the "shining pattern in the heavens" (*Republic* 592b), the virtuous soul will prove to the gods that it truly belongs to their celestial polity. Odysseus's often quoted observation in the *Iliad* regarding the undesirability of many rulers comes to mind here: human affairs should not be ruled by many mad masters.[38] The vision of the Good should preside over all human matters.

The image of weaving that both Cebes and Socrates used earlier also proves to be in harmony with this way of thinking. As Socrates said, it is of the utmost folly for the soul to free itself through philosophy and then, like Penelope, undo its own weaving at night (84a). It is through remaining faithful to the eternal order or *harmonia* that a soul may survive the scattering or disintegration of the body. To express this insight in the terms of the *Protagoras*, it is easier for a soul to stay good than to accumulate virtue over many incarnations. This doctrine also has important implications with respect to the theory of reincarnation: the doctrine of the unity of virtue means that such a harmony cannot be perpetually, disassembled and reassembled. Cebes' doubts regarding the persistence of any constant identity are justified in such an instance. My reading of the *Symposium* will show that through the alternation of *Poros* and *Penia* the soul continually goes through a process of regenerative education in one and the same life. Thus there is no need to postulate a process of reincarnation; the soul is continually reborn as it sloughs off objectified knowledge and grows in the spirit. We might observe that though Socrates has seen the death of many bright young souls, and "lost" many arguments, he has continually become reincarnated through each encounter with ignorance and hubris.

The reformulated theory just considered addresses still another weakness in Simmias's position, as Socrates indicated when he asked Simmias whether his materialistic model of the soul could differentiate between good and evil souls. Necessity being irresistible, it is impossible for any soul to be more or less of a soul, as Simmias frankly acknowledges. Yet if absolute measures of truth and justice are to be considered seriously, they must be the criteria by which a soul can be judged. Nor is Simmias' deterministic portrayal of the soul consistent with man's experience of how it functions. Socrates observes that the soul, far from being a passive shadow or reflection of the body's dispositions and powers, seeks to govern the body and direct its activities. As we discovered in the *Protagoras*, attunement is a lifelong process. The soul consolidates its liberation from carnality by ordering itself as a spiritual entity. It also resists the perverse inclination of the body to become part of the predestined order of generation and corruption.

Just as Simmias's earthbound theory of bodily harmony is transformed through recognition of the soul's attunement to transcendental verities, Cebes' nostalgic remembrance of the past glories of the fallen soul must also be turned around by Socrates, oriented toward the eternal standards that give meaning to the soul's *present* existence. Simmias's understanding of the soul was determined entirely by the materiality of the individual body. Likewise, Cebes must see that the soul as he perceives it is totally defined by external cosmological forces and thus utterly incapable of interacting with anything in the natural world in which it is exiled. The middle ground between these equally nihilistic extremes can be staked out only by means of the theory of the forms, which Socrates introduces with very characteristic indirection.

VI

We must examine Socrates' famous autobiographical statement very carefully to ascertain whether and how it serves as a response to Cebes' seemingly irrefutable skepticism concerning the soul's otherworldly prospects. Cebes must appreciate the grounds for Socrates' confident belief that *his* soul will happily survive its separation from the body. Although such an account does not respond to Cebes' challenge, which had to do with proving the *inherent* immortality of *all* souls, the beginning of Socrates' description indicates many profound weaknesses and inadequacies in Cebes' position. Socrates suggests that a cosmological account of reality is qualitatively indistinct from crasser versions of materialism in being unable to explain many matters that are essential to the human soul's quest for meaning and self-knowledge. Similarly, the partial theory of the forms that Socrates postulates here derives from his search for a transcendental moral superstructure. This spiritual order must be responsive to the soul's fundamental desires and insecurities. As was suggested earlier, what Socrates offers here is a very different approach to causality. This new approach must eschew determinism and recognize the soul's capacity for being-in-the-world.

Socrates' autobiographical account begins with a reference to his earlier fascination with natural philosophy. Through his failed scientific investigations he discovered that what Aristotle would call "efficient" and "material" causalities were incapable of providing a satisfactory account of the origins and purposes of things. Aristophanes' satirical account in *The Clouds* is partially vindicated when Socrates suggests that such studies could only have the effect of blinding the investigator and causing him to lose the little knowledge that he had (99d–e).

Socrates had previously believed that a man grew through absorbing substances into his body as food and drink (96c–d). Attempting to probe deeper into these processes, he inevitably progressed from material causality to efficient causality as he sought to understand *how* these various material transformations came about. It is easy to see how such a course of inquiry could have intellectually blinded Socrates' common sense. By endlessly probing into the origin of things he put himself in the position that Aristophanes lampooned so mercilessly. We can picture this pre-Socratic Socrates refusing to eat until he understood just *how* food was taken into his body. (One is reminded of his questioning Diotima about love without having any actual experience of eros himself.) These inquiries would generate endless chains of causal reasoning. As Socrates put it, the scientific materialist will not be content until he discovers (or postulates) an Atlas-like figure *on* whom all of the cosmos would rest and *from* whom all motion could necessarily be derived (99c). Further, such a process of analysis would inevitably unsettle one's commonsensical knowledge of the basic quantities and units of materialism, for these are also defined and determined by the mind— rather than residing in reality itself—the process must terminate in an ultimate mind from which these definitions may validly be derived.

That ultimate mind would also, presumably, be able to answer the *why* questions that represent the next stage in this cosmological inquiry. Answers to *how* questions are not sufficient without some explanation as to *why* these elaborate processes of causality are set in motion. This is why Socrates was so pleased to hear Anaxagoras's claim that the world is ruled and ordered by *nous* (mind): he hoped for an account of reality that would authoritatively explain *why* and *how* everything serves the good (97c); he would be willing to suppress his hankering for some other kind of causality if Anaxagoras could provide him with an explanation of how things are optimally ordered by this *nous*. Socrates expected that such an account would describe the good for all things, and place *each individual entity* in the best way possible for it (98a–b). These a priori expectations must be seen to be closely related to the spiritual concerns and expectations that Cebes, Leibniz, or any other human would have concerning a rationally ordered, best-of-all-possible worlds.

Much to Socrates' consternation, however, Anaxagoras failed utterly to satisfy his expectations. Far from explaining how the cosmos conserves the good of all things, Anaxagoras merely used *nous* as an ultimate efficient cause—as the ultimate agent. He failed to provide any account at all of how or why the world has reason or purpose. The justification of Anaxagoras's *nous* is ultimately theological rather than philosophical, because order is its own source of authority. According to Anaxagoras, the cosmos was previously an undifferentiated chaos of everything in all things. In the language of the Book of Job, the *nous* thunderously asks Socrates where he was when it ordered the universe.[39]

One major difficulty with such a view of reality is its inability to account for the integrity of individual entities: Anaxagoras's cosmology makes identity depend entirely on the ordering and differentiating motions of *nous*. Such a cosmology both corresponds to Simmias's materialism and confirms Cebes' worst fears of an omnivorous process of eternal recurrence which would literally pulverize the soul's integrity. Although (as Thales saw) all things possess a certain amount of soul, according to Anaxagoras's specifications soul can be no more than a capacity for self-consciousness in matter.[40] The soul 'knows' through recognizing like qualities in other quantities.[41] Soul likewise 'remembers' through preserving some parts, however infinitesimal, of its infinite previous identities. True reason or *nous*, through its total distinctness from the material continuum, is utterly separate from soul. Furthermore, according to these definitions, the rationality of *nous* consists entirely in its power to create, conserve, and destroy the 'truth' of various assembled entities. The nihilistic consequences of such a cosmology are evident.

So radical a disjunction between soul and rationality, stemming directly from Anaxagorean cosmology, makes it quite impossible either to explain human rational conduct or to justify Anaxagoras's derivation of this audacious transcendental deduction. Even if one tried to defend this perspective by assuming individual existence to be an illusion, Anaxagoras would still need to account for the various rational categories and moral concepts that guide human reasoning. Another problem: Anaxagoras claimed that extremes are not separated from each other.[42] As Socrates suggested in his discussion of quantity, this way of thinking undermines the integrity of such categories as largeness and smallness: 'the large' is infinitely small in the sense of being infinitely divisible; 'the small' can likewise be the sole constituent principle of the large. Even greater problems arise in the effort to explain the efficacy of moral ideas; they are not derivable through Anaxagorean cosmology.

Although Socrates had expected Anaxagoras to explain the individual and collective good of all things in his explanation of the cosmos, he soon realized that moral values are not derivable from a purely mechanical account of creation—an anticipation of David Hume's more celebrated claim that it is impossible to derive an 'ought' from a description of what 'is.'[43] In other words, one cannot derive the "Good" from *nous* or "Being." The god of the cosmologists cannot lead us to the God of Abraham and Socrates. The "Theory of the Ideas" results from this impasse between a bald description of the chaotic confusion of rationally unmediated reality and the practical requirements of thinking. The disjunction points toward certain categories or desires, inherent in the human intellect, which must be acknowledged and utilized. The second sailing is truly under way when one comes to realize that these a priori expectations are both the *cause* of his or her desire to understand reality and an essential part of the *response* to these desires.

The term "second sailing" had been commonly used to describe a nautical situation in which a ship was becalmed, and the sailors had to rely on rowing rather than the wind.[44] In such a situation the sailor is no longer facing the object of his motion. This stress on indirection is underscored by Socrates' famous warning that one should not repeat the errors of those who seek to observe an eclipse directly: "They sometimes injure their eyes, unless they study the sun's reflection in water or some other medium" (99d). Socrates feared that he would lose the sight of his soul by the practice of observing objects with his eyes and trying to understand them through his senses. For example, Phaedo is insufficiently prepared to observe the setting of his philosophical sun, Socrates; like the slave escaped from the cave, Phaedo runs the risk of blinding his soul to the significance of what has passed before him. Socrates is suggesting that we cannot understand what will happen to his soul by merely observing the fate of his body. He also implies that we should orient ourselves through the various heavenly constellations. These provide an eternal and constant pattern by which we may direct our wanderings. This method of navigation, toward which Plato directs our minds, has the advantage that the constellations are seen after the sun has set.

Socrates proposes "making a fresh start from these principles of mine that you know so well." In other words, he is "assuming the existence of absolute beauty and goodness and magnitude and all the rest" (100b). This statement discredits the notion that the ideas are a later Platonic invention. It is on the assumption that these principles exist that Socrates promises to develop a fresh account of causality and try to prove the soul's immortality; his intellectual and erotic awareness of these forms constitutes the basis of his belief in *his* soul's continued existence. Through the recollective causality of these principles the soul will be empowered to function at the level where it truly belongs. Although Socrates' account is, as he promised, rendered with all appropriate indirection, there is evidence to justify my interpretation. Instead of a monistic and arbitrary *nous*, which functions like the blinding sun,

Socrates' new approach indicates the way toward a constellation of ideas. Such a configuration orders the human understanding and allows for the making of free and moral rational decisions.

Alternatively, viewed in a literal manner, the laboriously developed fourth proof of the soul's immortality turns out to be no more than another invocation of discredited Anaxagorean causality. Socrates' interlocutors demanded that he preserve the integrity of the individual soul. Since Anaxagorean cosmology is incapable of responding to this request, our interpretation must proceed in a manner consistent with the stated objectives of the interlocutors and consonant with the direction of the argument.

Socrates claims that anything that is called beautiful is so by sharing or participating in the beautiful (100c–d). In other words, beauty is not explicable by its material constituents: a form is irreducible to a formula; it is the form of beauty that makes it possible for a thing to be deemed beautiful. We can further clarify the issue by asking the question in the terms that Socrates used in the *Euthyphro*. Is it by the beautiful that things are beautiful, or is it because things deserve to be called beautiful that they are called beautiful? The *Phaedo* suggests that in being a certain way, certain things are *discovered* to be beautiful. In other words, things are not arbitrarily called beautiful; it is through being oriented or striving toward the beautiful that a thing is found to possess beauty. This view is corroborated by the earlier mentioned criticism of Anaxagoras's theory that explained all cosmological matters by an appeal to despotic authority. While rejecting this worthless idea of an arbitrary *nous*, one must recognize the contribution that the human mind makes to this identification or judgment concerning the idea. It is through a thing's being a certain way that the mind *recollects* the idea of beauty.

It seems that a form's power consists in its being able to remind the mind authoritatively of certain transcendental ideas that regulate reasoning. Most men, however, rely on inadequate shadow representations that serve to dilute the erotic authority and heroic effort demanded by the true ideas. It follows that the best men hold steadfastly to their recollection of the ideas as they fight their way out of the labyrinthine cave of illusions. I am claiming that the structure of this dialogue sets up a very similar situation. The reader is challenged to resist the allure of the inadequate demonstrative proofs of immortality and reconstruct the true basis for Socrates' belief in *his* soul's capacity for continued existence. We will understand the profundity of Socrates' philosophical music only when we realize how artfully Plato wove the four strands of proof that accompany this swan song. It is his reader's task to retune this lyre.

In its untuned form the fourth proof of the soul's immortality is based on the unchanging nature of the form-in-itself; this form is unaffected by any vicissitude that may affect entities participating in its essential quality. For example, although Simmias is taller than Socrates, the fact of his simultaneously being shorter than Phaedo will obviously not detract from the integrity of the form of tallness itself. The proof suggests a parallel between the subaltern forms, which eternally retain an essential attribute of the form they are derived from (like the number five to oddness) and the human soul, which becomes a subalternate form of the idea of life.

The fourth proof of the soul's immortality sets out to blur the distinction between the individual soul and the form of life. This tendency is also reflected in the dangerous strategy of identifying the soul much too closely with the realm of the ideas. A more adequate model of participation must be provided before this problem can be resolved. The fundamental error committed here is the Anaxagorean supposition that a form functions like an efficient cause, acting arbitrarily and directly on the realm of being. Plato generally suggests that the forms operate indirectly by *reminding* the human soul of its powers and obligations.

According to this proof, since the soul has already been 'proved' to have existed before its bodily incarnation, and since the soul must be present for life to occur, it follows that the soul is the source of life—apparently by means of an unexplained connection to the form of life, *Zooes Eidos*, which is referred to only after the fourth proof has been accepted (106d). Since the opposite of life is death, the soul as the principle of life is inherently immortal. Therefore, because it cannot remain embodied in the presence of its contrary, the immortal soul merely withdraws from the body upon encountering the form of death.

The definition of the soul as the form of life represents a reversion to an older understanding of the soul as a life principle, rather than a human intellectual and volitional capacity. According to this biological understanding of the soul, either all living beings have immortal souls, or they are merely enlivened or ensouled by the form of life, which passes away when bodily conditions are no longer appropriate. For the latter possibility, Socrates gives the example of what happens when snow becomes too warm for the form of coldness to sustain it (106a)—yet another version of the questions of identity that plagued Simmias and Cebes earlier on. Although there is nothing unique about snow, how is there any assurance that the same identical snowfall or snow-flakes will return? How much less likely is it, then, that the same soul will be re-constituted? We cannot share Nietzsche's agonized belief in the eternal return of the same.[45] Existence is conferred (and taken away) by the form of life with complete arbitrariness. Life is given and life is taken away—blessed be the form of life!

To the extent that it is an eternal world-soul, the form of life is com-pletely indifferent to the tenets of morality by which an individual soul seeks to regulate its conduct. It is not just difficult to conceive of a sin-gle idea of life that will hold all the way from herbs to humans; it is also unnecessary. Unlike abstract categories such as tallness, courage, and beauty, which cannot be physically located in material objects, life is a self-evident biological phenomenon that does not need to be explained by the invocation of transcendental categories.

The alternative to these unattractive, unprovable, and unanswerable perplexities is to define *every* soul as a unique subaltern form of the idea of life. It does not suffice to derive the subalternate category 'human soul' from the form of life or soul. If every soul is an immortal form of life, then each individual soul must be deduced and derived, in all its uniqueness, from the form of life. This deduction would have the effect of making it impossible for the soul to grow or develop through its interaction with other souls in the world.

Outside the realm where opposites pass over into each other, it is dif-ficult to understand *why* such a soul must pass through this continual and meaningless cycle of birth and unliving. The problem results from the excessively intimate connection between the soul and the forms, and the concurrent removal of the soul from worldly existence. As noted earlier, an over-identification with the material world makes ethics redundant: the mad flux of materiality overwhelms the integrity of every thing; if each thing simply is, no soul is better than any other thing. Now, at the other extreme, over-abstraction from the world makes moral conduct equally unimportant. The soul is not susceptible to change at all. If everything is *essentially* good, existence is meaning-less, because no soul exists-in-the-world in any meaningful sense.

If the soul is *the* form of the body, the significance of its erotic con-nection with the moral transcendental ideas is minimized. Further, in dealing with ideas rather than factual realities, there must be some ac-count of how ideas are even capable of operating in the material realm. Ideas only 'exist' in and through the human mind, where they may ani-

mate the rational soul's actions in the material world; one cannot reverse this sequence and claim that concepts are the origin of the mind's
(and body's) *being*. The mysterious process through which an idea is
supposed to *generate* souls remains suggestively unexplained. Although his listeners seem to accept this proof eagerly, it is clear enough
that Socrates' definition of the soul as a form is, quite intentionally,
every bit as helpful as Anaxagoras's postulation of the *nous*.

This neo-Anaxagorean proof proves adequate to Socrates' desire that
his young audience should not succumb to nihilism in the uneasy twi-
light between the setting of the Socratic sun and the unforeseen ascent
of the Platonic dialogic constellations. It is equally apparent, however,
that this argument is not supposed to provide a dogmatic proof of the
soul's immortality. I venture to claim, however, that Plato provides his
readers with a subtext indicating the grounds for his belief that a truly
virtuous soul does survive death. Examination of the three previous
proofs has shown that each argument, although inadequate in itself, indicates important insights about the soul through the indirect method
of drawing attention to the shortcomings of the purported proof. The
proof *qua* logical demonstration is actually only a photographic negative or shadow of the truth.

The first demonstration of the soul's immortality served to draw attention to the soul's having no part in nature's cycles of generation and
corruption. The second reminded us that preexistence does not need to
be postulated to explain the soul's ability to see the archetypes and recognize its transcendental capacities. The third made us see that that although the soul is not an epiphenomenal harmony of the body, the eternal ideas constantly serve as the measures through which it may attune
itself to the transcendental realm. We must now try to discover what
the fourth proof contributes to this indirect process of pedagogy. The
soul's capacity for virtue is realized through its existential harmonizing
of the various transcendental moral imperatives. Likewise, the true
grounds for Socrates' belief in his soul's capacity for a second sailing
consists in the weaving together of these four subtextual strands. This
spiritual effort, which occurs after the shipwreck of the body, places a
high premium on the unifying effects of courage (a theme we examined
at some length when considering the *Protagoras*).

Although the fourth proof of the soul's immortality is clearly invalid
when taken at face value, it does provide a rudimentary account of the
ideas. It also suggests that the soul's capacity for life beyond the body
depends on how it comports itself toward these forms. We have already

seen that darkness at noon results from the direct approach described in the proof. It seems that the soul must find some way to steer a middle course. It must go below the high-flying hubris of those who would situate it high among the forms, and above the crass materialism of those who would drag the individual soul down to earth and deny its capacity for transcendence. The mythical dimension of the *Phaedo* responds to the perplexities that are caused by a literal and direct reading of it. Close attention to the subtext of this dialogue occasions a new approach to causality and brings the *theorian* of Socrates to a satisfactory conclusion.

VII

This approach overcomes the perplexities that beset both the unseeing soul, in its subterranean labyrinth of the body, and the naive reader of the dialogue, trapped beneath its surface. Apart from Theseus and his crew, the only others known to have escaped Minos's labyrinth were its designer, Daedalus, and his son Icarus.[46] Daedalus, with his customary ingenuity, attached wings of wax and feathers to the arms of his son and himself. He advised his son to fly neither too close to the sun, which would melt his wings, nor too close to the sea, which would dampen them. While his father succeeded in negotiating the flight home, Icarus disregarded his advice and, carelessly soaring too high, melted his wings and fell to a watery grave. Socrates seems to be Daedalus in this analogy (recall his claim in the *First Alcibiades* that Daedalus was his ancestor);[47] the high-flying Phaedo's inability to follow his master's path suggests that he is likened to Icarus. Alternatively, when Socrates plays Theseus, Phaedo becomes like Ariadne in loving Socrates but being excluded from the Platonic second sailing back to Athens. Although Phaedo sings the tale of Socrates' escape out of the labyrinth, it seems that he himself cannot follow his own story. His soul's wings are dampened by his tears and fears.

Phaedo's disastrous trajectory would bring about the blinding of the soul's faculty of discernment and cause the darkness at noon that Socrates warned against. One must not follow the example of Aegeus in prematurely supposing that Theseus / Socrates has failed in his *theorian*. Neither Socrates' nor Theseus's failure to *display* a comic second sail means that the second sailing was itself a failure. Theseus went on to become the founder of Athens. Similarly, and fortunately for us,

Plato rather than Phaedo successfully undertook the second sailing that ensured the immortality of the Socratic enterprise through the reinfusion of the Socratic spirit into the material remains that Phaedo (like the eponymous archon) buried outside Athens.

Remember that the second sailing has nothing to do with a sail but denotes a changed disposition: instead of passively depending on winds, the sailor decides to rely on the exertion of rowing. In the context of this dialogue the expression refers to the exertion of the human soul striving to extricate itself from an untenable situation. Similarly, a dialogue must always be reread with a view to recovering the powerfully suggestive erotic subtext that supplements the merely edifying surface teachings. Here, for instance, it is significant that unlike the sailor, who looks toward his objective, the rower looks in the opposite direction; he thereby finds protection from the danger of darkness at noon. This is yet another indirect clue that our investigation is moving in the proper direction. The same could be said about the deathbed of Socrates: Plato did not need to be physically present to understand its true significance; he was certainly there in spirit. Blessed are those who have not seen and yet have faith!

Socrates' last words, reminding Crito that he owes Asclepius a cock, suggest that he has discharged all his other debts.(This implies, surely, that he is not indebted to Pythagoras, since the Pythagoreans forbade the sacrifice of animals.)[48] Even more important, he believes that he has satisfied Apollo's command that he cultivate the Muses. This new-found musical ability allows Socrates to die conscious of *his* immortality. This is surely why he must sacrifice to Asclepius, the mortal who discovered the art of raising the dead.[49] More soberly, the sacrifice to Asclepius also indicates grave concern for his mortal companions. It is also well worth noting Diogenes Laertius's claim that Socrates learned to play the lyre in his old age.[50] Plato seems to depict this process in the *Phaedo*. Socrates has successfully cultivated the Muses through stringing the lyre of Apollo. The four proofs have been attuned to one another; they now sing in one musical voice.

Turning now to another mythological track of the subtext, we should observe that Plato's readers would doubtless have been acquainted with the traditional story of the swan song that Socrates feels compelled to restate. According to familiar Greek legend, swans about to die have sung sad songs since Phaethon's grieving friend, the musician Cygnus, was transformed into a swan by Apollo.[51] When Socrates tells Simmias that men utter lies about the swans because of their own fear of death

(85a), he draws attention to the need for a literary transformation of the swan's harsh tones into beautiful Apollonian music. In other words, the mistake seems to consist in supposing that the swan's harsh tones necessarily beget a sad song. Just as the harsh tones of a cock proclaim the beginning of a new day, we must not assume that Socrates' abrasive dialectical methods stem from a pessimistic outlook. Indeed, one could argue that it is Socrates' very confidence in the goodness of reality that makes him unafraid of using rough methods to bring men out of the cave into the sunlight. The very harshness of voice and body only serve to draw attention to the beauty of song and soul.

By drawing attention to the story of *Phaethon*, which also occurs between sunrise and sunset, Plato doubtless means his readers to draw parallels with the philosophical drama being recounted by *Phaedon*. Although Phaedo's attempt at rendering a demonstrative account of the soul's immortality does not stand up to rational examination, Plato transforms this tragic display of filial incapacity through his comic artistry. This is a part of the Platonic enterprise of making Socrates young and beautiful. By deftly juxtaposing the stories of Phaethon and Phaedon, *Platon* seems also to be suggesting that Phaedo's ongoing attempt to establish his credentials as Socrates' beloved disciple was about as successful as Phaethon's career as a charioteer. Like the unfortunate son of Helios, who could not handle all four of the Sun God's horses, Phaedo mismanages his proud legacy of the four Socratic arguments.

The comic character of this dialogue is maintained by Plato's subtle suggestion that it is absurd to recognize Phaedo as Socrates' chief legatee and mourner. The *Phaedo* suggests that it is Socrates who, after first attempting to prepare Phaedo for the ordeal that he has taken upon himself, laments his disciple's incompetence and then considerately provides souls of this type with suitably salutary stories. Thus Phaedo, who believes himself to be the narrator of a tragedy, unwittingly plays the role of straight man in the comic dialogue named after him. This is in keeping with the gently ironic tone of the banter that Socrates maintains throughout the dialogue. Socrates, like the Sun God, will inevitably rise up again when the cock crows; the question of his immortality is not of very much concern to him. His concern has rather to do with those like Phaedo who seem incapable of attending to the health of their souls.

Although no known extended account of Phaethon's story is contemporaneous with Plato, it is mentioned briefly in the *Timaeus*:

"Phaethon son of Helios yoked the steeds in his father's chariot and because he was unable to drive it along the course taken by his father, burnt up all that was upon the earth and himself perished by a thunderbolt" (22c). Euripides wrote a play called *Phaethon*, but only useless fragments of the work exist today. It is tempting to imagine that it contained something similar to his account of the disastrous chariot ride of Hippolytus, the eros-scorning love-child of Theseus and Hippolyta, who was killed when a monstrous bull (Minotaur?) approached his chariot. Here is the fatal scene:

> At once a terrible panic fell upon the horses. My master, who had lived long with the ways of horses, seized the reins in his hands and pulled them, letting his body hang backwards from the straps, like a sailor pulling an oar. But they took the fire-wrought bit in their teeth and carried him against his will, paying no heed to their captain's hand or the harness or the tight-glued chariot. If he held the helm and directed their course towards the softer ground, the bull appeared before them to turn them back, maddening the team with fear. But if they rushed with maddened senses into the rocks, it drew near and silently accompanied the chariot until it upset and overthrew the chariot, striking its wheel-rims on a rock. All was confounded: the wheels' naves and the axle-pins were leaping into the air, and the poor man himself, entangled in the reins, bound in a bond not easy to untie, was dragged along, smashing his head against the rocks and rending his flesh and uttering things dreadful to hear.[52]

For a full account of Phaethon's misadventure, however, one must depend on Ovid's *Metamorphoses*, in the hope that the Latin poet has given an accurate rendering. He relates how Phaethon disregarded his father's instructions to follow the celestial constellations and steer a prudent course between sky and earth, to "spare the lash . . . and more strongly use the reins, [for] the horses hasten of their own accord; the hard task is to check their eager feet. . . . go not too low, nor yet direct your chariot along the top of heaven; for if you go too high you will burn up the skies, if too low the earth. The middle is the safest path. And turn not off too far to the right, towards the writhing serpent, nor on the left where the altar lies low in the heavens . . . [but] hold on between the two."[53] If the four horses correspond to Socrates' four proofs, Phaedo is expected to hold them in harmony rather than allowing them to run away with his reasoning.

Lacking the strength to control his four spirited horses by the reins, Phaethon first sees his chariot (the Greek for chariot is *harma*) career toward the constellations: "When the unhappy Phaethon looked down from the top of heaven, and saw the earth far below, he grew pale, his knees trembled with sudden fear, and over his eyes came *darkness through an excess of light*."[54] This is quite literally the condition of darkness at noon that Socrates alluded to earlier; one should navigate *by* the constellations of ideas, not travel toward them. The place of the soul is between the forms and the natural world, between the forms and the earth. It is inevitable that darkness at noon will result if the soul loses this course and strays too close to the forms. The soul is not the form of the body as Aristotle asserts; such a definition puts it in the vertiginous position of playing *nous* over a world that it is too distant / abstract to relate to. The mind is not higher than the forms or even equal to them. The Platonic position seems to be that the mind can function *rationally* only when it maintains its proper *ratio* or *harmoniously* proportional relation between the intelligible forms and the natural order. Already terrified by the prodigious distance between the earth and his unharmonious *harma*, Phaethon "wishes he had never touched his father's horses. . . . Now, eager to be called 'son of Merops,' he is borne along as a ship is driven before a headlong blast, whose pilot has let the rudder go and abandoned her to the gods."[55]

This situation is obviously similar to that of Odysseus on the raft, which Simmias referred to earlier. Like Simmias, and unlike Odysseus, Phaethon decides to cling to his reins / raft and accept whatever fate the gods have assigned to him. This is no longer possible, however, when the fearsome figure of the Scorpion looms before him: "Dazed, he knows not what to do; . . . he does not even know the horses' names. To add to his panic, he sees scattered everywhere in the sky strange figures of huge and savage beasts. . . . bereft of wits from chilling fear, down he dropped the reins. When the horses feel these on their backs, they break loose from their course, and, with none to check them, they roam through unknown regions. . . . now they climb to the top of heaven, and now, plunging headlong down, they course nearer the earth. . . . the earth bursts into flame, . . . great cities perish, . . . and the conflagration reduces whole nations to ashes."[56]

Similar consequences could be said to ensue from Phaedo's attempt to establish himself as Socrates' designated legatee. Unlike Socrates, the previous sun figure of the *Republic*, his self-designated heir Phaedo will prove to be utterly incapable of "understanding his horses" and maintaining the appropriate distance between the transcendental forms and the real world. Read literally, the *Phaedo* makes impossible the adequate recovery of either the world of Socrates or its transcendental dimension. As we have seen, the four arguments offered are wildly contradictory: they make the soul out to be either impractically removed from all earthly affairs or related so intimately to the material processes of the earth that no individuality can be retained. Yet such are the interpretations we obtain if we preserve the material content of Socrates' teachings without any appreciation of the spirit.

To read the four arguments as "proofs" is to ignore the *spirit* of a Socratic dialogue and condemn ourselves to remain in Hades. A Platonic dialogue conceals its logos as it reveals beautiful myths. In effect, each of the arguments must be turned around like the prisoners in the cave and made to reveal what is true. Each Platonic dialogue attempts to remind the soul of the abiding presence and sustaining inspiration of the transcendental forces that enable people to lead a good and happy life. The process through which we learn to read a dialogue and to discern its marvelous underlying power and harmony may be compared with that by which a soul discovers the richness of the transcendental structures that surround it. In each instance it is the honest and courageous eroticism of questioning that takes us beyond the playful perplexities of the surface and leads to an apprehension of the truth. The beauty of the myth grants us the eros necessary for this adventure. Moreover, courage must be seen as part and parcel of a reader's virtue, but it is equally true that a thoughtful readerlike disposition toward life is an essential part of the virtue of courage.

Although it is subsequently impossible to reconstitute these revelations as objective proofs that may be circulated as information, they nevertheless are quite adequate. An essential part of the revelation consists in the soul's recognition that these revealed powers are apprehensible when the soul is itself. In other words, it is not through the equally inauthentic stances of either credulous gullibility or detached objectivity but, rather, by the thoughtful and harmonious exercise of its erotic potentialities that the soul receives confirmation of its true value. In a reciprocal process the soul displays excellence and demands / deserves confirmation of its value in the greater scheme of things. The process begins when eros inspires the soul to attune and orient itself toward the forms. The response from the forms will sustain this excellence. This process of challenge and response confirms the value of what the soul was—intuitively but not *irrationally*—reminded of.

The *Phaedo* has two levels and one rationally unified structure. Read superficially, it provides what seems to be (given Plato's rigorously evenhanded psychagogic approach) a more or less accurate caricature of Phaedo's teachings. Read more profoundly, with attention to its subtext, the dialogue goes on to provide a fascinating prediction of how the Socratic *corpus* decomposes when it is misappropriated and reduced to the status of dogma and proof by unworthy, self-appointed legatees. Accordingly, instead of serving as a literal disclosure of the structure of the afterlife, the elaborate cosmological myth with which the dialogue concludes provides a poetic reiteration of the life-affirming themes that we have already identified. This mythic corroboration confirms our identification of the themes subtly indicated by the incomplete logical structure of the dialogue.

VIII

While reading this myth and examining it for subtextual content, we can take as a starting ground Socrates' comments concerning the earth and humans' mistaken perception that they live on its surface. Socrates claims that they actually dwell in one of the many hollows of the earth; he uses the Greek word *kasma*, which means cave, chasm, or cavity (111c). This suggests that most men follow the sort of cavelike existence described so memorably in the *Republic*. The implication is that the two myths must be read in conjunction. As in the *Republic*, here Socrates is desirous of liberating mankind from its largely self-imposed illusions and bondage. Most humans are unaware of the true world, beyond the cave, that Socrates knows. Although some might claim that he lives in the clouds, the stunning truth is that only he is acquainted with the real world. Furthermore, he lives as one who knows that he is a part of this greater cosmic order; he refuses to behave like a prisoner in a cave.

To put it bluntly, what Aristophanes meant when he accused Socrates of living in the clouds was that Socrates inhabited the same space but did not live in the same world that other human beings occupied. Plato accepts this charge and inverts it. Other men cannot understand their humanity because they are imprisoned in their bodies by ignorance, fear, superstition, or carnality. Languishing in spiritually impoverished underworlds, they cannot be said to live at all! Instead of fearing death, they should ask if they have ever lived. It is because they understand and perceive themselves only through shadows that they are so afraid of dying. Socrates, who left the cave and saw himself in the light of goodness and truth, possesses adequate self-knowledge. Consequently, he does not fear death.

In this context it is helpful to consider the great myth of the *Gorgias*, since it sheds much light on both the *Phaedo* and the *Republic*. There is no need to read it as an account of the afterlife, for Socrates is really describing the damage that the intemperate soul inflicts upon itself. As in the *Republic*, the intemperate soul imprisons itself in a this-worldly prison of its own making: its unruly body. This condition seems to correspond to the spiritual suicide about which Socrates is so concerned. The point of these myths is simple and consistent: the soul that refuses to live virtuously is already in Hades. Thus there is no need to speak about sanctions in the afterlife; the evil man inevitably visits sufficient punishment upon himself through refusing to live virtuously in this life. The gods of the underworld merely observe what the soul has done to itself (324b–325a).

Socrates is like the escaped prisoner of the *Republic* in that he is free to travel between the cave and the real world. We are reminded irresistibly of the palinode from the *Phaedrus* when he says that like a fish coming up to breathe, a man can briefly poke his head up into the true world and contemplate its riches (109e). His body prevents him from dwelling permanently away from the cave (in this sense the cave is the body), but he does not return to the cave reluctantly. Eros, conspicuous by its absence in the *Republic*, and quite proudly present in the *Symposium*, empowers him to return joyfully to the cave.

I deal with eros in much greater detail in my study of the *Symposium*, but some preliminary observations can be made here. Since eros operates through the dialectic between *poros* and *penia*, the very wretchedness of the self-imprisoned soul enables it to burst free of its bonds and seek truth. The soul must first become aware of the extent of its self-deception, however, and this is where the abrasive processes of Socratic midwifery come into play. The soul must endure the death of its shadow self before it is prepared to become aware of its true identity. It must surrender all the false opinions and securities that it had clothed / imprisoned itself in. (One is reminded of the false cosmetic arts in *Gorgias* 465b–e and the final naked condition in which the soul is revealed to itself.) Further, because of the power of the body, the soul must endure spiritual death and reincarnation many times before it is ready to ascend beyond the bonds of the body. This seems to be what

Socrates meant when he said that those who study philosophy are engaged in training themselves for dying and being dead (63a).

The sophistic arts anaesthetize the soul and thus enable it to inflict grave damage upon itself, unthinkingly. Socratic dialectic, by way of contrast, helps the soul to heal itself, but it can do so only by first making the soul painfully aware of its sickness and disease. Socrates must tear the soul out of its womblike prison of false securities. Although this seems tragic (and even deathlike) to the yet unborn soul, such an exercise is comic from the vantage of the midwife.

The problem with disciples such as Phaedo and Cebes is their perverse desire to escape the physical world altogether. Although they wish to do so in order to ascend to a higher spiritual plane, they only deck themselves with false wings that have not sprung from the mysterious depths of erotic desire. In attempting to escape the labyrinth of Minos with its contradictory proofs and inefficient causalities, they end up, like Icarus, in Hades, where Minos waits to judge them. In other words, their pusillanimous denial of the world leads only to an even more perverse understanding of the ideal state. By denying the desires in their disgust at men led by their bodies, they only commit a different form of spiritual suicide.

In the *Republic*, we observed that the cave represented the refinement of the tyrannical ideas in Glaucon's soul. In other words the philosopher-king, instead of being at the top of the divided line, is the tyrant lurking at the very bottom of the line. Similarly, the underworld described at the end of the *Phaedo* represents the culmination of the flawed metaphysics and the life-negating philosophies espoused by Phaedo and his ilk. The myth of the divided line is remarkable for the fact that the second and third segments of the line will always be equal, suggesting that they could be collapsed into one. Their seeming difference, however, is in the respective psychic orientations they represent. The one looks away from the cave and toward the ideas; the other looks toward the cave and away from the ideas. The one represents an enlightened perspective on reality which enables it to participate in the field of eros generated by the ideas, whereas, the other depicts an impoverished view of reality which is the necessary result of the life-negating soul's perverse attraction to tyranny and its concurrent refusal to partake of the ideal realm.

It should now be apparent how Plato makes it possible for the *Protagoras* to be reconciled to the *Phaedo*. Socrates is not otherworldly in his dissatisfaction with those who live in the body; rather, his point is that materialism alienates men from the true world. In this sense he is the sternest critic of the otherworldliness of Phaedo and his kind. It is only by residing in the true world, not the impoverished realms of materialism and superstition, that one can experience the good life. Such a life, which depends on a man's knowing himself as a soul-in-a-body and a being-in-the world, will see through the illusions of pleasure and pain that pervade the various shadow realms.

Socrates would insist that the soul has much to learn through its tenure in the body. It is through the *via negativa*, of overcoming abstractly physical reality that the soul comes to understand many things about itself and its desires. It is through its dissatisfaction with the false reality in which it finds itself that the soul becomes acquainted with the structures of ideality. We learn from the *Phaedrus* that the soul needs the carnal power of the black horse to break out of its prison; the prisonhouse of the body must be transformed into a winged steed. In other words, it would be the utmost folly for the soul to seek to eliminate desire; rather, its task is to overcome the ignorance that leads desire blindly in search of material satiation.

The intermediary stage, as Diotima explains in the *Symposium*, has to do with the spirit (209a). Love of one's own, so tellingly caricatured as selfishness in the *Republic*, can turn into the loving and uncompetitive associations of friendship. It will then be possible to understand the transcendental conditions that sustain love and friendship. Thus, Socrates is not a hater of the body politic. He does not fear either the comic body he inhabits or the tragic political body that has sentenced him to die. He knows that neither body can destroy his identity. Indeed, in a spirit of *Amor Fati*, Socrates might well claim that his self-knowledge came through combining the tragic spiritedness of the body politic with the comic humility that his physical body taught him. It was through the erotic intercourse that he enjoyed with other citizens that Socrates became the wisest of mortals.

Taking a final look at the *Phaedo*, we see that four domains (corresponding to the segments of the divided line) are described by Socrates. These function like the four strings of a lyre; harmonized, they yield a cosmology derived from the various dispositional possibilities of the soul. The highest domain, the realm of the forms, has to do with the powers that sustain the virtuous philosopher. Although he does not expect to become one with these entities after his death, he obviously hopes to enjoy a closer and more permanent association with them. This true world, beyond all the caverns of the earth, is the basis of the truly human existence enjoyed by the philosopher. As a denizen of eternity he can be of much service to those who cannot see beyond the cave. Even though for the most part he lives in the caverns of the earth, he is not of them; his life bears testimony to the higher realities that sustain it. The world of everyday life is located, both physically and psychically, in these chasms; the task of those who dwell here is to turn body and soul around to contemplate the higher ground.

The lowest of the four domains, Hades, relates to the this-worldly effects of unrehabilitated sin (as described in the *Gorgias* and the *Republic*) or to the nihilistic ideals of pessimism and life denial that the *Phaedo* and its narrator have just described. Socrates' account of Hades is no more than a representation of all the randomness, uncertainty, and fear that the Pythagorean approach toward reincarnation engenders. Any soul that looks in this direction, instead of aspiring to the true humanness that the vision of the forms promises, will fall victim to discouragement and life negation.

As the image of the divided line indicates, the second and third domains occupy the same physical space but, by virtue of their very different views of reality, represent fundamentally different psychic dispositions. Most men are content to reside in the third region where they reason as slaves and live determined by false notions of causality and necessity. In attempting to escape the falsities of the third region, Phaedo and his kind flee in the wrong direction and consequently they fall even deeper toward the fourth region where, like Phaethon, they are doomed to be overwhelmed by the plunging horrors of chaos. Misology and misanthropy ensure that the selfish philosopher freezes in his own perverse Hades. He resembles the overheated sensualist in failing to understand that it is through the body and the desires that one learns how to enter the celestial realm of love.

Plato contrasts to this pathetic waste of human spiritual capacity the figure of Socrates, who lives in awareness of the true world. In the words of the *Meno* (100a), he walks around other men such as Tiresias among the dead; he is a solid reality among shadows. According to Odysseus, Tiresias was the only one in the underworld to retain his wits.[57] In the *Symposium* we shall see how this likeness to Tiresias persists through Socrates' successful synthesis of male and female spiritual qualities. Socrates may also be compared with his earlier alter ego in this dialogue: Heracles, whose true self feasted in Olympus while his wraith remained in the grim confines of Hades.[58]

There are many different ways to comport oneself toward a Platonic work. One extreme is simply assuming that the dialogue gives the literal truth, so that readers may harness their horses and go over the top without further ado; this leads only to an unwitting imitation of the sorry fate of Phaethon. The other exegetical extreme consists in being overwhelmed by pessimism upon encountering contradictory proofs; this leads readers toward the underworld described in the myth. Although superior to the first kind, such readers despair without understanding that the purpose of these contradictions is to reincarnate them in the text. They should continually reread a dialogue, with their minds and desires, until they finally discover its meaning within their souls. Instead of begetting an endless, Hydra-like proliferation of specious arguments, the labor pangs involved in reading a dialogue may effect a spiritual re-birth in the worthy reader. As was the case with the *Protagoras*, initial pain precedes the pleasure that follows the stringing the lyre. Like the bow of Odysseus, a dialogue is always a test of the reader's worthiness; it contains several built-in tests, devised to establish the identity and fidelity of the reader.

Socrates' daimon is the tuning fork that the reader must use to sound the matter of the text, as he explores its labyrinthine innards in search of secret harmonies. Simultaneously, Socrates' stonemason's hammer will perform its maieutic magic on the reader as it reveals and refines his soul matter. This process both resurrects Socrates and produces a soul that is properly appreciative of human existence. It is surely not too great an overstatement to say that we cannot have one without the other. It is the psychic disposition of the reader that determines whether or not Socrates is to appear before him.

Plato's *Phaedo* is many things: it is a comedy for Socrates, a melodramatic passion play for Phaedo, a definitive documentary for neo-Platonists, and a tragedy for the history of philosophy. By artfully weaving together these four possibilities, Plato says much about the importance that he attaches to his reader's psychic participation in the quest for Socrates. In other words, my reading suggests that Plato is willing to run the risk of misinterpretation in order to preserve for posterity the possibility of genuinely encountering Socrates.

The next dialogue to be considered, the *Symposium*, explicitly deals with the subject of blending comic and tragic elements. In the *Phaedo*, Plato studies the mystery of the continued existence of Socrates. In the *Symposium* he speculates about Socrates' even more enigmatic essence. While the *Phaedo* suggests that Socrates' quiet confidence in his continued existence derives from his personal relationship with the Ideas, the *Symposium* gives a memorable account of how the philosopher enters into this relationship and generously shares its benefits with his community.

4   Symposium I: The Battle between Comedy and Tragedy

The Uninvited Guest

My efforts at uncovering the soul of Socrates, and understanding the genuinely human condition that in the *Phaedo* he claimed to have attained, culminate in a discussion of Plato's *Symposium*.[1] Although Socrates' soul is unique and can only be discerned indirectly and momentarily through several veils and disguises, Plato is most explicit here about his own conclusions.

In this chapter, by way of approach, I contrast Socrates' spiritual disposition to two other politico-erotic possibilities: the hubris-driven optimism of the sophistic enlightenment, and the reactionary hubris of Aristophanes. The study of these extremes as bodied forth in the *Symposium* will prepare us to recognize the erotic moderation of Socrates. In his depiction of these two extremes of hubris, Plato suggests that Aristophanes is quite as dangerous as the young sophists from whom the conservative comic poet is so anxious to protect Athens. Whereas Aristophanes set out to create a natural order through artifice, and Agathon thought that nature should be overcome, the *Symposium* suggests that only Socrates properly apprehended the richness of reality. The hubris of Aristophanes and the optimism of Agathon jointly brought about the death of tragedy. Neither man knew how to go about the crucial task of educating human desire.

In Chapter 5 I turn to Socrates' contribution to the discussion. Diotima's speech suggests that eros must mediate between the divine and profane aspects in both the cosmos and the human soul. We will observe that the possibility of educating desire derives from Socrates' discovery of the feminine nature of the soul. And finally, Alcibiades provides valuable revelations that shed light on Socrates' own erotic education, explicate some of the more enigmatic parts of the *Phaedrus*, and decipher the intricate relationship between tragedy, comedy, and philosophy.

The *Symposium* provides crucial insights into the nature of love which could prove to be of the greatest value in understanding and resolving the erotic and political perplexities of our own age. Postmodernism urgently seeks an answer to the riddle of eros. With the opening up of the Pandora's box of technology, it seems no longer possible to suppress eros in a nontotalitarian manner. I have shown that Plato had already studied and refuted the totalitarian temptation with surpassing brilliance in the *Republic*; it now remains to be seen whether his resolution of the problem of eros is applicable to our age.

Plato's *Symposium* resembles Xenophon's *Symposium* in that both works draw attention to Socrates' status as an erotic object; however, there are striking differences both in the way they make this revelation and in the significance it is accorded. Whereas Xenophon's Socrates enters, albeit ironically, into a beauty contest with the much younger Critobulus[2] and claims to be proudest of his skill as a procurer,[3] Plato's Socrates merely asserts that eros is the only thing he understands (177d). It is left to the reader to tear aside this mask of irony and discover the connection between the procurer's art and Socrates' identity as an erotic daimon. Far from being a procurer, he is found to be an erotic emissary, passionately dedicated to elevating the polis from the subterranean state. The subtext of Plato's *Symposium* thus reveals a latent analogue to Xenophon's *Symposium*, but Plato's work is far more profound than Xenophon's curious report.

Many of the speculations and suggestions that emerged from the dialogues examined earlier are substantiated and corroborated in examining the *Symposium*. The philosopher attains a heroic state through his erotic activity.[4] His way of life is justifiable and rational, and it serves as its own source of satisfaction in the present and future. It thus turns out that Eros is not a mighty god who mediates independently between men and the other Olympians; eros is indeed a great power, but it functions in the truest fashion through the philosopher.

The erotic philosopher apprehends a vision of the Good and is obligated thereby to convey this good news to the cave. This communication is primarily through erotic deeds rather than by information transmission. Eros cannot be apprehended or transferred through efficient causality for eros is not an entity; it is more like an elemental cosmic force or grace that pervades all of reality.

I shall claim in Chapter 5 that the rulers of the cave set about reducing the transcendental archetypes to domesticated caricatures of their true and erotic nature. For the present, I shall describe how this approach is followed in the case of eros itself. Many of the speakers in this dialogue will attempt to portray eros in their own image, as a great power that they have harnessed and deployed for power and profit in the world. Socrates deviates from this pattern when he presents a significantly different portrayal of eros, one that he claims to have received from a wise woman. Although the content of his speech indeed highlights aspects of eros that are distinctively Socratic, the whole drift is away from the identity of eros. Socrates instead seeks to midwife an erotic vision for those who had hitherto been either tragically misdirected or comically deflated in their quests.

The similarities between this portrayal of eros and my interpretation of the *Phaedo* are obvious; here again the task is to eschew trajectories that are either too tragically high or comically low. Paradoxically, confirmation of Socrates' identity as the erotic mediator between the two extremes comes from a figure commonly perceived as the very personification of the highest Athenian hubris. Alcibiades' encomium to Socrates is characteristically erotic and yet untypical of his own notoriously egocentric nature; it abounds in humility and terror as he reveals the wondrous effects that this uncanny old man has had on his soul.

Alcibiades, who was accused of profaning the Eleusinian mysteries,[5] is quite as indiscreet in his identification of eros as Socrates himself. The revelation is, again, characteristically excessive, but as much as he confuses Socrates with the god Eros, Alcibiades does recognize the erotic personification that Socrates has achieved. Yet Alcibiades also illustrates the extent to which even the most promising of souls may be daunted and destroyed by its unwillingness to be properly receptive to the gifts of eros.

As noted, the *Symposium* is a contest in which Socratic Eros is compared with the other alternatives, comedy and tragedy. Tragedy is represented by as many as four different voices, each illustrative of a different facet of the sophistical enlightenment; the conservative force of comedy is embodied in its greatest practitioner, Aristophanes. Many close readers of the dialogues prefer to believe that Socrates was chastised and corrected by the encounter with Aristophanes that is chronicled in the comedian's unsuccessful play *The Clouds*.[6] An unprejudiced reading of the

Symposium, however, reveals the fundamental weaknesses and absurdities of Aristophanic antihumanism. The *Symposium* also displays Plato's prophetic anticipation of the subsequent triumph of the comedian, a victory so decisive that much delicate excavation is required before one may discern the alternative possibilities for the education of eros.

The erotic contest that takes place in the *Symposium* parallels the quarrel of the goddesses Athena, Aphrodite, and Hera over who was the most beautiful. It is important to bear in mind that each goddess represented a different form of eros. Hera's seems to be the tragic eros of the young sophists; they prefer power and glory to physical procreation, and Hera also typically attempts to take power into her own hands by overwhelming the will and plans of Zeus. Aphrodite, on the other hand, seems to be served by Aristophanes and comic eros; she prefers the pleasures and illusions of the flesh to the doubtful glory of storming heaven. Nevertheless, the unity of the soul makes it inevitable that some of the traits of comedy and tragedy should overlap and point toward each other.

This being the case, a subtler examination of the text suggests that the identification of Aphrodite and Hera with Aristophanes and the young sophists respectively is more than capable of being reversed. Indeed, the resultant identifications are, astonishingly, stronger than those that were superficially suggested. Since he defends the family and chthonic forces deeply resentful of the optimistic aspirations of democracy, tragedy, and humanism, Aristophanes well resembles Hera. He also seems to hate these forces as much as Hera hates Troy. Recall her celebrated attempt at defeating the plans of Zeus through seducing him on Mount Ida.[7] It was with this far from erotic intention in mind that she cynically used the charms of Aphrodite. We shall see that Aristophanes employs sex in the same fashion.

Conversely, Aphrodite and the young sophists are connected through the optimistic mentality of excessive and unenlightened eros that led, paradoxically, to such violent and tragic events as the Trojan and Peloponnesian Wars. The idea seems to be that internal repression or violence reduces the risk of war by encouraging the domestication of eros, whereas erotic self-indulgence is more likely to lead to actual strife outside the city. We shall find that this alternation of roles reveals the extent to which both the comedy and tragedy of the time are inadequate responses to the challenges of eros.

Whichever analogy we choose for Hera and Aphrodite, Athena certainly is followed by Socrates and his Homeric alter ego, Odysseus.[8]

Socrates resolves the dilemmas of eros by reconciling the earthy moderation of comedy with the infinite striving of tragedy. This formula for the education of desire seems far superior to the endless opposition of comedy and tragedy. The sophists represent a life spent blindly pursuing insatiable desire; Aristophanes merely offers immediate bodily gratification before the great force of eros is unarmed and put to bed. According to Plato, the salvation of Athens must consist in mediating between these warring factions.

As Martha Nussbaum has shown, this bitterly divided city is what the beginning of the dialogue re-creates.[9] Although the actual speeches are set in the year 416 B.C.E., and dramatically prefigure the night before the disastrous Sicilian expedition in 415, it is more difficult to set the dramatic date of the narration. It is some years since Agathon left Athens, and we know that Agathon was in Athens in 410; Alcibiades, who died in about 404 or 403, is spoken of as if he is alive; and Apollodorus, who did not become known to Socrates until several years after Agathon's departure, says that he has followed Socrates for three years. We can thus conclude that it is 405 or 404.

Other details support this dating. Apollodorus could hardly have enjoyed the freedom of movement necessary to walk regularly from Phaleron, a maritime location very close to the Piraeus, the stronghold of the democratic exiles, into the city if the Thirty had already been established. This means that the bitter civil war between the oligarchs and the democrats, which took place in 404–403, had not yet begun. Further, Apollodorus's questioner is a rich businessman, and the former does not speak as if the latter's economic activity has been suspended or curtailed by war (173c). This again suggests that the naval blockade, which followed the final naval defeat of Athens in 405 and reduced the city to starvation by early 404, has yet to take full effect.[10] Apollodorus speaks with the particular scorn that a poor man can display toward one much wealthier than himself in a time of general economic equilibrium; starving men do not address the wealthy in such tones. Apollodorus also speaks as if Agathon's absence precluded a meeting between Alcibiades and Socrates that he himself *could* have witnessed. Since, after his fateful departure for Sicily in 415, Alcibiades was present in Athens for only a few months in 407, we can conclude that Apollodorus was already a follower of Socrates in 407. Thus the outermost reach of Apollodorus's discipleship and the dramatic date of the dialogue is 404.

All these data serve to corroborate Nussbaum's dating of the dialogue. Just as the *Theaetetus* takes place against the background of the impending demise of that young mathematician, the *Symposium* has as its dramatic backdrop the looming death of Alcibiades and the fall of "violet-crowned" Athens.[11] Allan Bloom rightly points out that the *Symposium* combines references to the highest and lowest points of Athenian morale after the resumption of the Peloponnesian War; they represent its *poros* and *penia*.[12]

Apollodorus tells his unnamed interrogator that only two days previously, one Glaucon had also asked for details of those speeches about eros made so many years before. Glaucon's use of legal phraseology seems to suggest that his interest in these long-forgotten events was not occasioned simply by whimsy or curiosity. He has evidently been making extensive inquiries around town and country. These presumably had to do with the erotic connection between Socrates and Alcibiades for Agathon—the only other party named in his question—is hardly known to Glaucon. As Glaucon's ignorance concerning the year of Agathon's departure suggests, the poet is mentioned only because he was said to be the host of the discussion. This Glaucon is not very interested in the poets. In this respect, he resembles his namesake at the conclusion of the *Republic*.

Placing the dramatic date of the narration of the *Symposium* in about 404 suggests that these inquiries are *not* connected with the trial of Socrates, which took place some years later. Rather, the suggested time of the narration implies that the interest of Apollodorus's inquisitors had to do with an even more controversial figure. Alcibiades, who died in 404 or 403 shortly after the Athenian surrender, represented the last hope of the Athenians at a time when the downfall of Athens was imminent. Only the unbelievably resourceful Alcibiades, appearing as a deus ex machina could have saved the city from the Spartans. Conversely, the possibility of Alcibiades' return represented the greatest fear of the pro-Spartan landed gentry because only he could have divided their ranks and urged the more moderate elements toward a patriotic disposition. In fact, this was apparently why he was assassinated.[13]

Glaucon is the name of Plato's brother; whether or not the Glaucon of the *Republic* is also the Glaucon of the Symposium, the implication is that the latter is connected with Plato's reactionary family. At the time of this dialogue Plato's best-known kinsmen were Critias and Charmides, two rather prominent members of the infamous Thirty.[14] A group of rich businessman would have been more likely to associate with the Piraeus and pro-democratic elements. Whereas the oligarchs, as we have seen, would be identified with Aristophanes and comedy, the rich commercial interests were part of the hubris-driven imperialism that led to so much tragedy.

We seem to have identified two factions, with vastly differing political agendas, vitally interested in the erotic connection between Socrates and Alcibiades. As Aristophanes put it in a play written in 405, "The city longs for him, it hates him, and it wants him back."[15] Although Alcibiades, disgusted by the fickle populace, had voluntarily left Athens after his return from exile for a few brief months in 407, none could discount the possibility that he might again return. The great love that he reputedly still bore for Socrates could tip the scales toward this possibility. Such a homecoming might cause a dramatic change in the political balance of power, like Alcibiades' dramatic return just before the battle of Aegospotami to warn the Athenian admirals about their incredibly foolish deployments.[16] The hope was that this time the Athenians would accept Alcibiades, the only man who could simultaneously bamboozle the Spartans and Persians and possibly reconcile the warring factions within Athens itself. Alcibiades combines in his nature the seemingly disparate qualities of prodigal son and avenging deity; his belated appearance as Dionysus is far from accidental.[17]

Neither is the presence of Apollodorus as narrator accidental. Present at the deathbed of Socrates, Apollodorus distinguished himself by wailing loudly (117d). Here like Cygnus, the friend of Phaethon who was transformed into a swan, the harsh-toned Apollodorus conveys the most beautiful of the dialogues.

We also need to give further attention to the significance of the identity of Apollodorus's first interrogator, Glaucon. As I said earlier, Plato used this name-dropping device in the *Parmenides* to suggest how to read the *Republic*. Even if one is inclined to disagree with my take on how those gratuitous references to Cephalus, Glaucon, and Adeimantus are to be interpreted, it is clear that their names serve to draw attention to the *Republic* in some way. My reading of the *Republic* is supported by the fact that it is Adeimantus rather than Glaucon who talks to Cephalus in the *Parmenides*.[18] Glaucon will never speak again in the Platonic corpus; in the *Symposium* his words (if he is indeed the same Glaucon) are only reported. In the case of the *Republic*, however, the connection with the *Symposium* is very much more essential and suggestive; the *Symposium* completes the course of psychic education that the *Republic* pointedly left incomplete.

By using the name of Glaucon, Plato obviously intends to make his reader recollect the *Republic*. Leaving aside the question of his political affiliations, one must ask why Glaucon is so eager to know what Socrates and Alcibiades said about eros. The answer is obvious. Although the Glaucon of the *Republic* was a very spirited and erotic young man, his soul was divided against itself because his desires were misdirected. In the *Republic* he was made to see the problems with his own desires, but he was not yet ready to understand the orientation of Socrates' desires.

In the *Republic*, as we noted, Socrates did not provide the account of the perfectly just life that Glaucon requested; instead, he contented himself with dismantling the illusion of the life of perfect injustice that Thrasymachus had constructed. The desires of the so-called philosopher-king of the *Republic* were monstrous and tyrannical; Socrates contrasted them unfavorably and tellingly with the self-sufficient spiritual economy of the virtuous private citizen. Indeed, eros is portrayed throughout the *Republic* in an unfavorable light; the philosopher-king must disguise his own insatiable desires to lead his subjects away from the fever of eros and toward the prelapsarian or prelibidinal condition. There is some irony here; in order to construct the *Republic*, Socrates had to conceal his own erotic nature.

Although the *Republic* eventually refers to the truly philosophical vision of reality outside the cave, the description is couched in nonerotic language. This is the reason underlying Socrates' inability to explain why a philosopher would return to the cave. The philosopher is inspired by his erotic ecstasy outside the cave to return to the community and spread enlightenment. *Philo-sophia*, love of wisdom, is turned around and becomes the wisdom of love. Glaucon was not yet ready for this revelation.[19] But in the *Symposium* he is several years older; the idealized Glaucon now stands ready for the second installment of his philosophical education. It is not too rash to speculate that if Socrates had shared his most comprehensive vision of eros with anybody, it would have been Alcibiades. Indeed, it is Alcibiades who immediately comes to mind when we read in book 6 of the *Republic* Socrates' discussion of the destruction and corruption of the most excellent philosophic natures.[20]

Turning now to the dialogue itself, we must duly observe that its dramatic date is very close to the fateful departure of the Sicilian Expedition of 415. Many commentators have recognized this fact, and a few have even gone on to speculate that the famous desecration of the herms occurred on this very night. To the best of my knowledge, however, none have seen that this mutilation occurs within the structure of the dialogue itself.[21] Indeed, one could say that the fullest implications of the mutilation are revealed here. The mutilation of the herms is Alcibiades' tragicomic response to Socrates' rejection of his sexual advances.

It is also very important to recall Stanley Rosen's observation that all the speakers in the *Symposium*, with one notable exception, appeared originally in the *Protagoras*.[22] The *Protagoras* is set in the glory days of Periclean Athens, right before the beginning of the ruinous Peloponnesian War, and depicts Phaedrus, Pausanias, Eryximachus, and Agathon as students of sophistry.[23] In the *Symposium*, about twenty years later, the wind-eggs of sophistry have all hatched: these young men are now sophists and orators in their own right and prominent members of respectable Athenian society to boot. Alcibiades is a special case. As his timely intervention in the *Protagoras* demonstrated (336b–d), he was closer to Socrates than to the sophists.

Aristophanes is the one addition to the ensemble of the *Protagoras*. Although at first glance the archconservative comedian would seem to be at the farthest remove from Protagorean sophistry, one finds a startling likeness in many of the attitudes and expectations concerning human nature held by Protagoras and Aristophanes. The beginning and the end of history are not all that different. In the *Symposium*, Socrates once again finds himself occupying a precarious middle position between the materialistic optimism of the Athenian technophiles and the pseudotheological (but not less materialistic) pessimism of Aristophanes.

Socrates is met on his way to the house of Agathon by Aristodemus of Cydatheneum, one of the many enthusiasts who habitually kept his company. The name Aristodemus means "best of the many," and I argue that his conduct at the house of Agathon vindicates his name. Socrates is especially well groomed for the occasion; this is not inconsistent with his behavior in Xenophon's *Symposium*, where he boasted of his beauty and skill as a procurer. [24]

Aristodemus is reluctant to accompany Socrates to Agathon's party without a proper invitation, but he is soon persuaded to follow his master's bidding. Socrates then makes the casual observation that they would refute the proverb that the good go uninvited to the feast of an inferior; he proposes to restate it as "the good go uninvited to the feast of the good"—thus making a play on Agathon's name, which means "good." He adds that Homer would also disagree with the adage, since he makes the "limp spearman," Menelaus go uninvited to Agamemnon's feast (174b–c). Robert Lloyd Mitchell makes the very valid observation that these remarks concerning Menelaus represent a flagrant misreading of Homer, since they derive from a rhetorical provocation made by Apollo to rouse Hector when Menelaus successfully defended the body of Patroclus.[25] Aristodemus's meek concurrence with the distortion indicates that he is not a very good reader of Homer, but more interesting are the reasons underlying the better-read Socrates' deliberate misrepresentation.

Bear in mind that Socrates is comparing Aristodemus and Menelaus as uninvited guests. In fact, the best Homeric precedent for gate-crashing the house of a good man would be Telemachus's going incognito and uninvited to the house of Menelaus.[26] But it is crucial to the argument being set out that Menelaus should play the role of uninvited guest, not the host. The implications of this identification provide the key to understanding the entire dialogue.

Menelaus, for all his deficiencies as a warrior, is best known for his valiant determination to recover Helen. Since the temporarily beautified Socrates is Aristodemus's beloved, it seems as if the cuckolded Aristodemus / Menelaus is being lewdly hectored (by being called a limp spearman) to follow his beloved Socrates / Helen uninvited into the enemy camp.[27] Socrates / Helen has apparently been seduced by Agathon, so the tragedian would seem to be identified with Paris in Aristodemus's biased eyes—and like Paris, Agathon is characterized by effeminate prettiness. The likeness is illusory, however; in the ruling structure of the dialogue Agathon is Helen, the reigning beauty of the day, and Socrates is only the ugliest suitor in her court. Not until later in the dialogue does Dionysus overturn this decadent regime.

Why did Socrates go to the house of Agathon? Setting all punning aside, one can understand this action only in terms of erotic generosity, the kind of formal causality that would inspire a philosopher to go back to the cave. Socrates has not gone to worship the goodness of Agathon; he is going for Agathon's good. This is also why Socrates has gone to the extreme lengths of disguising / beautifying himself in preparation for this encounter between the two Helens: the duel between ephemeral and eternal beauty.

By combining these two disparate perspectives, we may see that Socrates far better resembles Odysseus in his familiar role of the beggar. He is either proceeding to the Trojan camp to spy on Helen or going into his own home to claim Penelope. In this latter capacity, Socrates the beggar is suddenly stripped of his ironic disguise by a god so that he may compete with the other suitors (including Agathon, the reigning beauty of the day) in the unlikely arena of beauty. The irony consists in the fact that Socrates, whom we previously supposed to have been a beggar at the feet of the other suitors, suddenly proves to be their rival and superior. Eros rises out of abject penury, endowed with well-feathered arrows.[28]

Alcibiades soon comments upon this stunning contrast between outer appearance and inner reality. He will judge this contest as an embodiment or representative of Dionysus rather than Athena, whose favorite Socrates / Odysseus patently is.[29] Indeed, Socrates represents the claims of Athena in what turns out to be a contest against Hera / Aristophanes and Aphrodite / Agathon over which of the three is the most erotic. Alcibiades, who at one time or another had great influence in Athens, Sparta, and Persia, was uniquely qualified to choose among the conflicting claims of beauty, power over Asia, and wisdom; he is thus fittingly chosen to judge this contest.

Although Aristodemus's reasons for accompanying Socrates have more to do with erotic need than with generosity, his master now uses another quotation from Homer to promote him to the stature of Odysseus.[30] The original lines from the *Iliad* describe Agamemnon's fear lest Diomedes choose Menelaus to accompany him on the night raid behind the Trojan lines. Diomedes set these fears at rest by choosing Odysseus for his resourcefulness. We must remember that the capacity for tenacious endurance is one that both Menelaus and Odysseus possessed in abundance; among other things, they were the last heroes to return from Troy. Aristodemus, the limp but faithful lover, likewise possesses this virtue of tenacity. His deficiencies as a speaker (which make him a limp spearman at this battle of words) do not prevent him from doggedly holding on and recalling all that was said about eros at the banquet. It is also worth bearing in mind that it was Menelaus, the so-called limp spearman, who recognized the voice of Odysseus and rescued him when the Trojans had separated Odysseus from the retreating Diomedes the day after the night raid.[31] Similarly, Aristodemus / Menelaus tenaciously protect the corpus of Odysseus / Socrates' remarks for posterity.

One final preliminary matter: why does Socrates have Aristodemus go ahead of him to Agathon's banquet? Since Aristodemus habitually dressed after the Socratic fashion, he apparently represents his master, while Socrates himself, disguised as he is, will appear in another persona. Aristodemus does not speak at the banquet; he emulates Socrates' professions of ignorance in this respect. Is this also why Socrates has his "Menelaus" play his own customary role of Odysseus the beggar? But where is Socrates and what has he become? At the more obvious level we could claim that he is Diomedes, who will go on to trounce both Ares and Aphrodite (tragedy and comedy)[32] and return, accompanied by Odysseus, with a team of heavenly horses.[33] But there are even deeper mysteries to be revealed. As would-be initiates we must return to the house of Agathon, take our seats with the side of the tenacious and un-invited Aristodemus / Menelaus, and watch for the disguised Socrates. In Socrates' own words, "This is like Proteus, the Egyptian Sophist. Let us follow the example of Menelaus and not let go until these men re-veal their real shape" *Euthydemus* 288c).

I suggested earlier that it is not easy to associate Menelaus with the practice of gate-crashing. Socrates' intentionally misreads Homer when he suggests that Menelaus was an uninvited guest at his own brother's tent during a strategy session (hardly a banquet) in a war waged to recover Menelaus's wife.[34] The all too patent absurdity of it is impossible would be hard pressed to find a Homeric instance where Menelaus makes an un-invited and disguised entry into another man's house. Isn't Menelaus the very model of hospitality? His violated hospitality is, after all, what occa-sioned the Trojan War. Further, he plays the role of gracious host to per-fection when Telemachus appears at his house.

Still, in one striking Homeric instance Menelaus does play the role of a disguised and uninvited guest. He himself relates the story to Tele-machus, who, like Glaucon, is seeking information about the absent Socrates / Odysseus. The incident in question occurred in Egypt when Menelaus, separated from the rest of the Greek fleet returning from Troy, was stranded on the island of Pharos. A sea nymph who be-friended him said that he would find his way back home only after cap-turing Proteus, the Old Man of the Sea, and compelling him to divulge the truth. She warned that although Proteus would change himself into many different earthly forms to evade questioning, Menelaus would have to grasp him firmly and not let go until the Old Man reverted to his own form. Menelaus duly clung to the Old Man as he went through six different metamorphoses and finally provided the information that was required of him.[35] If Aristodemus is to play Menelaus the uninvited guest, it follows that Socrates plays Proteus in the *Symposium*.

At this point it is worthy of mention that Apollodorus was incredu-lous when asked whether he had received his account of what tran-spired at Agathon's party from Socrates himself.[36] He did, however, admit to receiving confirmation of *part* of Aristodemus's account from Socrates. Why would Socrates be so reticent about *all* that went on at this party—what Eleusinian mysteries were profaned there? Is it simply the mutilation of the herms, or is something more going on? Further, since several important dialogues are narrated directly in Socrates' own voice, what sets the *Symposium* apart from those such as the *Republic* and the *Protagoras*? What parts of this dialogue would Socrates be unwilling to confirm?

All of Plato's dialogues investigate the souls of the various interlocutors; indeed, they are usually named after the soul that is being examined. The *Republic* and *Symposium* are exceptions to this practice of naming, and we have seen that the former is really a secret account of Glaucon's soul. Bearing in mind that someone called Glaucon is one of Apollodorus's questioners in the latter, and with a sharp eye for Plato's consummate artistry, we must ascertain whose soul is being revealed in the *Symposium*. Socrates, very willing to reveal the souls of his interlocutors, is remarkably coy about letting *his* nature be disclosed. I argue that the *Symposium* sets out to penetrate his own Protean defenses.

In the *Republic*, as already noted, Glaucon asked Socrates for a justification of the just life, an explanation of how Socrates justified his own life, and was instead provided with a brilliant account of Glaucon's own soul. At the time of the recounting of the *Symposium*, Glaucon, whether idealized or otherwise, is presumably ready for an account of the perfectly just life. He desires an account of Socrates' own soul, stripped of all appearances and illusions. Is it possible that this is what the *Symposium* is actually about? At one level, of course, saying so is restating the obvious: Alcibiades said explicitly that his speech would deal with Socrates. But the other speeches do not say anything at all about Socrates; all the other symposiasts are speaking of eros.

The respective identifications of Aristodemus and Socrates with Menelaus and Proteus may now be used to good effect. Eros turns out to be a polymorphously Protean figure who undergoes many metamorphoses before finally appearing as his own self. It would seem, according to Aristodemus's description in his capacity as Menelaus the faithful lover and stubborn interrogator of Proteus, that Socrates finally turns out to be identical with eros. Menelaus reported that Proteus underwent six transformations, becoming in turn a bearded lion, a snake, a leopard, a savage hog, running water, and a tree with towering branches, before finally resuming his own shape.[37] These changes correspond, at least numerically, to the six speeches given in praise of eros before Alcibiades appears and delivers his encomium to Socrates, which obviously corresponds to Proteus's far from voluntary reversion to his own form.

As Agathon and his guests start their dinner, Socrates is standing, as motionless as a herm, beside a neighbor's porch. Halfway through the meal he comes in and takes his seat beside Agathon at the host's request. Agathon, slightly annoyed by this intentional tardiness, claims to be desirous of receiving whatever wisdom Socrates has fastened on. The older man responds with withering irony, pointing out that it would be wonderful if the foolish could become filled with wisdom by merely coming into contact with those overflowing with it. Then would he joyfully keep the company of Agathon, hoping to receive some driblet of the wisdom that had won the full-throated acclaim of thirty thousand Athenians. In comparison to the kudos that Agathon has received for his dramatic depictions, Socrates says, his own paltry wisdom is fleeting as a dream (175c–e).

One is reminded of the escaped prisoner who returns to the cave and attempts to describe what he has seen to his chained comrades (516c–e). Agathon has just won a contest for creating shadows and received the praise of the entire cave; is it any wonder that he seems to have little regard for whatever Socrates might babble about? Agathon, well aware of Socrates' contempt for his popularity but confident that he is the favorite of the god, promises that it will be Dionysus himself, rather than the impressionable *demos*, who finally decides between them.

Eryximachus, who has just spoken of the harmful effects of inebriation, now suggests that the services of the flute girl (presumably sexual as well as musical) be dispensed with (176e), and it is unanimously agreed that the evening be devoted to conversation. All three of the excluded activities—drink, sex, and the sort of music associated with the flute—suggest Dionysus and excess—and all three are reintroduced by Alcibiades when he enters, very drunk and supported by a flute girl, giving us further evidence that he will play the role of Dionysus.

In assenting to Eryximachus's proposal that they speak in honor of love, Socrates states that he cannot disagree when the only thing he claims to understand is the art of eros (177d–e). Socrates also speaks for the other banqueters: he puts Agathon and Pausanias together and suggests that as lovers—of long standing: they had been an item twenty years earlier (*Protagoras* 315e)—they could hardly refuse to honor eros. Neither could Aristophanes, "whose every thought was about Dionysus and Aphrodite" (177e).

The significance of this observation, the only direct comment made by Socrates concerning Aristophanes, is well worth pondering. Does Socrates mean that Aristophanes is ignoring the other gods? Is it possible to regard Aristophanes' speech as a response to such a charge? Since Dionysus and Aphrodite are arguably manifestations of desire, Socrates could be alleging that Aristophanes is not sufficiently attentive to the other Olympians. Alternatively, and more daringly, he could be suggesting that the comic poet is so obsessed with desire that he does not acknowledge the existence of any other gods. Aphrodite and Dionysus can be viewed as the deities representing comedy and tragedy respectively. There is also the fact, observed by Leo Strauss, that Socrates seems to be immune to both sex and wine, through which Aphrodite and Dionysus become incarnate in the world.[38]

Finally, Socrates seems to enroll Aristodemus among the devotees of eros. We must keep in mind that Aristodemus's only connection with eros seems to be his great love for Socrates. Since Aristodemus does not speak at Agathon's dinner, we can conclude that his narration of the proceedings will constitute his tribute to both eros and Socrates. This is another anticipation of Alcibiades' advent: Dionysus will identify and pay homage to Socrates as Eros.

The Three Sophists

Eryximachus attributes his proposal that they honor Eros to Phaedrus, the first speaker, who has often complained that while so many lesser heroes had been singled out for praise, love had gone unhonored (177a–c). This clearly suggests that he has not yet heard Socrates' tribute to eros which appears in the dialogue named after him; the *Phaedrus* is thus dramatically subsequent to the *Symposium*—a fact not without its significance. The inference is also confirmed by Socrates' comment in the *Phaedrus* (242a–b) that Phaedrus has made and inspired many speeches and is surpassed in this respect only by Simmias the Theban.[39] The direct implication of Phaedrus's comment, however, is that the overwhelming power of love has much to do with the excellence manifested by a hero. (This attitude may also be compared to the disposition of Achilles in choosing the short, glorious life over the long, uneventful one.)

Phaedrus claims that Eros is the oldest of the gods; he is born of chaos and the earth "broad-breasted and safe" (178b). Eros would seem to represent something opposed to the "broad-breasted" feminine qualities of life and security. He is therefore the first masculine god, associated with the ceaseless striving for excellence, even if it results in death. Without this reason for a good death, life on earth would be perfectly secure and pointlessly stagnant.

Phaedrus thus espouses the most traditional and tragic view of Eros as the older lover who instructs his beloved in eros before dying a heroic death; this pattern is presumably emulated by the beloved when he is of sufficient age to love a boy. Phaedrus deprecates the value of the individual hero's life and stresses the nobility of the self-sacrificing lover who earns the eternal reward of the gods by choosing death over disgrace in the eyes of his beloved. Through glorious acts of this kind, the human condition would continue to improve with every passing-on of the Promethean torch from lover to beloved.

Like Hippias, with whom he is associated in the *Protagoras* (315c), Phaedrus has a prodigious memory and very little practical sense. The *Phaedrus* shows that much of his wisdom consists in learning great speeches by heart; he also follows Hippias in preferring the simple love of Achilles to the polytrophic perversities of Odysseus.[40] It is evident why the first of the Old Man of the Sea's metamorphoses, a bearded lion—representing the destructive force of tragedy, Achilles, and the older lover—should be used to symbolize the speech of Phaedrus. Yet somehow this passionate champion of tragic virtue has accepted a physician as his lover. Life and death must both exist, even if the terms of their coexistence turn out to be absurdly incongruous.

Phaedrus's speech, for all of its absurdities, is charmingly nonegotistical; he is, after all, speaking in his preferred persona of the naive beloved. The next speaker, Pausanias—whose name means "one who terminates sorrow"—is far from naive; he will abruptly dissolve Phaedrus' unreflective union of the masculine and feminine powers. The Terminator's reasons for this action are quite apparent, although they are clad in beguilingly moral words. The best men flee the security of earth and the shameful act of procreation through a woman; they go on to set up the more precarious institution of the polis which is based on the nobler kind of love. A sharp distinction may thus be drawn between the two kinds of desire. As Robert Mitchell has observed, the wholeness of eros has been terminated.[41] The two warring Aphrodites have eclipsed Eros. Aristophanes will go on to offer a different explanation for this act and even threaten further mutilations in the same vein. It is left to Socrates to restore the unity of eros, in both speech and deed.

Pausanias—who had studied with Prodicus, a celebrated rhetorician well known for the making of fine distinctions[42]—will attempt to effect a very clear separation here. Although Phaedrus has already cited Alcestis's love for Admetus as a remarkable exception, in Pausanias's eyes any possibility of genuine heterosexual love would be quite unacceptable; homosexual and heterosexual love are different in kind. Again, although Phaedrus has already distinguished between the earth and Eros, accepting Hesiod's word that the earth is the older of the two, Pausanias is not satisfied until he reverses this order of seniority. He claims that his love—intellectual pederasty—is of the heavenly Aphrodite and eternal, as opposed to the common bodily love that derives from Zeus's temporary liaison with Dione. Hesiod claimed that there were two types of *eris* (strife),[43] Pausanias will posit two kinds of eros.

Pausanias's claims to nobility are weakest when the pederastic act itself is considered; he attempts to evade this issue by claiming that the motive establishes whether a love is noble or base. We may use this very distinction to note that whereas Phaedrus' speech glorifies the love he demands from the older lover, Pausanias employs his powers of rhetoric to justify his own sexual preferences. As in the case of Protagoras, his verbal daring attempts to replace the genuine heroism and eroticism of a lover. One is reminded of the famous defense of the claims of the nonlover in the *Phaedrus* (230e–241c), an argument ultimately founded on the crass ground of utility. Pausanias himself is quite unabashed about claiming that the gods will forgive a lover who breaks vows made in the heat of passion (183b). Prodicus's student[44] will employ his guile and learning to defend the claims of an elderly sophisticated nonlover over a young and beautiful (un)beloved who, like Agathon, suddenly basks in celebrity.

It is not without reason, then, that the poisonous and hypocritical Pausanias may be identified as the serpent in our Protean analogy. Although he has drawn the important distinction (originally expressed by Prodicus)[45] between bodily lust and spiritual love, his loudly professed contempt for the body simply constitutes another form of hypocrisy, which will stand in the way of his ability to provide any true insight into the nature of eros and its connection with wisdom. As Stanley Rosen points out, the "unbeloved" of Pausanias must yield physically for two reasons: first, because it is noble to be deceived for the sake of virtue; second, because his lover is *au fond* a sophist who charges for his lessons.[46]

Pausanias's hypocritical distaste for the body would likely have exposed him to a withering retort from Aristophanes but is spared because the great comedian has been laid low by a devastating attack of the hiccups. It is possible that Pausanias's words have made him choke; alternatively, we could say that just as Socrates has prepared himself for the banquet by going into a motionless trance, Aristophanes retreats further into his body before making his speech. Eryximachus therefore changes places in the order of speaking with Aristophanes. In a sense, a comedian and a physician would be expected to possess similar views concerning a more harmonious and less dualistic cosmological order, but Aristophanes is a rather special case.

Eryximachus's name means something like "fighter of strife" and he is indeed placed in a situation where he has to mediate between Aristophanes' physical excesses and Pausanias's piously professed hatred of the body. As the lover of Phaedrus he is also required to frame a response to his beloved's implied lament that lovers of the present day are not more tragic and noble in their aspirations. By virtue of being a follower of Hippias and a believer in techne, Eryximachus is necessarily more optimistic in his outlook than a rhetorician (whose contributions to reality could only be superficial); he seems to believe that the medical art could transform and improve the disease-ridden cosmos itself.

Eryximachus points out that eros extends far beyond sexual preferences; Pausanias applied the wrong distinction in his understanding of heavenly and profane Aphrodites. Eryximachus, the Asclepiad, proposes to apply a simple preference for the healthy over the diseased. Since the role of medicine is to promote health and frustrate disease, the task of the cosmological physician is to foster attunement, love, and concord throughout nature. This means that nothing in nature is inherently bad; it can be said that evil was brought into existence by man's misguided attempts to create illicit distinctions and encourage either puritanical abstraction or excessive indulgence. Eryximachus's view of the cosmos does not exclude his own kind: the cosmos does not naturally exist in a harmonious state; it depends upon the ordering activity of a cosmic physician who serves as something like an Anaxagoraean nous.

Unlike that of his predecessors, Phaedrus and Pausanias, Eryximachus's cosmology says very little about the god Eros; he only distinguishes between healthy and unhealthy cosmic forces and attempts to mediate between them. Pausanias paid lip-service to the Uranian Aphrodite, although his cosmology was nothing but a transparent cover for his pederasty; Eryximachus, however, presenting himself as the "fighter of strife," does not seem to invoke the assistance of any divine force as he goes about his business. Although in the *Protagoras* (315c) he is associated with Hippias, his cosmology is in many respects reminiscent of that of Empedocles, who portrayed the world as a cyclical struggle between the forces of love and strife.[47] (It is amusing to note that Empedocles' poem "On Nature" was addressed to another Pausanias.)[48] Unlike Empedocles, however, Eryximachus does not appear to treat strife as anything more than a mere privation or lack of moderation which could easily be curbed by the proper science of love. The "fighter of strife" also presents himself as the "champion of love" and suggests strongly that the force of love depends on him more than he on it.

Eryximachus's character too can now be in the parallel with the Proteus episode: the leopard represents a compromise between the lion of Phaedrus and the spotted serpent of Pausanias. At the risk of sounding fanciful, I would suggest that the Greek word for leopard, *pardalis*, could be contracted to 'Paris,' who wears a leopard skin when he makes his first entrance in the *Iliad*.[49] Paris is also a technician (an archer) rather than a true warrior. The closest he came to being a fighter of strife was when he was asked by Zeus to mediate in the dispute caused by the goddess Eris (strife) after the wedding of Peleus and Thetis. Paris's experiences epitomize the inevitable succession of love and strife. Peleus's wedding (representing Love) is followed by Eris's gift of the golden apple, which is then followed by Goddess of Love's gift to Paris and the ultimate triumph of Eris: the Trojan War.

The identification of Paris with Eryximachus is also consonant with Phaedrus's wistful comment that lovers should display more heroism. Just as Paris defended Aphrodite's claims to the apple, Eryximachus defends the profane Aphrodite from Pausanias's attacks on her. By alluding to Paris, Plato means to portray Eryximachus's vainglorious claims with due irony. An effeminate aura is further bestowed upon Eryximachus if we recall Aristotle's observation (which reflects the conventional lore of classical times) that the leopard is one of the few animal species in which the female is more spirited than the male.[50] The implication is that Phaedrus, the beloved, is more spirited and leonine than his lover, Eryximachus. This little touch of feminism points toward one of the main themes of the dialogue.

The third speech represents a synthesis of the first and second speeches, which were made from tragic and comic perspectives respectively. Likewise, the sixth speech (Socrates') will strive to unify the more sophisticated renderings of these positions in the fourth (Aristophanes') and fifth (Agathon's) respectively. Both Eryximachus and Socrates present grand, unified theories of eros.

Their interaction in the *Symposium* suggests that Eryximachus and Aristophanes are interchangeable. This now seems more absurd than at first glance; how much similarity can there be between a hubristic technophile and the great utopian defender of comic order? Yet we will find their dissimilarity less striking than it seems on the surface. Aristophanes is very much more than a nostalgic poet of the golden age. He is, in his own way, a very skilled and hubris-driven technician.

Aristophanes

We have seen physical evidence (the hiccups) that underscores Aristophanes' human and embodied qualities; the good-humored poet would surely be the first to agree with this recognition of his own humanity. Yet as Robert Mitchell implies, Aristophanes seems to fear ridicule; he is far more at ease dishing it out.[51] He prefers the immunity from close analysis and the freedom from criticism that is usually accorded only to hoary ancient tradition. In fact, he speaks from his privileged position as the self-appointed defender of tradition. We must see that Socrates' old enemy is as pessimistic as Protagoras, as blasphemous as Euripides, and as innovative as Agathon.

I say this because my reading of the *Symposium* regards Aristophanes' speech in a somewhat more critical light than is usual among Plato scholars. Plato may be caricaturing Aristophanes as cruelly as the playwright treated Socrates in *The Clouds*. Whether or not the *Symposium* does justice to the historical Aristophanes, its implications must be carefully teased out if the speeches that follow are to make sense. Moreover, I suggest that the strategy of Aristophanes holds extraordinary interest for our own times.

It is worth noting that Aristophanes belongs to the same generation as Agathon, though his behavior is quite different. Socrates was old enough to be the father of the young man who criticized him so viciously in *The Clouds*.[52] Stanley Rosen points out that Aristophanes is so full of his bodily wisdom that he has the hiccups,[53] in contrast to Socrates' claim to be barren. As a physician, Eryximachus has suggested that the cosmic machine merely needs a regular checkup; Aristophanes prescribes far more radical surgical measures: he proposes to mutilate eros and exile it from the heavens in a subterranean chasm. In this, he emulates the actions of Kronos and Zeus against Uranos and Kronos, respectively. Aristophanes desires to restrict Eros to the blind and self-forgetful force of sexuality.

Aristophanes also emulates Protagoras in choosing to describe human nature through a powerful myth. The reader must remember that all myths are human creations. The gods do not need to create stories; they simply create reality. Unfortunately, they have not left an explanation of what reality means. Aristophanes suggests that it is for poets to build horizons of illusion, as they try to bring order and meaning to human affairs. Just as Pausanias's speech glorified eros from the perspective of a pederast, and Eryximachus's speech depicted Eros from the vantage of a physician and technophile, Aristophanes indirectly praises himself and his art through a myth about human nature and eros. By this device he goes about the poet's task of interpreting the world and re-forming human nature.

According to Aristophanes, human beings originally descended from the three main cosmological entities: the earth, sun, and moon. Pausanias has already spoken of the older gods; Aristophanes now traces man's descent from them (189d–e). But where one might expect a eulogy to human dignity and greatness, Aristophanes has different ideas. The comic poet explains that these beings had four hands, four legs, one head with two faces, and two sets of reproductive organs. These "egg-men" or "circle-men" were round and powerful; they attempted to scale heaven and overcome the gods themselves (190b). As punishment, Zeus had Apollo cut each of them in half to create mankind as we now know it. When it appeared that these sadly mutilated creatures would die out, he arranged that they would reproduce as they clung to their other halves. This is the origin of eros. Unlike the gods in Protagoras's corresponding story, Aristophanes' Zeus and the Olympians do not care very much for mankind; their concerns have to do with human sacrifices and the power of the gods in relation to man (190c).

Aristophanes' seemingly heterodox account of human origins has obvious parallels in standard mythology. Hesiod's account of the battle between the gods and Titans, the *Titanomachia*, described an unsuccessful counterrevolution against the newer Olympian gods involving the many-limbed children of the older cosmological divinities.[54] Humans, according to Orphic belief, were fashioned from the remains of the Titans.[55] In this context, the hundred-handed Titans may represent a primal tribal unity that preceded the individuated human state. Although aimed at a physical reenactment of a primal identity,

eros simultaneously recollects the psychic hubris of this earlier incarnation.

There are further profane implications to this story. Aristophanes has
conveniently glossed over the myth of the Zeus-led revolution that over-
threw the older cosmological beings and established anthropomorphic
and individual Olympian divinities in their stead.[56] Suppressing an earlier act of division through which the original primal beings were divided
into gods and men, he avoids admitting that the Olympian gods were anthropomorphic first! It was in trying to recover their former equality that
the circle-men stormed heaven and were defeated. As a punishment the
rebels were divided into male and female, and eros was created. Its purpose was to ensure that humans would never again be powerful enough
to challenge their betters. Hesiod's legend of Pandora's box conveys much
the same lesson.[57] According to Hesiod, man's life before Pandora was
idyllic: "Human tribes lived on this earth, without suffering and toilsome
hardship."[58] Pandora, the first woman, dispersed a multitude of grief and
cares. On the orders of Zeus, however, she kept Hope trapped securely
within her box; hence, the activity of sex is both an outlet for mankind's
tragic energies and the source of many vain hopes. It is in the same spirit
that Aristophanes piously points to eros as providing the greatest hope
that mankind shall be healed and restored to its ancient nature (193d).

Although Prometheus vainly warned Epimetheus against accepting
this gift of the gods, Pandora replaced Promethean foresight, or as
Rosen puts it, "sexuality replaces Logos as the principle of human wisdom."[59] The immediate Epimethean pleasures of sex obscure the capacity for forethought. Like Circe, Hesiod's Zeus uses sex as a drug to bring
about false self-knowledge. In his speech at the symposium, Aristophanes takes the place of Zeus. The self-knowledge that he imparts can
be expressed with Cartesian brevity: *Libido ergo sum.*

Aristophanes does not explain how the Olympians came into being,
but the inference is clear if we read between the lines: the poets created
the Olympians to explain and justify the monarchic rule of the strong
over the many. By claiming that the rulers were descended from the
Olympian gods they made tyranny legitimate in the eyes of the many,
and human affairs took on some semblance of order. Even unjust order
is preferable to the meaningless equality that exists amid anarchy. The
poets thus created nature to protect humankind from chaos.

Zeus, one must recall, was not a creator ex nihilo; he was a relatively
youthful imposer of order on an older more chaotic substratum. This
cosmology was derived from the prevailing conditions of governance in

archaic times: tyrants served as the model for the Olympians, not vice versa. Poets were related to tyrants as Homer was to Achilles. The story of a murderous warrior was transformed into a founding myth.

Aristophanes urges piety toward the gods for if humans become too arrogant again, they will be split up once more, sawed in half through the nose. Eros must be the means by which man may escape this terrible fate. Speaking against the background of the resumed Peloponnesian War and the looming invasion of Sicily, the creator of *Lysistrata* urges that the Athenians make love and not war. The suggestion is that if they embark on another disastrous invasion, they will be separated from their empire by the Spartans (193a).

To summarize, two mutilations or deformations of human nature are indicated here: one in the past and the other to come. The earlier mutilation generated the *oikos* (family or household) when individual man rose out of a natural but anarchic, undifferentiated state. Through the creation of love by the poets, men forsook the violence of the state of nature and the solidarity of the tribe in favor of domestic bliss in the *oikos* (household). Through the ideology of comic love, they became willing to sacrifice power for order. The second mutilation is threatened because the erotic power of the *oikos* has spilled out of the home. Paradoxically, comic love made men civilized enough to associate with one another beyond the *oikos*, in the polis, and this unexpectedly generated political love becomes a rival to familial prudence. Men begin to question the pious stories about the gods told to them by the poets. Through their comradely association they recollect an earlier incarnation and resolve to regain their lost glory. The circle-men reassemble outside the *oikos* and challenge the gods.

Aristophanes indicates that such a rebellion would culminate in men being "entombed" in the earth. (We might also note that the two-dimensional shape after the second mutilation would be consistent with the shadowy self-knowledge of the subterranean prisoners in the *Republic*.) When Aristophanes threatens that men would be sawed through the nose, he evidently has his sights set lower. He is warning the Athenians that if they wage war, they will be risking the pleasures of the flesh that at present they possess in abundance. In *Lysistrata* he will make this choice between sex and war, comedy and tragedy, even more explicit.

A democratic polis threatens the ascendancy that princes, priests, and poets enjoy in oligarchic society. Aristophanes feels that erotic political promiscuity threatens sexual love and its product: the family, the respective precondition and purpose of human existence. The poet would thus set out to destroy the still nascent polis in the name of piety, tradition, and the family. It is with this end in mind that all of Aristophanes' plays denounce the political and intellectual excesses of the present and extol an idyllic, god-fearing past or an ingeniously contrived peaceful future.

Aristophanes' speech is remarkable for its complete opposition to Phaedrus's belief in an invincible army of lovers (who could storm heaven), to Pausanias's dualism and praise of male pederasty, and to Eryximachus's aspirations for a harmonious ordering of the cosmos. All these outlooks share a common thread of optimism regarding nature and the cosmos; Aristophanes deploys many artificial devices to frustrate this optimism. Through his myth he has quietly conceded that even the family, that seemingly most natural of institutions, is artificial: it was fashioned to reduce human hubris and make primitive man more susceptible to indirect poetic governance in an inherently chaotic environment. The order of nature depends on poets to proclaim and promulgate the natural law. Familial piety and political strivings (that is, hubristic strivings) for excellence are essentially opposed to each other. The Olympian gods and the family were invented to curb original eros, broadly understood as man's aspirations towards his unmutilated original state of nature.

Aristophanes' speech thus suggests that although the origin and natural direction of human desire are tribal (species-oriented) and political, eros must be turned against itself and become sublimated through romantic love. This, again, is very much like the process through which the potentially most unruly and erotic elements in the cave are transformed into their complete opposites: the un-erotic (and indeed anti-erotic) auxiliary Guardians. Indeed, the desired result of Aristophanes' strategy—to the extent that it would mutilate and immobilize human desire to prevent the soul's tragic upward ascent—is similar to the conditions described in the *Republic*. Male homosexuality, which Aristophanes flatteringly refers to here as the condition of the most virile and hopeful of the youth, must be turned around (191e–192a).[60] Even though the motives of the Aristophanes of the *Symposium* and the Socrates of the *Republic* are as different as possible, both would take man away from unfriendly reality, into an artificial idyllic community. It is no accident that Plato borrowed many of the most bizarre features of the *Republic* from Aristophanes.

The difference between Socrates and Aristophanes concerns the future of man. From the Socratic standpoint, it is far more reasonable to see the *oikos* as a necessary but insufficient stage in human progress. Once man has become civilized, he can leave the womblike limits of the *oikos* and deconstruct the childish myths that facilitated the difficult transition from tribal being to individual. Although Socrates may be skeptical of the ability of the polis to combine the ethics of the family and the communal solidarity of the tribe, he believes in a divine order that will support man's intellectually erotic strivings toward it.

Aristophanes is deeply skeptical of enlightenment, either private or public. Whether Socrates corrupted the Athenians from the clouds or demagogues produced hot air in the assembly, both paths led to mob rule and decadence. In *Lysistrata* he proposes to set the *oikos* against the polis by pitting carnal desire against political eros. He seeks to make the centripetal gravity of the *oikos* far exceed the centrifugal capacities of the individual potential citizen.

Aristophanes concedes that sexuality does not reconstitute an original primal unity. If turned against the *polis*, however, it could alienate man from his tragic destiny. In his myth in the *Symposium* and many of his plays Aristophanes sets out to create retroactively the condition of infinite sexual craving that he purported to explain through his myth. He first contrives an artificial desire and then generously offers to make it necessary. This device is best illustrated by his account in the *Symposium* of Hephaestus's offer to join two lovers forever. Aristophanes cunningly says, in the tones of a procurer, that no lover on earth would refuse such an offer (192d–e). (The reader is immediately reminded of a less romantic scene in the *Odyssey* when the crippled god tied Aphrodite and Ares together as a punishment for erotic desire.)[61] In broader terms, he attempts to substitute temporal closure and seeming perfection for a lifetime of erotic striving. This motif recurs throughout the *Symposium*.

Socrates seeks to educate the tragic desires of Athens; Aristophanes denies that such an education is possible. As his description of Zeus's motives suggests, divinity and reality are basically hostile to man. Tragic wisdom causes man to tear his eyes out, like Oedipus. Accordingly, Aristophanes substitutes the lesser death of sexuality for the hubristic vision of the erotically moved cosmos that Socrates provides.

Further support for this accusation is found in Aristophanes' use of the myth of the three kinds of circle-men is to define humanity (reductively) according to sexual preference. The myth of male, female, and hermaphrodite (corresponding respectively to the mutilated descendants of sun, earth, and moon), can at best explain the erotic orientation of one generation. It cannot explain the gender and erotic disposition of *their* descendants. For one thing, the sexual longing of the descendants of the original amputees can never be truly satisfied. Halves are no longer halves per se but psychically mutilated nonindividuals. Wholesale promiscuity and incest would seem to be the most efficient ways by which the old yearnings for wholeness could be even partially satisfied. As long as the regulative illusion of a perfect partner exists, however, mankind will be unable to pursue more adequate and less exclusive forms of political union. This "retro-sexual" state of affairs is what Aristophanes desires.

Further, since the continuance of the human species is ensured through heterosexual intercourse, the descendants of the mutilated circle-men would necessarily turn out to be heterosexual. The heterosexual nature of the act of procreation (rather than the homosexual orientation of either parent) would decisively settle the gender of the offspring. By Aristophanes' own reasoning, human sexual behavior can only be an attempt to replicate the necessarily heterosexual act of generation by which the actual parents of the sexual partners involved gave birth to them. If anything, their sexual yearnings would be for the parent of the opposite sex. Homosexuality and friendship cannot be explained in these terms; they can only be understood as attempts to reconstitute the original pre-sexual solidarity of the circle-men.[62] Since this association is primarily erotic and political, it smacks of hubris and impiety in Aristophanes' eyes. Homosexuality, however, is only a venial offense if the goal is sex and not eros; he would far prefer discreet and guilty private acts of homosexuality to chaste political expressions of the undomesticated erotic impulse. According to Aristophanes, then, Socrates is a particularly dangerous and promiscuous intellectual pederast.

The manifest contradictions in Aristophanes' story indicate that his romantic tale of the circle-men is not natural but artificial. It is an illusory self-knowledge custom-woven by the poet to make men humbler. Aristophanes is like Sigmund Freud in offering reductive explanations of sexual conduct as a desire to return to the material principle. The projects of both seem to be undertaken with the specific desire of overturning any supernatural understanding of eros. Indeed, Dr. Freud seems to combine the technical authority of Eryximachus with the poetic ingenuity of Aristophanes.

If we go by Aristophanes' myth and his scatological spirit, the original position of the sexual organs suggests that reproduction, for the circle-men, was a process akin to defecation. This is what it means to say that the circle-men planted their seed in the earth like farmers. The circle-men were not concerned with reproducing themselves; they sought immortality through heroic tribal deeds (inevitably violent, without a polis to preserve memories of excellence) rather than through reproduction. Their impersonal copulations would have been blind, brutish, and short. At best, reproduction would be a casual action; at worst, it would be an admission of shame or failure in the sense of passing on to the future a task that one could not perform. The circle-men might relate tragic eros and comic reproduction in the same proportions that Socrates accords to speech and writing in the *Phaedrus* (274e–278d). He vastly prefers the former; regarding the latter as merely a residual afterthought and shadow of the original. Socrates would not, however, see eros as egotistical violence; this is why he will emphasize the feminine aspect of the soul.

The Socratic possibility of spiritual recollection stands midway between the tragic, purely masculine, hubris of the circle-men and Aristophanes' single-minded concern with the reproduction and preservation of the *oikos*. Until this redemption comes about through the combination of the tragic and comic powers of the soul, comic reproduction must continually preserve the possibility of going beyond tragedy. In other words, all that writing can do is preserve the possibility of speech. Aristophanes, however, threatens to use reproduction to destroy the possibility of anything but reproduction. This is the opposite extreme of Aristotle's unmoved thinker: instead of thought thinking itself, reproduction is intent only on reproducing itself.

Aristophanes seems to believe that natural man is, in Freud's memorable expression, polymorphously perverse. Curiously, however, his perversity has to do with man's political nature rather than with his sexuality. It is Aristophanes who turns this unformed infinite erotic desire toward carnality. He reverses the Athenian priority of the public over the private, claiming that the private is sacred, the public evil.[63] This is one of the most important prophetic aspects of his speech. In today's society, where sexual comedy rules over erotic tragedy, even the word "tragedy" means only something with an unhappy romantic ending. In such a world, one might say that snivelry gallops along while chivalry has been unhorsed and unmanned.

Equally important to society's present predicament is Aristophanes' comment that the true hermaphrodite no longer exists (189e). This observation may be a relatively banal detail of his fantastic vision, but it provokes the question of whether male and female qualities can be

fruitfully combined—not in one body but in a single soul, for it is evident enough that Aristophanes' myth pertains to the gender identity of
the soul rather than the body. By saying that no true hermaphrodite exists, he argues that since all human beings are dependent on sex, they
are not erotically self-sufficient. Socrates would agree with the second
claim but emphatically reject its derivation from the first. It is precisely
by rising above bodily necessity that humans can give adequate expression to their erotic nature.

Socrates takes up Aristophanes' challenge by stressing Diotima's role
in his education. His enigmatic nature actually represents an Athena-
like synthesis of male and female spiritual qualities; this allows for
speech *and* writing, eros *and* reproduction. It must be distinguished
from the violence of the circle-men and the scarcely less hubristic Periclean emphasis on the glorious and short-lived polis.[64] Aristophanes'
belief in human depravity cannot allow for a more moderate view of the
spiritual desires. He thinks that this very belief in moderation would
serve only as a kind of Trojan horse to make enlightenment respectable
and smuggle in the more dangerous variety of nihilism. Accordingly,
the poet-theologian, refusing to distinguish between Socrates and the
sophists, collectively denounces all these political propensities. In this
respect he reflects Protagoras's earlier lumping together of Socrates and
the sophists.

In our Homeric parallel, Aristophanes corresponds to the Proteus's
fourth metamorphosis, into a savage hog. For one thing, Odysseus received his first wound—in the inner thigh—from such an animal while
he was hunting with his grandfather Autolycus.[65] Aristophanes likewise, in his play *The Clouds*, is the first to attack Socrates. Moreover,
the deep lair of this hog, impervious to the rays of the sun, recalls the
chthonic powers with which Aristophanes identified himself.

Like the young Odysseus, Socrates has presumed to invade the underworld of Gaia (the domain of the Eleusinian mysteries) and ask questions about the time-honored rituals and norms of life. Through his
erotic midwifery Socrates seeks to rescue the Titanic soul from its justly
deserved subterranean incarceration. Aristophanes, in his advocacy of
extreme measures to control the raging fever of eros, functions in a manner not dissimilar to that of the Guardian of the cave. In this capacity he
stoutly resists the attempts of an enlightened escapee to reenter the cave
and infect the prisoners with his insatiable erotic curiosity. According to
the model of the divided line, Aristophanes moves away from reality and
toward fantastical *eikasia* (imagination) to protect humanity.

There is also the matter of the location of the wound inflicted by the great boar. The area of the groin corresponds to Aristophanes' comic region of concern, as well as his threat that the gods (or poets) will carve up humanity (with jagged tusks or sharp pens). These deities will refuse to let men abide within the broad-bosomed earth if they persist in hubris and impiety toward the gods and their creators. Indeed, in view of Socrates' supposed indifference to the body and reproduction, the threat of castration is an instance of the punishment fitting the crime. Alcibiades' double castration of Socrates and the herms seems also to be prefigured here.

Before we consider the speech of Agathon, the banquet's youthful host and the most beautiful man present, several points of contrast between Aristophanes and Agathon are worthy of mention. Whereas Aristophanes' speech expressed a doctrine of chronic cosmic pessimism, Agathon's contribution is a eulogy of unbridled optimism dedicated—in no particular order—to eros, the coming new world order, and himself. Further, Aristophanes deliberately tries to conduct himself like an older man; Agathon, though of the same generation, sets out to emphasize his youthfulness. And although Agathon is renowned for his innovative stagecraft,[66] Aristophanes' far more creative dramaturgic endeavors are totally subsumed in the service of his desire to evoke nostalgic allegiance toward a mythical past order.[67]

Socrates is not the only person present at this banquet who has suffered an attack by Aristophanes. The comedian's *Thesmophoriazusae*, which came out a few years after the dramatic date of this dialogue and a few months after the *Lysistrata*, depicts Agathon as a mincing effeminate who dresses in feminine apparel the better to understand his female characters. The play tells of Agathon being urged by Euripides to disguise himself and spy on sacred feminine rituals[68]—ceremonies resembling the Eleusinian mysteries, which several of the symposiasts were alleged to have profaned on that very night. In the light of Aristophanes' own fascination with women, and his continuing preoccupation with the gynocratic theme, one wonders why he is placing Agathon in this situation. Why should Aristophanes, a self-professed feminist, make so great a fuss about Agathon's effeminacy?

The chief difference between Agathon and Aristophanes seems to be that the former *is* effeminate, the latter is merely intellectually committed to feminism, driven to pose as a feminist because of his hostility to the overweening masculinity of the democratic polis. In other words, whereas Agathon is naturally effeminate and enjoys dressing up as a woman, Aristophanes is politically and intellectually committed to making political use of feminism. He decks himself out in the trappings of gynocracy because he dislikes the (homosexually oriented) hubris of Periclean manliness and will go to any absurd lengths to inspire a reaction against it. Aristophanes is a cross-dresser because he is cross with the erotic excesses of the male Athenian democracy. It is in much the same spirit that many atheistic political reactionaries of today "cross-dress" in the sense of allying themselves with religious fundamentalists.

Aristophanes is undeterred by the absurdity of many of his schemes; for him, the human condition is such that the order generated by obviously arbitrary authority is to be preferred over a striving for justice. The latter effort causes men to be optimistic and believe that their condition can become more rational. It is only when oligarchic authority casts off its ridiculous professions of rationality and affirms its (continually re-poeticized) tradition that an oasis of order is created in an irrational sea of chaos.

To restate several crucial points made earlier: we are at the midpoint of a struggle between two very different varieties of feminism here. What the reactionary Aristophanes most fears is the optimism and hubris that Agathon's variety of feminism represents. Agathon's feminism is typified by the thoughtless and erotic impulsiveness of Aphrodite, which inevitably leads to such massive armed deployments as those in Troy and Sicily. In this sense, Ares and Aphrodite naturally belong together.

Aristophanes is like Hera in her adamant opposition to such *nouveau* divinities as Heracles, who start off as humans but wish to recover their divinity. Aristophanes, as we have seen, concedes man's divine ancestry (since there is nothing higher than man) but is implacably hostile to any effort that man might make to recover his exalted original state. This original desire / sin is essentially perverse and thus needs stringent external coercion and restraint. Through the valorization of carnality, Aristophanes seeks to suppress this sinful original desire.

Unlike Agathon's optimistic vision of the future, Aristophanes' view is utopian only to the extent that he hates the present; his plans for the future are resolutely committed to the complete dismantling of corrupt modern optimism. Aristophanes also deeply suspects Socrates' lack of due respect for tradition and sexuality. He will strive mightily to prevent Socrates from leading the desires out of the cave.

Unlike Aristophanes, who was preoccupied with Aphrodite and Dionysus, Agathon confuses the two and enthusiastically invites

Dionysus inside the city. The older tragedians had used tragedy far more prudently to balance the two powers and keep the potentially destructive force of Dionysus at bay. As Allan Bloom suggests, Agathon represents the end of tragedy; he would substitute "happiness" for the learning about reality that is gained through tragic suffering.[69] After his time, comedy became the more popular genre. Neither the pessimism of Euripides nor the escapism of Agathon could ever recreate what Aeschylus and Sophocles had wrought.[70]

It should be noted, however, that Aristophanes' strategy is even more dangerous and perhaps just as responsible for the death of tragedy. Though warning against the consequences of divine wrath, he proposes to anticipate this very sanction. The end result of his proposals will be the destruction of the tragic element in man with a view to protecting the comic. Aristophanes attempts to imprison man's potentially daimonic nature in an artificial state of rustic bestiality; he will not allow divine *poros* to penetrate the penury of *penia*.

Agathon

We should first point out what is commonly acknowledged: Agathon's oration gives every sign of having been inspired by Gorgias, the famous Sicilian-born sophist.[71] Socrates himself calls attention to this when he remarks playfully at its conclusion that he feared that Agathon would cause the Gorgon's head to emerge out of the underworld and turn him to stone (198b–c). On another level, Socrates is ironically praising Agathon for his Medusa-like (deadly) beauty, which could cause involuntary erotic arousal even in one as old as himself. We should keep this in mind when considering Alcibiades' subsequent testimony regarding Socrates' amazing powers of physical self-restraint. Socrates is apparently capable of being excited by attractive ideas.

Since Aristophanes, the comedian, has painted a tragic picture in defending his comic (albeit deeply pessimistic) definition of eros, Agathon will heed Gorgias's advice and defend political eros by fighting tragedy with comedy.[72] If Aristophanes sheds the tears of a clown, Agathon the innovative tragedian will steal Aristophanes' clothes to sing the praises of peace.

Since Agathon is celebrated as the great tragedian of the hour, it is appropriate that we should consider his teacher Gorgias's teachings. Especially significant are his treatise *On the Non-existent* or *On Nature* and his celebrated speech defending Helen. In the latter Gorgias set out to prove that Helen was not to be held responsible for deserting her husband or for any of the terrible bloodshed of the Trojan War. Likewise, we could playfully exonerate Agathon for his subsequent desertion of Athens for Macedonia and turn to the more serious charge that overweening rhetoric led to the unprecedented bloodshed of the Peloponnesian War.

Gorgias's basic ontological stance is strikingly similar to that taken by Aristophanes, but the ethical doctrines derived from his teachings by Agathon are very different indeed. Aristophanes based his pessimistic anthropology upon an understanding of man as something alienated from nature and generatively sustained by the radical creativity of the poet-theologian. Agathon derives his extremely optimistic doctrine of man from an essentially identical ontology: Gorgias's celebrated teaching that first, nothing exists; second, even if it did, it would be incomprehensible by man; and third, even if it were comprehensible, it would be incommunicable.[73]

Whereas Aristophanes used various professions of piety and conservatism to disguise his own radical creativity, Agathon is utterly unabashed about his nihilistic Gorgian presuppositions (one can see another reason why Socrates referred to the head of the Gorgon) and using this nihilism to license the most unbridled creativity.

Aristophanes' bawdy comedy is a means by which the credulous demos could be made to attend to things of the body and the *oikos*, and distracted from dangerous political actions and intellectual speculations.[74] Agathon, on the other hand, is unheedingly and irresponsibly optimistic; he seems genuinely to believe that a new world order based on eros will bring about the end of history and conclude all strife and turmoil. Agathon desires to run away from ontology in the hope that what is forgotten or outdistanced will disappear. Perhaps he believes that mankind will have a much easier time of it if liberated from the dangerous illusions of being and presence, hazardous notions that can only cause ignorant and deluded armies to clash by night. After all, according to Gorgias, the logos has no access to or connection with a noumenal realm of things-in-themselves; in other words, words are related only to other words and have no connection to being or beings.[75] Mankind cannot escape from the sticky web of language; nature is wholly inaccessible to humans, and the sooner they understand this state of affairs the easier it will be for them to dwell securely in the logos. The antimetaphysical Agathon depicted by Plato is the first postmodern.

Agathon's speech paints a glowing picture of the healthy state of affairs that will ensue once the cruel rule of necessity is overthrown. This necessity consists in the superstitious belief in nature and mankind's necessarily violent efforts to make human affairs conform to an inaccessible and incomprehensible natural order. Unlike the older gods, who were created as part of the impossible attempt to relate man to nature, the newest god will be a celebration of man's liberation from his false belief in necessity and nature. To be sure, Agathon is also responding to Aristophanes' desperate attempts to protect man from what is now called the fifth-century enlightenment. Unlike Aristophanes, who reacted to the cultural and religious crisis by inventing increasingly imaginative and fanciful myths about the gods in their absence, Agathon boldly proclaims the poet—more specifically, himself—as the presiding deity of the new enlightened age.

Aristophanes alienated man from himself by telling him that he was incomplete, and that his other half was to be found in nature. He threatened human beings by telling them that if they rejected the artificial nature of the cave, the priests and poets would further handicap and restrict the human spirit. Agathon relieves man from these artificial and perverse restrictions by announcing that the guiding principles of the new age will be positive rather than negative.

In the terms of Empedocles' basic metaphysical categories, Agathon wants love to reign; then things would come together, instead of being divided from themselves and one another.[76] The unity of the logos would be recognized, and humanity would be delivered from its artificial alienation from nonbeing. Eros would no longer be a punishment, a never-to-be-satisfied desire similar to the sufferings of the doomed in Tartarus. As an enlightened force of unity and wholeness, eros would conclude the painful odyssey of suffering humanity. Man would discover that his true destiny is to reside in language, the tent of nonbeing.

This emphasis on form rather than content, on words rather than being, marks the very beginning of Agathon's speech when he states that before actually speaking he would consider how he ought to speak. His next comment, that the previous speakers have dealt with the benefits of Eros rather than the god himself, suggests again that he is not dealing with an external being, since such knowledge—granting his Gorgian epistemology—would be impossible. Agathon continues in this barely concealed confessional vein when he says that Eros is the happiest, the best, the most beautiful, and the youngest of the gods (195a).

Agathon is not unwise in placing emphasis on the form rather than the content of his embarrassingly sophistical speech, but his encomium will reveal much more about the sophistical optimism that he represents in this dialogue. He places great emphasis on the youthfulness of Eros and his great hatred of old age (195a–b). Eros's headlong flight from old age and necessity are indicative of his hostility to tradition, history, and nature and consistent with his (and Agathon's) great delicacy, which renders him unwilling to come into contact with brute facticity. Eros is content to keep the company of Aristophanes' clouds; he hovers above and beyond reality while delivering splendid orations. Of course, Agathon's timid attitude toward reality suggests that this itinerant deity will have a hard time in any situation that brings him into contact with reality. Agathon is like Humpty Dumpty (another egg-man), who famously boasted that when he used a word, it meant what he chose it to mean—neither more nor less. All the Great King's horses and men could not repair the damage done by the time Spartan deeds had finished with Athenian speeches.

It should be noted that the respective positions of Agathon and Aristophanes represent equally objectionable extremes. Aristophanes insists that man be restored entirely to the state of nature and a prelapsarian state of servitude; Agathon proclaims that man must be separated entirely from the nonexistent natural so that a brave new world of the future can be established at the end of history. Aristophanes suppresses the human spirit in the name of nature; Agathon reverses this order and seeks to destroy nature in the cause of humanity. There is clearly room here for a middle position between the two extremes, for a better and less adversarial relationship between man and nature.

There are many political contrasts to be drawn between Aristophanes and Agathon. According to the Protean model, Aristophanes is connected to the earth and the darkness of the boar's lair. This youthful traditionalist is associated with the land and the landed power of the old oligarchy. Agathon, on the other hand, is connected to the fifth metamorphosis of Proteus, running water, which is irresistibly associated with the hubristic ways of democratic Athens.

If the angry old boar is an Athenian knight defending his land, the running water stands for the democratic force of the navy. Service in the army required expensive military equipment and a horse, whereas one needed only a strong back to serve in the navy. The trireme constituted the vehicle for the imperialistic aspirations of the Athenian demos. The massive maritime empire of Athens, held together by trade and tribute, brought in much new wealth, disrupting the stable land-based economy of the old order, which had been dominated by the oligarchs. Of course, wealth was not the only thing brought to Athens by the running water; many different ideas—and teachers of ideas—flowed into the city including the sophisticated relativism of the likes of Agathon's teacher, Gorgias. The motif of running water is also reminiscent of the famous teachings of Heraclitus that "everything flows" and that "one cannot step into the same river twice."[77] On close examination, one finds Agathon's speech continually evoking this theme. In his encomium he says that Eros is "balanced and fluid" in his nature and possessed of a "fluid supple shape" that will enable him to touch the hearts and the souls of men (196a). Eros thus reigns over mankind through his rhetorical skills and power over words, which enable him to paint dazzling pictures and persuade anybody of anything. Gorgias, Agathon's teacher, soberly described how a practitioner of his art could defeat a specialist in the assembly (Gorgias 456a–c).

The problem with this effort to substitute demagogic rhetoric and thought pictures for reality was that ultimately it left the great Athenian empire hanging together by nothing more stable than bombastic oratory and a fickle populace. The fact that the dramatic date of the Symposium coincides with the departure of the ill-starred Sicilian armada over water to Syracuse, a project inspired by the captivating rhetoric of Alcibiades, is a dramatic irony deeply woven into the text.[78] This illustration of the might of the orator is clearly recognizable as an instance of the Gorgonic power that dispatched many brave men to Hades before their time. In his defense, Agathon could offer the words of Gorgias himself in his Defense of Palamedes: "Nature, with a vote which is clear, casts a vote of death against every mortal on the day on which he is born."[79]

This quotation recalls the wisdom of Achilles and his inevitably tragic life. Even though Agathon's Eros is an unlikely Achilles figure, a very strong case can be made to support this identification. Like Agathon's Eros among the gods, Achilles was the youngest, best, and most beautiful of the Greeks (as Agathon claims to be the best and most beautiful in the room). It could even be said that he had soft or vulnerable feet, and Agathon's account is weakest when it comes into direct contact with the earth or nature. Agathon also claimed that Eros could inspire all the other gods and make them serve him. Likewise, Achilles could demand favors of the gods (Hephaestus, for instance) and make Zeus alter the course of the Trojan War. Just as Eros was the youngest god who (according to Agathon) became their king, so too was the son of Thetis originally destined to supplant Zeus and rule in his stead.[80]

Agathon goes out of his way to contrast himself, in all of his youthful beauty and eloquence, to the ugly and ironic Socrates. He thus hubristically poses the celebrated Homeric question as to whether Achilles or Odysseus was the better man. It suffices to point out that while Agathon / Eros runs away from death and ugliness, Socrates regarded his life as a not unsuccessful effort to outstrip injustice (38e–39b).

Despite his bold Achillean subtext, however, Agathon explicitly portrays Eros as a great peacemaker. Perhaps his Eros can be understood as an Achilles born of a divine father, a "kinder, gentler" Achilles who will end the divisions and quarrels of gods and men by "filling us with togetherness and draining our divisiveness away." Speaking as the host of the symposium, Agathon says that such gatherings were convened by Eros himself (197d).

The kind of amicable unity that Agathon describes stands in striking contrast both to the rationally dictated formal unity of the Eleatics and to the violently enforced conformity of the past. Running away from strife, however, hardly seems the best way to resolve faction and disruption. We have already noted Agathon's fear of natural reality. If nature is governed by strife, peace and harmony may be generated only through the convening of a wholly artificial world. As I suggested earlier, the community described by Agathon seems in many respects to resemble the cultural milieu of Periclean Athens viewed from a rose-tinted perspective that ignores the Peloponnesian War.

In Nietzschean terms, one could say that Agathon is illicitly separating the Apollonian superstructure of the School of Athens from its Dionysian substratum.[81] Alternatively, he is like Paris in choosing Helen and ignoring her dowry: the Trojan War. Agathon himself supplies the best simile here when he says that Aphrodite has a powerful hold on Ares (196d). Although Hephaestus (techne) believes that he is the master and possessor of Aphrodite, strife-filled Ares will always follow her. Irresponsible young love may flee, but age-old necessity and strife will always find him. In a poignant vein, we can recall that Agathon himself eventually fled Athens, when discord entered the city after the troubles of 411, and sought refuge in the Macedonian court. After all, Eros "never settles in anything . . . that cannot flower or has lost its bloom" (196b).

Agathon states that the stories told by Hesiod and Parmenides about the violence of the gods concern events that happened under the harsh rule of necessity: the unity of the past was brought about by "violent deeds of castrations and imprisonment" (195c). While we have seen that Hesiod certainly recounted events of this sort, no surviving fragments of Parmenides deal with this theme. It is more likely that Agathon is hostile to Parmenides because Monism serves as the metaphysical foundation of the austere regime of necessity and nature—the regime that Eros is about to overthrow. The ideas of Gorgias concerning the nonexistence, unintelligibility, and incommunicability of being constitute a direct rejection of Parmenides' theory of the unity of being, a perfect and unchanging unity that resides in the bonds of inflexible rational necessity. Although Aristophanes claimed to look back to an older Golden Age, this is not identical to the changeless and eternal unity proclaimed by the Eleatics. And yet the two attitudes are similar in an essential respect: both seek to liberate mankind from the curses of freedom and individuation. Agathon loudly proclaims Eros, and Aristophanes subtly deploys Eris.

Contra Parmenides' statement that "it is the same thing to think and to be,"[82] Agathon's speech contrasts Eris (strife), who "walks upon the heads of men," to Eros, who has the softest feet and settles only on soft and gentle souls and characters. After having previously praised Homer, Agathon gently contradicts the bard's statement that Eris's feet are soft because she walks on the heads of men, pointing out that men's skulls are not really soft at all (195e). Eris, identified with the hard science of rationality, is opposed to the gentle ways of Eros and rhetoric. This also means that the harsh duo of thought and being are opposed to the gentler magic of eros and nonbeing.

Aristophanes opposed Socratic rationalism because it was too artful and devious alongside the hardened necessities of time-honored tradition. We now see Agathon reject reason because it is inflexible, in contrast to the infinitely malleable ways of rhetoric. Of course, since tradition was originally rhetoric anyway, we can see reason being sandwiched between the new and the old ways of rhetoric. In effect, then, the structure of the dialogue suggests that Socrates is identifiable only when he stands between Agathon and Aristophanes.

Both Aristophanes and Agathon incorporate aspects of the unfortunate Pentheus of the *Bacchae*. Aristophanes resembles Pentheus in his earlier obdurate refusal to acknowledge Dionysus or let him into the city; Agathon unwittingly mimes Pentheus's later desire to give himself up completely to this terrible beauty. Only Socrates knows how to deal with Dionysus when he appears at the banquet. Indeed, it is Dionysus, ably represented by Alcibiades, who will claim to be erotically torn apart by Socrates.

Agathon's frivolous optimism thus stands in clear and extreme contrast to Aristophanes' chronic pessimism. Aristophanes defines the good in terms of the separation of man from god and even goes on to separate man from his own nature and potential. Conversely, Agathon suggests that the new god Eros combines all the other virtues, thus providing a curious version of the celebrated Socratic doctrine of the unity of virtue. Agathon puns about the unity of the good in himself: he is both *eros* and *agathos*. His boast that anyone, "even the most uncultured," who touches love (that is, himself) becomes a poet prepares us for Socrates' own poetic discourse on love. This claim also embodies both the previous and subsequent banter among Agathon, Socrates, and Aristophanes concerning the physical communicability of virtue. In other words, the very virtues themselves become unified through coming into contact with love. Thus, Alcibiades' subsequent identification of Socrates as Eros is supported by the Socratic unification of the moral and intellectual virtues. As our earlier examination of the *Protagoras* suggested, this Socratic reconciliation of speech and deed occurs through a redoubtable combination of evocative words and courageous deeds. However unwillingly, Alcibiades' speech will complement Socrates' winged words by bearing testimony to his beloved's equally notable actions.

5 Symposium II: The Secrets of Silenus

The Place of Socrates

At last we are ready to study Socrates' personal contribution to the *Symposium*. Socrates had earlier claimed to know nothing but the things of eros (177d), thus suggesting that eros is known differently from all other things. Now he confesses that he was instructed in eros by Diotima, a wise woman of Mantinea (201d). Since the reference to Mantinea seems to be in response to Aristophanes' anachronistic comment about the Mantineans (193a), there is a strong possibility that Socrates is personifying his own manic or prophetic soul. Further, through the mouthpiece of Diotima, Socrates completes the female drama of the second triad of speeches in the *Symposium*, complementing the voices of the feminist Aristophanes and the effeminate Agathon (451c). Aristophanes and Agathon, however, offered mankind different forms of closure and perfection, at the beginning and end of history, whereas Socrates describes the loving *imperfection* of a life of infinite striving.

Socrates sets out to mediate between the reductive cynicism of Aristophanes and the undiluted hubris of Agathon. He likens the Eros described by Agathon to the beautiful and terrifying head of the Gorgon, which could turn men into stone.[1] Apart from the obvious sexual jest earlier alluded to, Socrates suggests that Agathon's view of eros is both beautiful in itself and terrifying in its consequences. Like Perseus, one cannot afford to look directly into the face of this Gorgon because darkness at noon will surely result.[2] Socrates will instead look into a reflecting surface and speak about eros in more humanly comprehensible terms. In other words, he will not speak directly of the uncanny force that Agathon has blindly invoked but, rather, speak of an ironic but beneficent daimon, delivering recollections of eros out of the souls of men. The practice of viewing eros indirectly, through the eye of the beloved, is reiterated in two other dialogues we shall turn to: the *Phaedrus*[3] and the *First Alcibiades*.[4]

As in the case of the *Republic*, readers are not provided with a comprehensive vision of the good itself but only of its offspring. This time, however, we pass beyond the mediated image to receive a skeletal account of the cosmic order that the soul recollects through eros. In other words, we progress from the consideration of eros / light to an intimation of the origin of eros: the Idea of the Good and Beautiful. This idea generates eros just as the sun shed light on the *Republic*.

We never really pass fully into what is good and beautiful in itself. Instead, we are shown the first step in the reverse direction, from the vision of the good and beautiful to the cave. It would seem that the world is created for love, rather than for perfection. This means that the journey, from the good to the cave, matters more than the prospect of eternally lingering in perfection, the vision of which could only blind us; a beatific awareness of the good may be gained only indirectly, through that second sailing of the soul referred to earlier. We must remember the lesson of the *Phaedo* that the laws of efficient causality do not apply at the level of the ideas. To put it differently, Eros chooses to forgo divine pleasure in order to serve humanity. Happily, it seems that his very choice and activity make the erotic messenger more godlike.

The ascent of speeches in the *Symposium* ends with Socrates' account; the descent, a matter of deeds, commences with Alcibiades' description of Socrates' conduct. Speech and deeds have to be woven continually together if any contact with the Idea of the Good and Beautiful, however tenuous, indirect, and sporadic, is to be maintained. Moreover, the best look at the good and beautiful is won by understanding and observing the daimonic conduct of one possessed by this vision. It is not inappropriate that this account of the soul's descent is provided by one who, for all of his godlike potential, was himself stricken by darkness at noon. Our own second sailing will profit much from observing what Alcibiades would not recognize. Like Glaucon, Alcibiades sought information from Socrates, but he failed to see that he needed to live a Socratic life to understand his lover's secrets. We, however, may yet profit from his undigested observations.

Socrates' nature emerges through the weaving together of the speech put in the mouth of Diotima and the deeds that Alcibiades is compelled to testify to. The preceding chapter located the Socratic enterprise in the no-man's-land between Aristophanic comedy and Agathon's tragedy. This chapter sets out to reveal the soul of Socrates through close study of the dialectic between the *poros* of Diotima and the *penia* of Alcibiades. Ultimately, Plato challenges the reader to occupy the daimonic space that opens between the various pairs that emerge from the *Symposium*: Comedy and Tragedy, *Poros* and *Penia*, Reason and Desire, Soul and City are four prominent examples. Like that of Dionysus, the nature of Socrates will flash forth, momentarily, before it is torn apart by these various categorical oppositions. Plato used much the same technique of writing between the lines in the *Protagoras*, to reveal the Sisyphean nature of Protagoras between Tantalus / Prodicus and Heracles / Hippias.

Returning to the immediate context of Socrates' speech, we see Agathon quite unaware that instead of praising Eros, he has in fact invited a terrifying Dionysian force onto the stage—though the very purpose of honoring Dionysus *on* the stage in Greek tragedy is to keep him *off* it. From the standpoint of Platonic irony, Agathon's speech is an open invitation for Alcibiades to attend his celebration. Fortunately, Alcibiades, though invited by Agathon to play Dionysus, has become aware of the presence of Socrates and pays homage to a greater and more powerful erotic than himself. Agathon is blissfully ignorant of the forces he is playing with. His playful reference to the soft feet of delusion and mischief serves as ironic self-testimony to the extent of his own delusion (195d).

Aristophanes was clearly not altogether wrong in warning against unbridled optimism and invincible ignorance. Agathon is drawn irresistibly to Dionysus for his beauty and girlish prettiness; he quite fails to see the darker side of the wine god. Agathon refuses to see the connection between literary license and literal violence. By destroying the Apollonian conventions enclosing the human community and offering protection from nature, he supposes that he can free man from necessity—but he has actually invited unbridled necessity into the very heart of the city. It is as if the Athenians or the Trojans were to suppose that their fortified walls were the biggest obstacles to enjoying the pleasures of peace. When Agathon boastfully claims that reality is up for interpretation, he fails to see that nature, red in tooth and claw, would brush him aside and destroy what the statesmen and tragedians of yore had built with so much effort.

Agathon loudly denies any difference between the gods and man; the ironic, albeit erotic, relation between the human and the divine that Socrates will strive to articulate is completely foreign to him. But so promiscuous a coupling of human and divine could only promote narcissism and cultural chaos; timebound men can only strive vainly and absurdly to emulate the infinite creativity and playfulness of the Homeric gods. As described in Euripides' *Helen*, a terrible phantasm of beauty is born in Athens, one that will inevitably lead many brave men to the tombless quarries of Syracuse and the bloody beach of Aegospotami.

Throughout his speech Socrates tries to avert this looming disaster by restoring the separation of man from deity and articulating the role of the daimon who must mediate between them. There are ten years between the disaster at Syracuse and the ominous time at which the high jinks at Agathon's are recollected. We might infer that, like Diotima with the plague, Socrates was able to postpone this disaster for only ten years (201d). He did so by trying to use the rough magic of *penia* to expose the hubris-ridden rhetoric of *poros*. Although eros is the mediating term between the human and the divine, it is not the essence of divinity; this means that man cannot become divine by identifying with *poros* and engaging in narcissistic conduct. The premise of such narcissism is that self-love is the essence of divinity; the resulting conduct alienates men from true eros itself. Genuine virtue will do no more than remind them of their true dignity and worth as human beings.

Alcibiades will identify Socrates with the god Eros, but this claim must be modified by Socrates' prior explanation that Eros is not a god but a mediator between the divine and human realms. If eros is the god, it becomes contentless or in Socrates' terms, love of nothing (199e–201c), for eros is an activity and not an identity. Instead of the intellectualism of the Aristotelian formulation of thought thinking itself,[5] we have the equally solipsistic exercise of eros desiring itself; both models have a nihilistic attitude regarding the ultimate value of the external world.

Aristophanes' position represents the other extreme attitude toward eros; he regards love as a demonic force that is inherently hostile to order, tradition, and nature. Just as the circle-men were progressively carved up by the poets and gods, the domesticated denizens of Aristophanes' pseudogynocracy would mutilate and dismember Dionysus, to their ultimate peril. A more moderate position is needed. Eros is not *the* good, but neither is it evil personified. Socrates says that eros is *of* the good and offers mankind the opportunity to participate in the activity of goodness.

In short, Socrates' position is that eros delivers intimations of a transcendent order of goodness from the soul to a self-forgetful subterranean polity. Erotic activity is recollective rather than generative. The erotic daimon discovers and helps reveal the good to the world; he does not create it. The erotic deeds of the daimon must point beyond him, in the direction of the good; self-reference is not the end of such activity. Socratic self-irony is required by this emphasis on the good as the source of erotic prowess. The madness of Alcibiades will shortly illustrate the tragic limitations of the self-referential approach.

Socrates' questioning of Agathon, which precedes his speech, begins the process of restoring the objective (if transcendental) ground of eros. Agathon is forced to concede that it makes no sense for Eros to desire if, as he has maintained, the god already possesses everything he desires (200a–d). An eventual reappraisal of the notion of divine generosity is in order, but Socrates must set the stage for it. For the moment, Agathon must recognize that the erotic is, in some sense, deficient.

Of course, awareness of deficiency is itself a kind of manic possession. Diotima admonished Socrates for believing that one who desires is contrary to that which he desires (201d–202d). Right opinion without the ability to render an objective account is neither knowledge nor ignorance (202a). Once the sophistical presupposition of an excluded middle is refuted, it is possible to postulate the intermediary position between *poros* and *penia* which the erotic can occupy. Ironically, the very exclusion of the erotic man from the plenitude of possession has also liberated him from the dangers of narcissism and intellectual materialism. Socrates' last words to Agathon underline the way in which eros has now been transformed into a relation. He will soon give an ecstatic account of a cosmos constructed according to formal and "inefficient" causality.

When Agathon acknowledges that he cannot contradict Socrates, the older man replies that it is truth that he cannot contradict (201c). The self-proclaimed god of linguistic creativity has to acknowledge the primacy of truth. Now that eros is viewed as a relation, we may see how the sixth metamorphosis of Proteus, a mighty tree mediating between the earth and the heavens, symbolizes Diotima's speech. This image also prefigures the stoutly rooted bed of Odysseus and the union of male striving and female resourcefulness that Socrates will extol.

Diotima

Socrates has claimed that his instructor in erotic matters was Diotima, a Mantinean prophetess. Martha Nussbaum points out that the name Diotima (god honor) stands in direct contrast to the name of Alcibiades' mistress, Timandra (man honor).[6] Unlike Diotima, Timandra was real. She represents Alcibiades' choice of a courtesan over the intangible divine, and his inability to incorporate the feminine element into his own soul. By a strange irony, when Alcibiades was shot to death, Timandra dressed his naked body in her own garments.[7]

I have remarked that Socrates' reference to Mantinea comes seemingly in response to Aristophanes' anachronistic reference to the dispersal of the Arcadians (more specifically the Mantineans). This device directs our attention to the Mantinean Alliance that Alcibiades formed—a provocative alliance with a city-state within Sparta's sphere of influence, which caused the resumption of the Peloponnesian War and the Athenian defeat at the battle of Mantinea.[8] Socrates' erotic association with Diotima thus seems to reflect the very hubris of the circle-men who stormed the heavens. His choice of a Mantinean mouthpiece is provocative enough; even more disturbing is his proposal of a spiritual equivalent of the Mantinean Alliance between the gods and nature. Although Agathon sought to become divine through tragedy, and Aristophanes tried to reduce man to a natural being through comedy, both poets rejected the possibility of restoring cosmic order through human Eros.

Socrates uses his alliance with the manic Mantinean to advocate such a synthesis, promising genuine spiritual procreancy. He rejects both the mimetic reproduction recommended by Aristophanes and the vaingloriously barren lust praised by the various pederasts in the room. Socrates also indicates how to transmit virtue across the generations. Though Aristophanes and the pederasts have also made a similar claim, it is fairly clear that the absence of the possibility of genuine spiritual friendship will negate such an attempt. By contrast, Plato's framing of the dialogue shows how the erotic bond between Socrates and Alcibiades could still fascinate Athenians who were quite unconcerned about Agathon's current whereabouts and oblivious to Aristophanes' presence at the banquet.[9] It is, moreover, no accident that the *Symposium* provides those of us possessed by the hope of educating eros with the clearest transmission of Plato's thoughts on this subject.

I am also suggesting, of course, that it is the Platonic intellectual congress with Socrates, though it may well have been as one-sided and frustrating as *poros* mating with *penia*, that has produced so much of Western civilization. We can note in passing that most other Socratic interlocutors or readers of the dialogues see only themselves. This is clearly the case with the earlier speakers in the *Symposium*, who ended by describing their own souls instead of praising Eros. We must remember, however, that the purpose of the labyrinthine structure of the dialogue is to enable its readers and participants to see their own souls and hidden presuppositions through the erotic midwifery of Socrates. It is only after this harrowing ordeal that divine madness may cause a few of these battered participants to gird up their lacerated loins once more to see something of their daimonic midwife.

Although Socrates (through Diotima) seemingly restates the Pausanian doctrine of a distinction between divine Aphrodite and profane Eros, his speech ultimately describes the vital role played by Eros in holding together the heavenly and earthly realms. In spite of this crucial role, however, Eros is always a clownish herald and never an august plenipotentiary with power to bind and loose. In other words, Eros will always be a man with a donkey's head babbling somewhat incoherently about "a most rare vision" which "eye has not heard and ear has not seen."[10]

I make these allusions to *A Midsummer Night's Dream* to suggest that the escapee who returns to the cave does not always find it easy to speak with precision and felicity. As he reenters the underworld and resumes the language of the shades, this worthy not only is aware that he is incapable of describing the gratuitously unveiled transcendental truth (Titania); he also knows that he is equally incapable of seeing anything true in the staged shadow rituals of nothingness that he has returned to. It is an accurate description of his condition to say that he is only aware that he knows nothing. This knowledge of ignorance makes him the wisest of all mortals, but it also makes him a natural scapegoat.

Although the parallel with Shakespeare illustrates the intermediary status of eros, we still need to understand the decided separation between man and the divine that seems to be set up here. Why is the greatest human wisdom no better than the babbling of a rude mechanical? Why is the divine so relatively uninterested in human affairs? The first of these questions is the easier one to answer, since we can see how the statesman's task of stage-managing shadows in the cave is perceivable in all its banality when one returns from outside the cave. The second question is far more difficult. The poet-puppeteers set about reducing the divine ideas to a series of easily manipulated shadows. Although the cave rulers, by this means, try to ensure that no intimations of the transcendental truth are allowed into the cave, it is hard to see how the divine could allow itself to be excluded from the human realm by profane and tyrannical mortals.

Socrates would answer with the counterquestion that he raised in book 6 of the *Republic*: namely, why are the many so perverse? (490d). Why do men so adamantly resist Eros? Although the cave is emphatically *not* the true realm of humans, the sin of falling into the cave cannot be blamed on their rulers, their ancestors, or their inherently fallen nature. Man seems to imprison himself and his descendants in this subterranean domain through his own willful ignorance, vain skepticism, and chronic insecurity. As we saw in the *Protagoras*, there seems to be a collective guilt that all the prisoners in the cave participate in through their cowardice. The skill of the puppeteers consists in using these propensities to self-deception.

We have seen in our examination of the *Phaedo* that the forms or ideas do not operate on man through the efficient causality of the material world. Formal causality operates through recollection, not contiguity; it wells up from within the soul, though it cannot flex sinews and muscles in any physical sense (*Phaedo* 99a). Through understanding the irony of erotic maieutics, one may better understand how the Good is both physically impotent and graciously omnipresent. The good makes itself felt through erotic intermediaries and midwives like Socrates, who remind other human beings of who they really are. Indeed, it is through this spiritual deliverance of others that Socrates, like eros, is continually reborn or re-collected. An erotic daimon must continually empty himself of ossified knowledge so that eros may speak through him.

According to Xenophon, Socrates prided himself most on his skill in pandering (*mastropeia*), which we may understand as a reference to his facility with desires not approved of by the authorities.[11] The cave-state is a gigantic effort at reducing the Hyper-Uranian divinities to politically governable shadows of their true selves; men seek to possess and control the highest things and, in the process, let virtue slip through their fingers. Socratic pandering thus has a very important role in recalling men to their true identity. It does not aim at bringing lovers together for sexual procreation or flattering the many but, instead, strives to free human beings from vain desires so that the recollection of divine things in the human soul may result. This kind of pandering is the only honest response to a natural desire in the human soul for a meaning greater than anything the cave can offer. The philosopher will educate the soul toward its natural habitation on the true terrain of the earth.

We must remember, from our earlier discussions of the *Republic* and *Phaedo*, that the "cave" is a (tyrannical) mind-set, not a spatial location. Thus, returning to the cave has to do with an erotic disposition to share the beauty of the true earth. This disposition actually preserves (and is the only way of preserving) the ecstatic experience of authentic human existence that it strives to communicate to others. In other words, the experience of transcendental beauty and goodness require the released prisoner to participate in the activity of erotic generosity. He must recognize that the existential transmission of eros is the essential condition for remaining liberated and enlightened. The newly reborn prisoner is keenly aware of the distinction between static perfection and erotic vulnerability. Both Aristophanes and Agathon exploited the desire for perfection to seduce men away from the true world and the difficult path of erotic vulnerability.

Of course, like Penia after her mating with Poros in Olympus, men cannot remain in this state of ecstatic awareness forever. The subterranean obligations thrust upon them by eros require that they experience the heartbreak of failure and rejection. Because Eros is the child of *Poros* and *Penia*, one could argue that like Sisyphus he never succeeds in rolling the rock over the hill: one can never really transfer virtue from one soul to another. Like Protagoras, humans can *appear* to be virtuous contemplatives while actually refusing the arduous burdens entailed by the conscientious practice of virtue. Yet, paradoxically, by refusing to go down to the cave, they only entomb themselves in a cloudy cave of solipsism.

The appropriate Socratic response to the pose of high-minded world-weariness is that the activity of virtue, and the knowledge of having done one's utmost, is the best way of remaining outside the cave and most efficacious way of teaching. Put differently, those who fear injustice more than they love daimonic generosity never leave the cave anyway. For to repeat, the cave is an acquisitive and insecure state of mind; it is not spatially located.

In the eyes of the marketplace, where everything has a price and nothing has value, the activity of the virtuous erotic may seem absurd to the extreme. Socrates is an unbelievably ridiculous figure out of a Kafka story. He is a ragged and impecunious smuggler who uses the torturous paths of irony to convey laboriously a noncommodity (his knowledge of ignorance) to a completely unrestricted marketplace, where anything could be bought, or sold, at a price.

Protagoras also taught knowledge of nothing by denying nature and asserting that all is conventional. Yet he had the decency to charge a hefty fee for explaining how this nonwisdom could be used for great profit in the marketplace. He may not have hawked a commodity, but he did sell the equivalent of an M.B.A. in retail salesmanship.

Socrates outrages all the conventions of this perfect free-market economy not merely by refusing to sell his nonwisdom but also by giving it away to customers of his own selection. He compounds the outrage by throwing in himself into the bargain, as a sort of lifetime guarantor of the impracticality of his gift. In this regard especially, he is different from the itinerant sophist who would sell to anyone and take the greatest pains to distance himself from his customer the moment money changed hands.

The smuggler becomes dangerous to the marketplace precisely because his conduct seems to provide strong grounds for believing that he is sustained by forces that violate all the fundamental assumptions that sustain the economy of the homogeneous world marketplace. Camus's hero Sisyphus possesses a dignity suggesting that he is not simply an absurd character, an aberration in an otherwise rational world.[12] Sisyphus somehow implies that the ones who are absurd, or at least hindered by a very limited perspective, are those unable to understand the import of his actions. There is a dimension or quality to his world that cannot be apprehended through the two-dimensional shadow logic of profit and loss that governs conduct in the cave.

In the *Republic* the prisoners would argue from their selfish perspective that if the escapee were really privy to the incredible bliss of the transcendental realm, it would make no sense at all for him to return to the cave. Why would he spend an inordinate length of time trying to convince everybody else to join him outside? The selfishness that imprisons the many in the cave cannot comprehend such conduct. The way they see it, the escapee's very need to return to the cave suggests that it cannot be so wonderful out there. If they, sensible and prudent men that they are, were to discover any such wonders, they would never be stupid enough to risk losing them by returning to the cave, where they might have to share their treasures with other people. They dare not trust the judgment of someone so stupid. If anything, they suspect that he is trying to lure them out in order to secure a better position for himself within the cave—perhaps a better place on the couch, closer to the munchies and the TV set. Hegel put it well when he pointed out that it is this way of looking at things that ultimately makes the hero a hero and a valet a valet.[13] The cave is nothing more or less than the absence of a certain generosity in one's disposition toward reality and grace.

The escapee's constant travels to and from the cave would certainly seem to be every bit as absurd as the labors of Sisyphus. He is engaged in a never ending task of dragging himself in and out, over the steep rocks guarding the mouth of the cave, with nothing tangible to show the cave dwellers. He has no gems or treasures that would convince them of the value of what awaits them outside. In the terms of our earlier image of the smuggler, it is as if all that Socrates can smuggle into the cave is his generosity.

Yet this intangible quality is a great threat to the cave economy. Besides his manifest lack of means, one has to contend with the equally apparent fact that Old Socrates, one of the ugliest and poorest citizens of Athens, is also the happiest of men. This inexplicable but manifest happiness is the gravest threat to the stability of the subterranean market. One can see why the Athenian equivalent of accusations of witchcraft were made against Diotima's student.

Eros's strangely mixed ancestry corresponds well to his absurd predicament. Although he is the son of Poros and richly endowed with all the goods of the realm of quality, this very condition will, paradoxically, make him the poorest and most imprudent of all beings when he enters the subterranean market world of his mortal mother. Socrates is well aware that both Eros's ancestry and his Sisyphean contempt for the Olympians will excite the deepest suspicions of Aristophanes and his ilk. Poros was the son of Metis, and this means that he was destined to supplant Zeus and the Olympian regime set up by the poets in their attempt to make man forget his divine origins. Recall from Aristophanes' speech that this was done by telling of the hellish punishments and mutilations wreaked by jealous and capricious gods on those who ventured outside the cave. Like Dionysus in the *Bacchae*, Eros represents a grave threat to the rigidly enforced artificial stability of this world. No wonder Socrates claimed that Aristophanes' every thought was of Aphrodite and Dionysus; these divinities are clearly the Uranian forces that conservative poet-creators of political gods fear greatly. This is why Aristophanes found it necessary to channel the erotic desire for goodness toward the fleshly and familial.

The beginnings of the philosophical adoption of Eros are evident in Socrates' claim that Eros is a philosopher, a lover of truth, and a lover of beauty. The subsequent substitution of goodness for beauty as the goal of all desire (204e) also means that the desire for beauty is readily comprehensible. The eudaimonistic Greeks were not burdened with an abstractly moralistic definition of goodness; they saw the good as that which is intrinsically worth possessing because of the happiness bestowed on its possessor. Diotima, retracing the theme from the *Republic*, defines eros as a universal wish for happiness and love (205d), common to all men, though certain misdirected varieties of this desire may be referred to by other names. The goal of eros is not changeless personal immortality, love of one's own, or doing good to friends and evil to enemies; one can leave the cave only through the recognition of a universal desire for the good in all men. That recognition leads toward participating in an erotic principle that created the world out of a desire to share eros, not perfection. Eros, humans must learn, cannot be transferred as a commodity; its nature is such that it can only be discovered and chosen freely. Socratic midwifery is the closest they can get to sharing this insight with one another.

Eros must be chosen freely, for its own sake and not for selfish reasons, but unfortunately, original desire is blind and seeks shadowy specificity instead of the good. The other, truer, desire for the divine ideal "that dares not speak its name" is persecuted mercilessly in mankind's original subterranean condition as something that leads only to horrifying punishments and the disintegration of the cave community. Somehow, men must learn that the erotic impulse is only seduced through sexual catharsis. Its true destiny is to retrace the ascent of Penia toward the plenitude of Poros, where the (feminine) soul may be impregnated with the idea of the good. It must then return to the earth, where it will assume the role of a physically abstinent midwife and direct beautiful young souls toward the heavenly abode of Poros. This seems to be the real origin of Aristophanes' tale of the hermaphrodites who stormed heaven. Those beings posed a threat to the false but safe mythology of the Olympian regime, which was supported by the poets in their traditional role as statesmen and supporters of tyrants. To put it differently, it is not man's destiny to be a death-fearing mortal who lives literally fearing his own shadow.

Diotima makes the crucial point that eros is not of the beautiful but rather of procreation and begetting in the beautiful (206e). It does not suffice to ascend toward and selfishly lose oneself in the beautiful. Fortunately or unfortunately, man cannot possess the goods of the soul; they must possess him. Once impregnated by the god, men will recollect their true identity. They will see the need to return to the cave and undertake the task of pandering for or smuggling the good. We have seen Socrates reject the notion that once one leaves the cave, he should never return. A man thinking this way can conceive of nothing better than to gate-crash the feast of the gods and stuff his empty belly with their leftovers. The disguised Odysseus, Socrates' preferred alter ego, had more satisfactory aspirations; only *disguised* as a beggar, he had designs on supplanting Agathon, the reigning beauty of the town. We can now resume our examination of the Homeric subtext of this work and follow the adventures of the disguised Socrates.

Odysseus and Helen

Ten years after the Trojan War, Helen tells a tale of a strange encounter she had with Odysseus, one in which she saw through his disguise but did not disclose his identity to the Trojans.[14] Telemachus is deeply moved by this story, but Helen's long-suffering husband, Menelaus, is not deceived for a moment. He, in turn, tells how Odysseus prevented the Achaeans from falling victim to Helen's uncanny ability to mimic the voices of their loved ones when they lay crouched in the Trojan horse.[15] By combining the tales of Menelaus and Helen one may form a more accurate notion of what really happened when Odysseus encountered Helen in Troy. It would seem that he successfully overcame her efforts to have him disclose the Achaean plans while he was on his way to steal the Palladium from Troy. This very erotic moderation led him to choose circumspect Penelope over Helen.

To put it bluntly, Odysseus would not exchange the Palladium for Helen's sexual favors. As her treacherous conduct before the Trojan horse suggests, Helen had no illusions as to the fate that rightfully awaited her once Troy was taken.[16] It was very much in her interest that the Palladium, the symbol of Trojan invulnerability, remain safely within the citadel; with this objective in mind, Helen would save her hide by seducing the brains of the Greek army. If Odysseus were on her side, Troy would never fall. (Compare the effect that Alcibiades' defection to the Spartan camp had on the Athenian fortunes.)[17]

Nevertheless, it is clear that Odysseus and Helen possessed the ability to recognize each other immediately. She knew him at once despite his beggar's rags, and even from within the belly of the wooden horse he identified her Siren-like voice and polymorphously deceptive ways. There is obviously a sense in which Odysseus's own far from negligible skills as a liar made his recognition of Helen possible; this suggests that the enigmatic relationship between the two was governed as much by sameness as by difference.

The significance of this extended analogy is not that Socrates does not understand eros because he is too ugly to be affected by it; rather, the suggestion is that he is too erotic to desire eros itself. Robert Lloyd Mitchell makes the same point when he says that Socrates did not act any differently when drinking wine, because he was always drunk.[18] Socrates is immune to the sexual blandishments of an individual beauty such as Alcibiades because he is already in love with beauty itself. He does not confuse Alcibiades, the beautiful messenger, with the message.

Odysseus and Helen, the children of Poros and Penia, have too much in common for any further intercourse to be necessary. Helen was the daughter of a swan; Socrates, though an ugly duckling, becomes swanlike on his deathbed. Likewise, Odysseus (though likened to a huckster by the Phaeacians)[19] must undergo a similar transformation and sing his way back to Ithaca by charming his hosts. It is not sufficient for him to find consolation in the nubile beauty of Nausicaa; he must become beautiful himself. As we shall see, the other alternative is for Nausicaa (that is, Alcibiades) to become wise, but unfortunately this is not a commodity that a storm-tossed seaman can easily bestow. In order to be impregnated with wisdom, Alcibiades must undergo the ugly process of spiritual rebirth himself. Having sex with Odysseus would not guarantee Nausicaa the husband she yearned for. Likewise, Alcibiades is in the even more difficult situation of seeking to incorporate the Poros of Socrates into himself, without acknowledging the Penia in his own soul.

As Albert Camus states (echoing Goethe) in his famous essay "Helen's Exile," the Trojan War was fought for the sake of beauty.[20] Yet the suggestion is made in the *Symposium* that the Greeks were deceived as to the identity of beauty. Supporting evidence for this claim lies within the *Odyssey* itself. The Proteus episode to which we have found so many parallels also suggests that Menelaus may return home only when he recognizes that Helen is not really what she signifies. Her ability to mimic the heart's desires of many suggests that she has no real identity of her own; she is nothing without the erotic recollections of her victims. This quality makes her the perfect beloved. It is her very shallowness that makes her seem so profound: she can perfectly reflect her lover's innermost desires.

Of course, Menelaus is not the most impressive character either; in the *Iliad* he is regarded as a valiant but rather pathetic cuckold. Menelaus must undergo the ritual of a simulated mating with that other polymorph, Proteus, before his heart is freed from bondage to Helen's shameless phantasm. Only then may he find his true identity as the splendid figure of the *Odyssey*. It is also clearly significant that Odysseus is the comrade that Menelaus is last informed of by Proteus; Odysseus, that other sea-tossed exile, is the man with whom Menelaus has most in common—another reason why he grieves more for Odysseus than any other comrade. We are reminded of Aristophanes' circle-men when Menelaus states he would have emptied an adjoining city for him, so that "nothing would have separated us two in our friendship and pleasure."[21] It seems indeed that Menelaus would prefer his mortal friendship with Odysseus to the prospect of spending an eternity in the Blessed Isles with Helen.[22] He would surely reject Hephaestus's offer to weld him to his profane and dearly bought Aphrodite. Like Aristodemus, who assumes his persona, he would rather be joined to his Protean male comrade-in-arms. Odysseus has already made a similar choice in preferring the mortal prudence of Penelope to the effortless knowledge offered by Circe and Calypso. He thus stays constant to the choice made earlier, when he alone among all the Greek princes refused to court Helen.[23] He has chosen love, and a lifetime of erotic striving, over the illusion of perfection.

We have seen that Proteus's penultimate form is a tree; *dendritis* was Helen's ancient name in Sparta, and it was in this form that she was carried off into the earth.[24] Menelaus may leave the underworld of erotic desolation and deception only when he sees how the polymorphous nature of his imagination is both responsible for his exile and capable of effecting his liberation. Thus, he must become Odyssean to be freed from the terrible beauty of Helen.

Such an interpretation of the figure of Menelaus is confirmed in Euripides' *Helen*. According to that play, Helen is spirited away to Egypt by Hera, while a phantasm is sent to take her place in Troy. Proteus is the king of Egypt who serves as Helen's chaste protector during the time of her exile. When Menelaus finally arrives in Egypt and discovers the true Helen in Proteus's palace, her "shameless phantasm" disintegrates. Euripides wrote *Helen* shortly after the terrible conclusion of the Sicilian expedition; the irresistible inference is that both the Trojan War and the Sicilian expedition were fought over illusory prizes.

Plato implies that only Socrates / Proteus, through his self-knowledge, understands the truth about Helen. Because of his truly erotic / Protean nature, he alone is immune to the blandishments of her phantasm. He knows the truth about the divine images that Alcibiades tried so hard to barter for. We shall soon see Alcibiades come close to saying that he left for Sicily because he could not stand to live in the same city as Socrates. This was because Socrates reminded Alcibiades of the paltry character of the goals that his fevered desires craved. The false Helen was but a beautiful floating signifier; Alcibiades was convinced that the truth was to be found within the stony heart of Socrates.

Alcibiades

Alcibiades enters the *Symposium* as a wrathful god, a Dionysus who will not submit to Athens or Athena. Although Socrates claims to be the dirty old man who loves him (213c), Alcibiades indignantly denies it; he asserts that Socrates never loved another man in his life (216e). Socrates, his Silenus, is the beloved while he, Alcibiades, is like Dionysus merely the hapless victim. He will attribute his madness to Socrates' hubristic refusal to grant him satisfaction. Dionysus will drive Thebes insane because Pentheus, although sexually fascinated by him, will not acknowledge his divinity.[25] Alcibiades threatens to visit a similar fate on Athens because of Socrates' maddening conduct toward him. Pentheus was torn to pieces by Dionysus while hiding in a tree; likewise, Alcibiades proposes to open Socrates up and reveal the secrets of his Odyssean tree bed. It was with much the same amazement that Circe and Calypso could not see why Odysseus preferred the fading beauty of a mortal woman to their eternal pulchritude. It was not what Penelope possessed that captivated Odysseus; it was what she reminded him of. Here again is the choice between perfection and love. While the eternal feminine lures with the promise of perfection, mortal love leads one to be imperfect and heroic in generosity. Alcibiades cannot understand this; like Aristophanes, he proposes to treat eros as a material commodity and remove it from the herm, surgically.

When Alcibiades, in his capacity as Dionysus, is asked to praise Eros, he refuses on the trumped-up grounds that Socrates will not allow him to praise anyone else. He proposes to praise Socrates instead (214d). Socrates' speech contained many elements of self-identification in its description of eros; notably, however, he claimed that Eros was not a god, but a mediating daimon, one of many such beings who mediate between humans and gods (202e). Alcibiades, who has not heard this speech, suggests instead that Socrates is identical with the god Eros. He dwells on Socrates' lack of desire; this lack, understood in terms of Socrates' cross-examination of Agathon, could only mean that Eros does not desire what he already has. Socrates already has the bounty of Poros, the divine images, within his soul; these are revealed when his two halves are pulled open. The suggestion is that Socrates already has both male and female attributes, tragedy and comedy. In the language of the *Phaedrus*, Socrates' team of horses is divinely temperate. In the language of Aristophanes, however, Alcibiades has shown Socrates to be the last of that dangerous race of circle-men. Socrates expressed the matter differently when he claimed that Eros was the child of Poros and Penia. Alcibiades, however, claims that Socrates unites these principles as appearance and reality: he appears to be needy but is completely self-sufficient.

In his anguish, Alcibiades warns Agathon and all other beautiful young men not to heed Socrates' siren song. This reminds us of the famous episode Plutarch relates, in which Alcibiades reputedly mutilated the fine plumelike tail of his expensive dog so that it would not be more attractive than he![26] The dog was supposed to attract attention to its owner, not to be admired for its own sake. Alcibiades warns the rest of Athens that if he cannot have Socrates as his lover, no one can. Appropriately, he takes on the voices of Helen (220c) and Menelaus (222b) as he recounts his woes. In the tones of Menelaus, that limp spearman, he straddles the body of his beloved and warns the Trojans that they may not bear it away.[27] Quite apart from the ironic reference to Socrates' reputed erotic deadness, Alcibiades also reminds us of, and implicitly confirms, the Proteus analogy developed earlier. Like the cuckolded Menelaus, he has clung doggedly to the Protean Socrates and revealed his true nature. It is surely not coincidental that Silenus, like Proteus, was regarded as one who would only prophesy truthfully under duress.[28]

Just as Menelaus warns the Trojans that they should learn from the experience of others and not be as victims of dumb suffering,[29] Alcibiades urges Agathon to distinguish between true and false beauty.

Socrates is the genuine article, and this is why Agathon, who merely seems to be beautiful, is warned to beware of him; Socrates will strip him of his beauty as mercilessly as a Siren will devour her prey. When Alcibiades used Helen's voice as he talked about Odysseus / Socrates' heroism, he spoke as one whose own beauty was of no avail when it came to seducing Eros. We have already noted that Helen's tale of Odysseus tacitly accepts the distinction between his true beauty and her mimicry. Just as Helen is an echo of Aphrodite, so Alcibiades, for all of his gifts, is only a shadow of the truer beauty that Socrates embodies. Though Alcibiades claims that Socrates is sexually indifferent, the truth seems to be that Alcibiades is spiritually barren. This is the truest reason why he cannot serve Athens and Athena.

What *did* Socrates want with Alcibiades? This investigation must commence with the recollection that the purpose of an erotic encounter with a philosophical midwife is realized in the quickening of the spirit. Intellectual intercourse fills the initiate's soul with an awareness of the ignorance that it must give birth to. Through dying in the flesh the spirit is freed to follow a life of philosophical virtue. This is the context of Socrates' liaison with Alcibiades. We shall see that although Alcibiades is racked by labor pangs of the soul, his pride forbids the necessary birth. (Compare Zeus's literally splitting headaches before he gave birth to Athena, the child of Metis whose son was destined to supplant him.[30]

Alcibiades' proud spirit has been cloven in two. He will seek revenge by splitting Socrates' Protean image of Eros (as a mighty tree) in two with the erotic thunderbolt that he bears as his crest.[31] As noted earlier, one of Helen's names was *dendritis*, and we could speculate that Odysseus was immune to the beauty of the Trojan phantasm because of the stability of his own tree-anchored marriage bed.[32] Like the true identity of Socrates, this secret of Odysseus was one that could not be taken out of the bedroom / soul and openly communicated in the marketplace / city as an object of profane beauty. It is Alcibiades' fate to reveal the hidden meanings of both the arboreal image of Eros and Socrates' corresponding identification with a mighty tree. Diotima described eros as a mighty force, firmly rooted in the earth but reaching to the heavens. Through his marriage with the Diotimean or feminine element in his soul, Socrates may be seen to possess the treasures of Helen / Eros.

Socrates has sought to transform the tyrannical masculine ego of Alcibiades into a more feminine or truly androgynous soul. In other words, Timandra (honor of man) must become Diotima (honored of God). Alcibiades, instead of trying to play the role of Poros toward the polis, must assume the submissive posture of Penia toward the truth. Though willing to assume this position temporally and sexually toward Socrates in order to gain the knowledge necessary to further his ultimately masculine designs, Alcibiades is unwilling to give birth to a humbler new self, for doing so would entail acknowledging a good higher than, and beyond, his own appetite for self-perfection and domination. (Remember Nietzsche's proof that there is no God: if there were, how could he bear not to be Him.)[33]

We could say that Alcibiades accuses Socrates of wanting to do to him what he, Alcibiades, was accused of doing to the herms. His spiritual contumacy is illustrated by his refusal to play the flute, which Socrates refers to in the *First Alcibiades* (106e); Plutarch supplies the amusing datum that Alcibiades was unwilling to distort his beautiful face by subjecting it to a mouthpiece.[34] This may be compared to the distortion of the body that a woman suffers in being pregnant and giving birth. Socrates wants Alcibiades' soul to emulate the feminine Penia in its humility, but this is very much like wishing that Coriolanus, Alcibiades' Plutarchan twin, would humble himself and canvass votes.[35] It is not accidental then that the drunken Alcibiades arrives to refute Diotima supported by a timandrous flute girl.

Alcibiades will use only the alluring speech of Poros; he refuses the abrasive humility of Penia. The unexpected presence of Socrates forces him to give birth to an image of his beloved. Unfortunately, he does not do so in deed; he cannot bring a spiritual pregnancy to term. The image of Socrates that Alcibiades crafts must be regarded as the most splendid of the wind-eggs brought to light in the works of Plato.

In his encomium to Socrates, Alcibiades compares him to the satyr Marsyas, an *aulos* player who bested Apollo's performance on the lyre and was flayed by the god for his hubris.[36] Alcibiades seeks to emulate this punishment by exposing Socrates' divine innards in revenge for his erotic humiliation. He does not appreciate Socrates' deficiencies in the art of demotic music. One who hears the music of the forms is rarely attentive to the rigors of demonstrative proof.

We must bear in mind that although the *aulos* (a pipelike instrument that sounded like a clarinet or oboe)[37] is associated with Dionysian music, it was invented by Athena, who threw it aside for the same reasons that Alcibiades dropped the flute.[38] Socrates, like Athena, discovered the perfect instrument, Alcibiades, but could not play it himself.

Socrates will not play the *aulos* for Alcibiades; he instead wants Alcibiades to accompany him on the *aulos*, to set his teachings to music. But Alcibiades prefers to intoxicate the demos with the songs of Poros, he refuses to incorporate the ugly and abrasive sobriety of Penia into either his soul or his song.

In other words, Alcibiades' hubris consists in his refusal to give birth to spiritual beauty *qua* feminine psyche; he refuses to serve the city by employing his oratorical skill for pedagogic purposes. Socrates was willing to lay down his life for the city sacred to Athena. Alcibiades, however, would neither submit to her justice nor sacrifice his beauty for her glory nor discount his personal ambitions for the greater good of the city. A *Roi de Soleil*, Alcibiades prefers to identify himself with Athens—which he greatly resembles in choosing short-lived glory over self-effacing virtue: Achilles trumps Odysseus. He values his position in Athens more than Athens itself. He values eros more than the feathered wings (*pteros*) that it has to grow; he will not set it free and thus rejects Socrates' position that eros is a means to enlightenment and should not be used for physical gratification or political aggrandizement.

Plato suggests that it was Alcibiades who first awakened eros in Socrates and made him set foot on Diotima's ladder. This encounter is guardedly recalled in the *Phaedrus* when Socrates makes his great palinode to eros. By comparing the palinode with Diotima's speech in the *Symposium* and the *First Alcibiades*, we shall see that Socrates is in fact describing *his* version of the events that Alcibiades has recounted in his speech about Socrates. Ultimately, Alcibiades means no more to Socrates than Nausicaa did to Odysseus, yet the palinode in the *Phaedrus* shows that just as Odysseus promises to remember the youthful beauty who saved him from the waves, Socrates cannot forget the divine emissary who saved him from the clouds of cosmology.

In the *Phaedrus*, Socrates warns us in advance that he is not at all interested in mythical stories for their own sake. His concern is with self-knowledge and with whether he is a complicatedly Typhon-like monster or a kinder, gentler, and simpler creature (230a). Structurally, Plato is sounding a warning to all his readers that they should not regard his myths only as beautiful pictures expected to provide pleasure without edification. Rather, they are intended to supplement his pedagogic concerns; they express meanings that lie beyond the limits of language. Their function is to make our interpretations of Plato's works both richer and more difficult as we strive to find a fundamental unity organized around the theme of self-knowledge.

Any reading of the *Phaedrus* can and must be oriented from this very basic concern; even Socrates' own investigations into eros find their ruling beginning in it. I argue that it is indeed the power of eros that results in the shift from Socrates' initially competitive response to Lysias's speech to his humbler and yet far more beautiful palinode. One may go so far as to claim that the shift represents his own turning-away from disputation and natural science. The vengeful reparations of cosmology are replaced by the generosity of eros. Socrates' original speech does not, as Phaedrus required, actually champion the claims of the nonlover; he contents himself with condemning the lover in his hubris, selfishness, and irrationality. The implication is that even Socrates was not originally erotic; he was, rather, a disinterested rational observer who was equally amazed at the beloved's folly and the lover's madness. (This structure is paralleled by Socrates' well-informed unfamiliarity with the countryside; like Immanuel Kant, he could converse very learnedly about places that he had never visited.)[39]

One may even argue that Socrates' very interest in talking on such matters derived from his wish to demonstrate the superiority of the objective and dispassionate intellect. His ability to make the more disinterested argument the stronger was reflected in his own lack of monetary interest in speech writing; contrast Lysias's professional reasons for advertising his skills. Socrates was merely trying to show off his superior intelligence and technical prowess as a child would; consequently, he would win honor among men by sinning against the gods. It is Alcibiades who precipitates his delayed erotic maturity and delivers him from his absentminded hubris.

We can now see why we should encounter Socrates outside the city. If we were to ask him the question he asked Phaedrus at the beginning of this dialogue, "Where are you going and where have you come from?" (227a), Socrates' ironic answer would surely be that he is descending from the clouds to enter the city. He might even add, sotto voce, that he is bringing philosophy with him under his cloak. Although his interlocutor is Phaedrus, just as the beloved reminds the lover of his god, so too is Socrates truly reminded of his encounter with Alcibiades when he delivers the palinode before Phaedrus. Socrates' subsequent career could be seen as an attempt to purify himself from his involuntary but nevertheless arrogant disregard for eros. Diotima's speech anticipates this: she doubts Socrates' ability to receive her teachings because he has not fallen in love with a beautiful body (209e–210a)—the necessary first step on Diotima's ladder.

Alcibiades' testimony on this matter is deeply ambiguous. One could see it as conclusive proof that Socrates could not speak of eros because he had never fallen in love, or one could regard Socrates' meeting with Alcibiades as the decisive turn in his education as an erotic philosopher. I advance here the latter position, and in order to do so I argue that Alcibiades has typically given his own perspective of these soul-shattering events: it was not accidentally that his crest bore the emblem of Eros wielding a thunderbolt. We may reconstruct Socrates' own version of their encounter, however, from the *Phaedrus*, the *First Alcibiades*, and the obvious references to Alcibiades in the *Republic*.

Alcibiades claims in the *Symposium* that Socrates is really a monstrously ironic nonlover, and we have already examined some of his complex reasons for making this claim. But we must also see that Socrates defends himself against this charge in the palinode. Alcibiades claimed that Socrates was a quasi-divine being who drove men mad through his seductive rhetoric and stoic conduct: the promise of Poros and the practice of Penia. Socrates' own concealed version of their intercourse lays great emphasis on the beneficial effects of erotic mania on his otherwise austere soul.

In discussing the *Phaedo*, I suggested that the pre-Socratic Socrates approached eros as he studied digestion: just as he paid less attention to eating the more he strove to understand the phenomenon of digestion (96c–d), it seems likely that he tried to understand eros without really experiencing it. All of this changed through his encounter with Alcibiades. Whatever force (or Theages-like bridle) it was that rendered him immune to eros suddenly relaxed its prohibition. The very description provided of the black horse seems intended to suggest that Socrates, unlike Phaedrus, was not merely a Platonic lover of fine speeches.

To read a Platonic dialogue, we have to be readers possessed by the passion of the black horse; we cannot be content until we have stripped the text bare of all of its ironic trappings. In this respect, we must emulate the erotic / maieutic conduct of Socrates himself as he ruthlessly exposes the youthful soul of his interlocutor to the light of the good. In other words, we cannot leave the dialogue regarding it as a monster more complex and ill constructed than Typhon. The *Phaedrus* is actually a more gentle creation, possessed of a subtle unity. Paradoxically, the dark horse turns out to be the key to revealing this simpler nature. Before becoming acquainted with the power of the black horse, Socrates was trapped in cloud-cuckoo-land, between the subterranean and hyperterranean realms. Once he was moved by the power of eros, it was possible for him to travel between the two domains instead of remaining becalmed in the in-between.

After his antierotic first speech in the *Phaedrus*, Socrates is warned by his daimon that he must make atonement to Eros for his blasphemy (*Phaedrus* 242b–c). This structurally compares to the effect of Alcibiades' speech in the *Symposium*, in which he seems to confirm Diotima's misgivings regarding Socrates' potential for erotic ascent. A dichotomy is set up between Socrates' very intellectual account of Diotima's ladder, which takes the soul beyond fleshly cravings, and Alcibiades' Dionysian version of his stoic conduct toward bodily beauty. In Aristophanic terms, heavenly *pteros* and bodily eros are essentially opposed: the one is a repetition of the tragic career of the circle-men beyond the cave; while the other is its comic remedy. This quarrel between comedy and tragedy is what Socrates urges Aristophanes and Agathon to resolve at the very end of the *Symposium* (223d); he will try to carry out this resolution himself in the *Phaedrus*.

We have already seen that the figure of Proteus is crucial to the *Symposium*. Proteus and *pteros* are virtual anagrams of each other; in other words, by holding on to the Proteus analogy, our study of eros may start to sprout feathers (*pteros*) and yield awareness of transcendent truth. This position is directly opposed to Aristophanes' position that bodily eros is a great benefactor precisely because it turns us away from the mad flights of *pteros*. Plato suggests that eros naturally grows feathers. Where Aristophanes threatens to chop limbs off disobedient mortals, Plato promises to make man grow divine wings. It is also ironic that this well-feathered rejoinder is aimed at the author of *The Birds*.

Instead of birds, Socrates speaks of horses in the *Phaedrus*; his task is to reconcile the very different muses of comedy and tragedy. His first speech is made *qua* white horse. It is clearly inspired by Phaedrus himself who both resembles this steed and embodies the limitations of its perspective. As I suggested, Socrates made his first speech as the cosmologist and scientist that he was before eros brought him down from the clouds and into the city. It is the erotically transformed Socrates who, in the palinode, is not ashamed to depict himself as the black horse. His ultimate aim, however, is to point Phaedrus toward a synthesis that integrates both natures / genres. The erotic power of the unruly horse is indispensable for any ascent to the Hyper-Uranian realm of true beauty. Only Socrates represents this position.

In the *Symposium*, Alcibiades and Aristophanes, albeit in very different ways, both champion the black horse as they accuse Socrates of disregarding the body. Phaedrus and Agathon view matters from the abstractly romantic perspective of the white horse (toward which the pre-erotic Socrates himself had inclined). We could say that whereas the partisans of the black horse would use Dionysus to serve their ultimately destructive and tyrannical ambitions, those on the side of the white horse believe that the Dionysian can easily be controlled. They underestimate the power of the black horse and thus, unwittingly, admit Dionysus into the hapless city.

Quite obviously, Socrates' position is that this integration of horses must take place within the soul. Only such a resolution can overcome the terrible political consequences of the struggle between the adherents of tragedy and comedy, a quarrel that would eventually tear Athens apart. Socrates' defense is that he incorporated the black horse within his soul through Alcibiades. His refusal to conduct himself *qua* black horse, as Alcibiades would like, does not mean that he has rejected divine madness; rather, he has received this prodigal power within his soul and acknowledged it. In contrast, Alcibiades would alternately seek to use the black horse and then, inevitably, end up being used by it. The erotic black horse functions with all the ambiguity of a *pharmakon* (drug): properly used, it brings the greatest gifts, but proper use requires the erotic moderation of a Socrates (244a). The checkered career of Alcibiades well illustrates the results of its misuse.

Socrates claims in the *First Alcibiades* (103a–b) that he approached his beloved only after his daimon freed him to do so. His daimonic sign, since it functions only in a negative capacity, thus performs as a kind of charioteer giving the reins to the unruly black horse. Accordingly, Socrates had the time to observe Alcibiades, and he evidently studied his subject very closely indeed—quite as diligently and objectively as the nonlover of the *Phaedrus*. Socrates makes it very clear to Alcibiades that he is not at all awed by the younger man's talents, ambitions, and connections. Indeed, he says that he would not have been interested in the beautiful youth had Alcibiades been content to rest on his laurels and hide his insatiable ambition (104e–105a).

This means that Socrates' own resemblance to the black horse is not accidental; the *First Alcibiades* chronicles the conversation between the respective black horses of Alcibiades and himself. In the *Symposium* (216a), Alcibiades describes the struggle in his own soul between his lust for the approval of the demos and his love of Socrates; these might almost be the two horses in his own psychic configuration. Socrates, on the other hand, must reconcile his love of the clouds—an

Apollonian abstract, impersonal love of truth—and his Dionysian desire for Alcibiades. As Socrates ascends Diotima's ladder, his desire for the erotic youth soon becomes a love for the Dionysian soul of violet-crowned Athens itself. This love for Athens, to which he pays testimony in such works as the *Crito*, leads him back into the cave. It is in this way that intellectual and physical appetites are reconciled. We could even speculate that his daimon allowed him to approach Alcibiades only when his love had grown beyond the proportions of purely physical desire. Conversing with Alcibiades will now help Socrates to better recollect Hyper-Uranian mysteries and to further the education of the subterranean polity.

Added confirmation of the change in Socrates may be gained from the fact that the pre-Socratic Socrates was guilty of the very error that the Socratic midwife was so opposed to. I have emphasized many times that information transference is not the way a soul learns about things higher than itself; it can learn about these matters only through erotic recollection of an idea. Yet as we have seen in our reading of the *Phaedo*, this was the position that the Pre-Socratic Socrates assumed towards unions of both the physical and the spiritual varieties.

Returning to the *First Alcibiades*, we find Socrates employing the techniques of erotic suggestion. He will try to make Alcibiades openly acknowledge the full extent and implications of his boundless ambitions (105a–d). These are contrasted to Alcibiades' paltry actual accomplishments and sexual attractions. This is Alcibiades' first encounter with the *penia* and *poros* of the human condition, the struggle between the black and white horses jostling for ascendancy over his own soul. Socrates first enables him to apprehend the enormity of his desires and then, abruptly, makes him aware of how ill-endowed he is in comparison with these imperial fantasies (*First Alcibiades* 121a–124b).

We see evidence supporting Alcibiades' complaint against Socrates here. He is put in the position that Socrates in the *Phaedrus* (230d–e) claimed to be in: he is the hapless donkey who could be led around, willy-nilly, whenever Silenus dangled his carrot and sang his Siren song. Just as the Sirens lured Odysseus with their instant recognition of him and promise of complete knowledge,[40] so too is the egotistical Alcibiades captivated by the golden images that Socrates discerns within his soul.

Here again, the resemblance to Helen is evident; she knows what men desire, or at least she reminds them of this long-forgotten self-knowledge that slumbers within their souls. Like Socrates, or a Platonic dialogue, Helen is a mirror in which men see the innermost desires and mysteries of their souls; the image of a mirror is one that looms large in the *First Alcibiades* (132c–133c). There, Alcibiades is forced by Socrates to acknowledge that all he has said has derived from his (Alcibiades') soul and not from Socrates'.

In the *Phaedrus*, the eyes of the lover are referred to as a mirror in which the beloved sees himself (255d)—further evidence that Alcibiades is the concealed beloved in the *Phaedrus*. Alcibiades, on the other hand, reminds Socrates of his own erotic identity as a lover of wisdom. Socrates stresses in the *Phaedrus* that each lover uses the beloved to fashion a living statue of the god he follows (253a). It is not without significance that whereas Socrates is speaking as a onetime professional stonemason, Alcibiades speaks of cheap stone images of gods which are available at every statuary's (literally, herm-maker's) shop (215b).

Socrates says that those who are philosophers will seek a Zeus-like beloved, one who is by nature disposed to be both a lover of wisdom and a leader (252e). These qualities are clearly those of Alcibiades. When the beloved is found, the lover encourages him to realize these qualities in his nature and will set out to learn about these qualities himself. He will draw on all available sources, including his own recollected awareness which is revived by the vision of the beloved. Bacchant-like, the lover will pour this knowledge of the god in great draughts into the soul of the beloved to create the best possible resemblance to their ruling deity (253a–b). This image recalls the scene in the *Symposium* (213e–214a) where Socrates and Alcibiades each drained a half-gallon portion of unmixed wine; there is also an echo of Thrasymachus and his great torrent of words as he attempts to seduce Glaucon (*Republic* 344d). In the *Symposium* Socrates greatly discounted the chances of passing his wisdom on, through physical means, to Alcibiades (218e) and Agathon (175d–e). Now, in the *Phaedrus*, he says that as lover and beloved progress in their friendship, the flow of passion that surges in the lover overflows into the soul of the beloved through their eyes (255b–c). What is imparted here is not wisdom but passion: a flood of erotic energy that is bounced back to its mediate source via the lover.

I referred earlier to Alcibiades' shield emblem of Eros bearing a thunderbolt. It is not too fanciful to claim that just as Socrates saw himself through Alcibiades, Alcibiades is now depicting who Socrates really is. This is especially fitting since Socrates had once saved his life (*Symposium* 220e). As a lover he will craft a divine image of his onetime lover and immortal beloved. He will bear his shield as Perseus did, to watch the reflection of the Gorgon and be protected from being maddened by its monstrous beauty. The crest of Alcibiades is also a two-dimensional revelation of the nature of Socrates; it represents objectively, albeit symbolically, what he expressed in his speech. According to the love-dazzled Alcibiades, Socrates is none other than Eros himself. Plutarch points out that crests on shields were customarily used to depict famil-ial descent,[41] but Alcibiades' device goes against this practice by reveal-ing his erotic relation to Socrates. Understood from the standpoint of the *Phaedrus*, Alcibiades' mistaken identification of Socrates with Eros itself is easy to understand: he is merely repeating the mistake, made by any lover, of confusing the sign with the signified. This parallel also serves to underscore the close connection between the *Phaedrus* and the *Symposium*.

Just as Alcibiades illustrates the unhappy plight of the black horse, Phaedrus represents the inadequacy of the white horse apart from its spirited counterpart. Though he loves speeches, he has received only in-adequate accounts of them; his passions have never really been en-gaged. That is, although he has a great hankering for speeches about Eros, this emotion has never become passionate enough for him to go beyond the written word. He has certainly had lovers but he has never really been in love in any concrete sense and therefore has yet to ascend Diotima's ladder. None of his lovers has overflowed with eros and com-municated this divine madness to him. Phaedrus is, in some sense, aware of this deficiency and expresses it through his insatiate need for speeches about eros, but he is in love with speeches only and has never really felt the vicious cravings of the dark horse. We might ask him whether it was only a rolled-up speech he carried under his robe (228d) or if he was really erotic. Writings about Eros are inadequate supple-ments to or substitutes for the insatiate bite of Eros itself. The white horse can help the prisoner hate the illusions of the cave but it cannot really take him outside. Without the power of the black horse soul is becalmed in a cosmological cloud-cuckoo-land; one is tired of living and afraid of dying.

There are thus two different energies here: the more intellectual and voluntary on the one hand, and the more passionate and involuntary on the other. These might also be likened to the two horses: the white horse, or the more intellectually disposed drive, looks like the beloved—it is a divine image that the lover has voluntarily imparted to the beloved—whereas the black horse looks like the lover. Since this image is less mediated and more passionate, it cannot impart to the beloved the fact that the lover is not its origin. The beloved associates the picture of the lover with this passion because it was imparted through the eyes and look of the lover, even though the passion itself was inspired by the beloved himself and is of cosmic origin. The black horse is thus the less self-aware and more powerful of the pair. It is far more susceptible to mimetic suggestion.

To put it differently, the immortal yearnings originally inspired in the lover become divided by the very attempt to understand them and then impart them to the beloved. The soul matter of the beloved cannot adequately receive the infinite image that the lover proposes to represent upon it; the very wisdom that he proposes to transfer falls on ill-prepared ground. Since the lover himself cannot adequately understand the infinite import of what he is trying to express through necessarily finite means, raw passion is more easily imparted. This means that passion becomes separate from knowledge within the soul of the lover himself. In this form it is the black horse, and it naturally communicates with the confused and unformed capacity of the beloved in this guise. The beloved is made more immediately aware of the infinite potential of what the lover had hitherto struggled to express through finite language; the awareness of the disparity between eros and logos makes passion more attractive than reason.

Under the strain of expressing the awesome perfection and simplicity of the unbounded One, the finite souls of both lover and beloved buckle and become complex; this is a "fall" of sorts and must be how the soul is divided into white horse and black horse: intellectual awe and carnal desire. The power of the black horse is immortal—it even sustains the infinite striving undertaken by the doomed souls in Hades—but the problem with this power is its tendency to confuse the sign with the signified. In the language of the *Republic*, it confuses the shadow with reality. As a result, it seeks sexual fruition with what is merely a sign of that which is truly desired.

The white horse, on the other hand, would merely languish before a divine vision of loveliness; it cannot act on this knowledge. Only by properly combining this respect for beauty with the energy of the black horse can the soul wrestle with the reality of the sign and apprehend the reality of the signified. Both aspects are essential to the process of pedagogy. The lover conveys what he has recollected *through* the glorified beloved, *to* the phenomenal reality of the selfsame beloved. In other words, it is by mediating between the *penia* and *poros* in the beloved that the lover learns more about the dazzling reality that he glimpsed as beauty. This principle of pedagogy is diametrically opposed to the laws of scarcity and quantity that rule the marketplace.

Beauty leads to the recovery of all the other Hyper-Uranian qualities. As we saw in the *Protagoras*, the practice of these virtues enriches one's intellectual awareness of them; speech and deed sustain each other. Such praxis surely demands the courage and power of the black horse. The soul must continually mediate between the Hyper-Uranian ideality above and the erotic potential of the beloved reality below. The feminine soul is possessed by this *poros*-driven vision which it then imparts to the *penia* of the beloved. Although in doing so, the soul of the lover seems to act out a masculine role, it is always aware that its task is midwifery and not *poiesis* (making). It is discovering what is already present as potential; it is not creating in its own image and seeking to further its own greater glory. Yet this humility must be possessed with a fervor and a madness that other men can derive only from the very masculine lust to procreate. These two seemingly disparate aspects must somehow be unified in one nature which, like the noble puppies of the *Republic* (375c) must be both erotic and self-effacing. Like Socrates, it must combine the lusty energy of the stonemason with the reverent humility of a midwife.

This is why the white and black horses have to be synthesized within the soul. The soul must retain the masculine capacity for striving even though it is essentially feminine in its motivation and method. It must accordingly give pride of place to its vision of Hyper-Uranian reality. It is this ecstatic vision that saves maieutic philosophy from becoming nihilistic poetry; the soul's receptivity toward truth preserves it from the extremes of hubris and despair. As in Aristophanes' circle-men, the psychic elements of tragedy and comedy are present in every human nature. The goal is a Caesar with the soul of Christ, an Alcibiades who can play the *aulos*. Only so can man become truly human, and preserve an erotic relationship within the soul that mediates between the gods and the earth, and thus be able to become a denizen of that true world which Socrates described in his swan song at the end of the *Phaedo*. Aristophanes would regard Socrates' attempt to combine these natures as a resurrection of the circle-men who stormed heaven, but Socrates is much the humbler man, since he is not claiming to be either of divine origin or a maker of gods.

The white and black horses may also be seen to correspond to tragedy and comedy respectively. The contemplative understanding that the white horse gains through viewing sublime but tragic events can be enjoyed only through the pathos of distance. What is observed becomes far less pleasant when any personal involvement is factored in. The more satisfactory carnal knowledge of the black horse, however, occurs beneath the level of tragedy and does not provide any insight into the cosmic economy.

Socrates consistently points toward what could be called an Odyssean midpoint which resides between and beyond the tragedy of an intellectual overachiever and the comedy of a sexual underachiever. One does not have to choose between studying the gods' response to hubris and sharing in bestial incontinence. Although it is hubris for a mortal mind to seek to linger eternally in the *poros* of the heavens with the forms, it is disgustingly bestial for its body to wallow contentedly as a subterranean prisoner of Aristophanes. Man must combine the two halves of his nature, tragic and comic, for the healing of both city and soul to occur. Put in terms of the escape from and the return to the cave, we could say that while the black horse is the difficulty on the way out of the cave, the white horse proves equally reluctant to return to the subterranean realm. It prefers to languish impotently before Hyper-Uranian beauty. The black horse moves the soul to share its knowledge with the prisoners in the cave.

A proper combination of *poros* and *penia* is thus essential if the heroic soul is to rise beyond the unhappy end of tragedy. As illuminating as the sanguinary lessons of tragedy may be, they are always bought at the expense of one who might have gone beyond their ultimately pessimistic teaching. The problem with the tragic hero is that although he has transcended the cave and is in a position to bring great benefit to humanity, he believes that these powers inhere in him and are not gratuitously expressed through him. In other words, he cannot acknowledge or understand the sustaining power of eros. As a result of his lack of self-knowledge, like Dionysus in tragedy he comes into being in a divine state momentarily and then is torn to shreds through his hubris. This hubris may be understood as the incapacity of the finite soul to bear the infinite burdens that it has presumed to bear.

Under the joint influences of *poros* and *penia*, so dangerous a cataclysm is averted. The soul understands that its power of *poros* is only a channel, a receptivity that it does not possess in itself, and this humble self-awareness comes through the rough ministry of *penia*. Left to its own devices, however, *penia* would merely administer the pessimistic lesson of Aristophanes that any transcendence or human excellence is both sinful and impossible. The Socratic spirit of irony and humility, although fully aware of the teachings of *penia*, is also awestruck by the beauty of *poros* as reflected in the beloved. Thus, it will not repeat Aristophanes' blasphemy of denying the transcendent. The philosophic soul understands that though not itself divine, it is sustained by a transcendental order of goodness. Just as it knows that it does not know, it possesses sufficient grace to circulate the greater grace that surrounds it.

This humility is the greatest of the benefits that the philosophical soul successfully brings back to the cave. Indeed, this very humility helps it to see that eros is not governed by the laws of quantity, whereby whatever is possessed *qua* object can be held only at the expense of others. It sees that it may continue to be sustained by eros only as it freely imparts this grace to others. Instead of comic humility administered externally to preempt the heroic ascent of the soul, ironic self-knowledge ensures that *poros* and *penia* act in tandem within the economy of the soul as it rises out of the cave: *poros* participates in eros; *penia* prevents this grace from becoming objectified or treated as a possession.

As we learned from that unlikely philosophical comedy the *Phaedo*, the soul must eschew the two extremes of comic pessimism and tragic optimism. Even at its best, comedy conveys the impression that grace can only come up from the earth and will never come down from the heavens; it teaches that one should forsake the transcendent to find bestial happiness. Tragedy, on the other hand, can be overwhelmed by the bounty of *poros*; it is worth remembering that it was Dionysus who gave Midas his deadly golden touch, for restoring Silenus to him.[42] The human soul must learn to be graceful; its schooling consists in learning how to receive eros and dwell in the element of divinely derived grace. The scriptural image of Peter trying to walk on water comes to mind; he had to learn to trust in a grace that he could not possess.[43]

The lesson of the *Symposium* is that just as the real Helen—that is, true beauty—never left for Troy, the true salvation of Athens has never left the city. Alcibiades could never rescue Athens; this deus ex machina had too ill-trained a team of horses. Athens should instead have tried to do what Alcibiades understood literally but was unable to perform spiritually. The Athenians should have held on to Socrates who, unlike Alcibiades, never left Athens. Alcibiades cannot understand that it is the striving after the transcendental which brings mortals into a proper relationship with it. Those who try to carry off the truth *qua* commodity will forever repeat the tortures of Tantalus in Hades.

Put differently, it is precisely a god who cannot save mankind. External intervention through efficient causality cannot bring about the necessary spiritual growth and self-knowledge. Human beings already possess the key to salvation in their own souls, in their *poros*-derived capacity for apprehending the very element of eros or grace in which they dwell unwittingly. Socrates' practice must be the model. One must learn to pry apart the subtle wrestler's grasp of Plato to glimpse those marvelous divine images that both Alcibiades and he discerned. As we observed earlier, Socrates never left the polis. More daringly, we might say that it is impossible to re-create a polis, a genuine humanistic community, without Socrates. One cannot separate the Hyper-Uranian vision of the philosopher from his robust sense of reality. It is the very psychic unity that Socrates gained within the cave that takes him beyond its confines to the vision of the good, inspires him to return, and continually sustains his daimonic mission between the two realms.

It is time for us to return to the case of Alcibiades. Although Socrates, as we have seen by his own account, is a follower of Zeus and is attracted to those with the ability for philosophy and leadership, it is noteworthy that in the *Protagoras*, Socrates likens Alcibiades to Hermes (309a–b). We have seen that he came to Socrates' assistance at a crucial juncture in his dialectical duel with Protagoras (who also claimed to be Hermes), appearing as a gift from the gods. And Alcibiades played a crucial role in transforming Socrates' pre-erotic courage into full-blown eros. In other words, Alcibiades reminds Socrates of Hermes' promise to Odysseus: the gods would ensure that his courage would not go unrequited.[44] Alcibiades unwittingly echoes this view in the *Symposium* when he describes his initial perception of his beauty as a gift from Hermes before going on to sculpt and mutilate his own image of that stony-hearted herm, Socrates. Alcibiades could never understand the sense in which gifts were given by the gods. Because he could understand a gift only as a possession or object, rather than as a grace that sustained and worked together with courageous heroism, Alcibiades was unable to see why Socrates could not bestow his wisdom upon him. He could not understand the difference between efficient and formal causality.

This very disparity between the personae of Zeus and Hermes, ruler and ambassador respectively, sheds further light on what went wrong with Alcibiades. Socrates was clearly attracted to the younger man's royal and philosophic nature, as evidenced by his swift revelation of Alcibiades' imperial ambitions in the *First Alcibiades* (105c). He tried to make his beloved into a Hermes, a philosophically schooled Pericles who would mediate between divine law and erotic ambition. Alcibiades, however, had some grounds for expecting that Socrates came to anoint him as the successor to the Great King (121b–124b).

All this revives the age-old question whether Achilles or Odysseus was the better man. Socrates sought to graft some of his Odyssean qualities onto the Achilles-like soul of Alcibiades. Alcibiades wanted the power of Zeus and the golden arms of Achilles; he discovered, to his chagrin, that he was expected to be an erotically inspired messenger of a kingdom that was not of this world. When he found out that the gods preferred Odysseus, like Sophocles' Aias he went mad. He would not exchange gold for bronze; he preferred the golden armor of the gods to the brazen ironies of Odysseus the beggar. As Aias slaughtered sheep, Alcibiades mutilated herms.

In other words, Alcibiades would not distort his lips to suck out the poetic poison of Protagoras: the belief that the ruler was not the servant of the gods but their maker. The lines Phaedrus quoted from Euripides' *Hippolytus* (199a), that the lips promised but not the heart, can be reversed here: in the case of Alcibiades, the heart promised but not the lips. He refused to accompany Socrates on the *aulos*.

The implications of his refusal can now be studied. Socrates clearly does not need Alcibiades from the standpoint of his (Socrates') soul, now that he has been reminded of his nature. Alcibiades has roused the black horse within Socrates' soul and turned him around toward political philosophy. In a sense, however, the fate of Athens also depends very much upon statesmen such as Alcibiades to preserve the possibility of Socratic humanity. I mentioned earlier that the *Symposium* combines references to the highest and lowest points of Athenian morale during the war; both points are connected to the reception of Alcibiades, who, through his eros, convinced the Athenians to embark on the Sicilian expedition.[45] With his dismissal, the invasion was doomed and so, eventually, was Athens. We are told by Plutarch that Socrates was opposed to the expedition.[46] Likewise, the refusal of the Athenian admirals to heed the advice of Alcibiades before Aegospotami led to the final disaster of the war.[47] Socrates' only public political intervention in the war concerned the treatment of the victors of Arginusae; although he was the presiding officer at the time, his protests were completely ineffectual (*Apology* 32b). As a result, Athens lost probably its last competent fleet commanders.[48] Socrates, as he well knew, was impotent before the many; it required the eros of an Alcibiades to sway the assembly.

We must remember that it is Plato who has provided us with a Socrates made young and beautiful, a Socrates who has learned music. Athens had to deal with the real Socrates, a rather more abrasive person who was difficult for those lacking the genius of an Alcibiades or a Plato to grasp. Socrates, the old weaver of the *Phaedo*, will not change the rough texture of his rhetoric. This is why Athens seems to need an Alcibiades to set the teachings of Socrates to music—yet, we have seen that this is precisely the role Alcibiades will not play. Although only he can lure souls to submit to his eros, Alcibiades will not learn the art of gymnastics; he will not strip souls naked and expose their ignorance under the pretext of revealing his own ugliness. Dionysus may confess privately that he is the lover of Silenus, but he will not publicly submit to him. He needs the secrets of his Proteus-like beloved so that he may intoxicate the world into worshiping him as Poros, just as much as Socrates needs his seductive gifts to enshrine philosophy in Athens.

Neither Socrates nor Alcibiades, then, would submit to serve the purposes of the other. Though Odysseus hailed Nausicaa as a young palm tree he had observed at Delos, the shrine of Apollo,[49] her presence, however serendipitous, was ultimately accidental. She merely served to remind him that he was supposed to incorporate the gifts of Apollo into his own soul. Socrates viewed Alcibiades in much the same spirit. Although Alcibiades reminded him of his need for eros, he practiced seductive rhetoric only once in the entire Platonic corpus: in the *First Alcibiades*, when he mesmerized his beloved with the promise of *poros*.

Apollo, whose oracle had previously deemed Socrates the wisest of men (*Apology* 21a), reminded the philosopher many times of his need to cultivate the Muses (*Phaedo* 60e). Unlike Odysseus, who had to move from manipulative lies to poetry, Socrates was asked by Apollo to make his truthful rhetoric less ironic and more musical; philosophy must become more immediately attractive to erotic young men. Socrates refused to practice flattery, however. In his defense, he could possibly adduce the case of Alcibiades who, by his own account, was driven mad by a glimpse of the divine images that Socrates flashed before him briefly. Ever since then, Socrates seemed to have used more *penia* than *poros* in his pedagogy.

Plato, however, did receive the gift of philosophy from Socrates in a more indirect but untainted manner. This is why he is able to transmit the wisdom of a Socrates, albeit one rendered young and beautiful, to us. The Platonic second sailing is thus more successful than the direct approach used in the case of Alcibiades, who was only maddened by the direct vision of divinity. The problem is that the paths of dialectic are as torturous and devious as the voyages of Odysseus. Nevertheless, at the end of the day it is through Plato that the qualities of tragedy and comedy are reconciled. It is therefore significant that the *Phaedrus*, the dialogue in which these seemingly disparate psychic powers are reconciled, takes place outside Athens in the shade cast by the leaves of a *platonos*, a plane-tree with wide spreading branches (230b).[50] This alternative is clearly to be preferred over the darkness at noon experienced by Alcibiades. It is also worth noting that the name of the narrator of the *Symposium*, Apollodorus, means "gift of Apollo." Is it too far-fetched to suggest that through writing this dialogue Plato completely discharged Socrates' obligations to Apollo? Just as the *Phaedrus* takes place outside of Athens, so too does Plato's musical transfiguration of his master make it possible for the legacy of Socrates to be passed on to another age in desperate need of his uncanny presence.

One final observation. The teams of horses driven by the gods in the *Phaedrus* (246a) do not differ essentially from those possessed by humans, since the human teams are capable of receiving a proper training. Furthermore, the Olympians themselves are not the highest powers in the cosmos but merely the best-mounted spectators of Hyper-Uranian truth (247c). It follows, then, that they are themselves only demigods and not much better than the daimons of the *Symposium*. We must remember Diotima's comment that Eros was not the only such daimon or intermediary between absolute beauty and the human realm (202e–203a). This means that a soul with a properly trained team of desires will become a daimonic companion of the Olympians as an angelic messenger of Hyper-Uranian truth and a lover of the ultimate wisdom. Although there can be no ways of demonstrating such an implication, this does seem to be the ultimate reward for the philosophic life. I argued from the *Phaedo* that it was the temporary experience of this vision in his embodied state that sustained Socrates' faith in the afterlife. Likewise, it is Plato's Pauline vision of the cosmic Socrates that inspires him to address us across the ages. For ourselves, we must find comfort in the power of the living presence of Socrates to animate philosophical discourse, and to resurrect dead souls, twenty-four centuries after his death.

Notes

Preface

1. Søren Kierkegaard, *Concluding Unscientific Postcript*, trans. David Swenson and Walter Lowrie (Princeton: Princeton University Press, 1941), 180.
2. Stanley Rosen, *Plato's Symposium*, 2d ed. (New Haven: Yale University Press, 1987), xvi.
3. Jacob Klein, "Plato's *Phaedo*," *Journal of St. John's College*, January 1975, 1–10.
4. *Meridian Handbook of Classical Mythology*, ed. Edward Tripp (New York: Meridian, 1970), 52–53.

Chapter 1. Glaucon's Republic

1. For the Greek text of the *Republic*, I have used the Loeb Classical Library edition, trans. Paul Shorey (London: William Heinemann, 1963). All English translations are from *The Republic of Plato*, 2d ed., trans. and ed. (with an interpretive essay, and a new introduction) Allan Bloom (New York: Basic Books, 1991).
2. Leo Strauss, *The City and Man* (Chicago: University of Chicago Press, 1964), 65; Xenophon *Memorabilia* 3.6, 7.
3. Plutarch *Life of Solon* 15.
4. Homer *Iliad* 9.410–16.
5. Herodotus *Histories* 1.8–13.
6. Homer *Odyssey* 10.488–91.
7. See Leo Strauss, *Socrates and Aristophanes* (Chicago: University of Chicago Press, 1966), 270–82; and *The Rebirth of Classical Political Philosophy*,

sel. and ed. Thomas L. Pangle (Chicago: University of Chicago Press, 1989),
125–26.

8. Aristophanes *Ekklesiasuzae* 877–1111.

9. Niccolò Machiavelli, *The Prince*, Norton Critical Edition, trans. and
ed. Robert M. Adams (New York: Norton, 1977), 72.

10. Hesiod *Theogony* 740–44.

11. Hesiod *Works and Days* 110–99, 293–97.

12. Cited in *The Oxford Dictionary of Quotations*, 3d ed. (1979), 151.

13. Homer *Iliad* 6.234–36.

Chapter 2. Protagorus and the Myths of Sisyphus

1. For the Greek text of the *Protagoras* I have used the Loeb Classical Library edition, trans. W. R. M. Lamb (London: William Heinemann, 1924).
English translations are from *The Collected Works of Plato*, ed. Edith
Hamilton and Huntington Cairns (Princeton: Princeton University Press,
1961).

2. Of course, I am thinking of Aristotle's *Ethics* and his distinction between intellectual and moral virtue at the conclusion of book 1.

3. See Plato *Gorgias* 518e–519a. For a more favorable view of Pericles, see
Donald Kagan's excellent *Pericles of Athens and the Birth of Freedom* (New
York: Free Press, 1991).

4. Plutarch *Life of Pericles* 24.

5. For a fine treatment of the subject, see Donald Kagan, *Outbreak of the
Peloponnesian War* (Ithaca: Cornell University Press, 1969).

6. See *Meridian Handbook of Classical Mythology*, ed. Edward Tripp
(New York: Meridian, 1970), 256–57.

7. Homer *Odyssey* 9.601, 582.

8. Hippias, amusingly, claims that he is superior to all the wise men of
the past but he habitually praises them because he fears the wrath of the
dead (*Greater Hippias* 281e–282a). It is fitting that he should be very much
at home in the underworld.

9. Prodicus himself was reputed to have orated on the subject of Heracles
and easy virtue. Like Tantalus, however, he seems unable to practice what
he preaches. According to Prodicus, Heracles had to choose between the
paths of virtue and vice as personified by two women. Vice says that her
real name is pleasure. She extols the value of a sensual and opportunistic
life. Virtue then tells Heracles that the gods give no real benefits or honor to
man without struggle. Vice claims that this is a long and arduous path, unlike her short and easy route (Xenophon *Memorabilia* 2.1.21–33). It is
surely not coincidental that these themes loom large in the discussion between Protagoras and Socrates.

10. Patrick Coby, *Socrates and the Sophistic Enlightenment* (Lewisburg,
Pa.: Bucknell University Press, 1987) comes *tantalizingly* close to getting
the meaning of this point. He recognizes that the shade of Sisyphus is posi-

tioned between Tantalus and Heracles, but he only infers that "to pursue wisdom, knowing only that one does not know, is akin to Sisyphus's repeated (and presumably endless) efforts to roll a stone over the crest of a hill" (190). Coby ignores his own insight that "courage . . . holds the key to the character of Protagoras" (13).

11. Prodicus was no stranger to these doublings. He is reputed to have said that desire doubled was love and love doubled was madness (Stobaeus 4.20.65).

12. See *The Older Sophists*, ed. Rosamond Kent Sprague (Columbia: University of South Carolina Press, 1972), 5–7.

13. See, e.g., Robert Graves, *The Greek Myths* (Harmondsworth, Eng.: Penguin, 1960), 216–20. The story goes that when Autolycus, Odysseus's grandfather, stole Sisyphus's cattle, Sisyphus took revenge by seducing Autolycus's daughter. This post-Homeric legend could well account for Odysseus's strained relationship with his father (why is Laertes not the king of Ithaca? why does he not rule even in his son's absence?) and his need to converse with his mother in Hades.

14. As noted in Chapter 1, Glaucon is a not atypical example of a rich young man unwilling to go about receiving a proper education.

15. See Tripp, *Meridian Handbook*, 499.

16. Diogenes Laertius *Lives of the Philosophers* 9.50. See also Sprague, *The Older Sophists*, 4.

17. Given a marked similarity to Aristophanes' speech in the *Symposium*, it is no coincidence that Aristophanes is the only speaker in that dialogue who is not present in the *Protagoras*. He seems to take Protagoras' place. See Stanley Rosen, *Plato's Symposium*, 2d ed. (New Haven: Yale University Press, 1987), 24–25.

18. See Thucydides *History of the Peloponnesian War* 2.41.

19. Hesiod *Works and Days* 85–91.

20. Ibid., 78.

21. See Nietzsche, *Beyond Good and Evil*, no. 150 in *Basic Writings of Nietzsche*, trans. Walter Kaufmann (New York: Modern Library, 1968), 280.

22. See Leo Strauss's commentary in *On Tyranny* (New York: Free Press, 1963) for valuable insights into Simonides' character. See also the translation of Simonides in vol. 3 of the Loeb Classical Library's *Greek Lyric*, trans. David Campbell (Cambridge: Harvard University Press, 1982).

23. Hesiod *Works and Days* 287–92.

24. *Greek Lyric*, 3.292.

25. Plutarch *Life of Pericles* 36.

26. Homer *Odyssey* 10.321–24.

27. Of course, the most famous formulation of this position is found in Aeschylus *Agamemnon* 176–78: "Zeus . . . has laid it down that wisdom comes alone through suffering."

28. Socrates knows that he does not know; this knowledge makes him wise. Protagoras knows that virtue is impossible, and this is supposed to make him the best teacher of virtue.

29. We saw Thrasymachus follow a similar tack in the *Republic*. For both men, professional interests necessitated that the nihilistic nature of their beliefs not be publicized.

30. See *Greek Lyric Poetry*, trans. Richmond Lattimore, 2d ed. (Chicago: University of Chicago Press, 1960), 55.

Chapter 3. Phaedo and the Socratic Mission

1. For the Greek text of the *Phaedo* I have used the Loeb Classical Library edition, trans. H. W. Fowler. English translations are from the *Collected Works of Plato*, ed. Edith Hamilton and Huntington Cairns (Princeton: Princeton University Press, 1961).

2. Ronna Burger, *The Phaedo: A Platonic Labyrinth* (New Haven: Yale University Press, 1984), 1–2, says that the *Phaedo* is an exposition and defense of the twin pillars of Platonic philosophy: the theory of the ideas, and the immortality of the soul. As a result, she adds, it is accorded the distinction of having inaugurated Western metaphysics.

3. Ibid., 213.

4. Plato *Symposium* 173b; Plato *Theaetetus* 143a.

5. Kenneth Dorter, *Plato's Phaedo: An Interpretation* (Toronto: University of Toronto Press, 1982), 10.

6. Diogenes Laertius *Lives of the Philosophers* 2.9.

7. *Meridian Handbook of Classical Mythology*, ed. Edward Tripp (New York: Meridian, 1974), 470–71.

8. Athenaeus *Deipnosophistae* 9.505e.

9. Jacob Klein, "Plato's Phaedo," in *Journal of St John's College*, January 1975, 1–10.

10. Diogenes Laertius *Lives of the Philosophers* 2.9.

11. Athenaeus *Deipnosophistae* 9.507c.

12. Ibid.

13. Diogenes Laertius *Lives of the Philosophers* 2.47.

14. Plutarch *Life of Theseus* 23.

15. Burger, *The Phaedo*, 17.

16. Tripp, *Meridian Handbook*, 51.

17. Plutarch *Life of Theseus* 36.

18. Burger, *The Phaedo*, 28–29.

19. Tripp, *Meridian Handbook*, 52–53.

20. G. W. F. Hegel, *The Phenomenology of Spirit*, trans. A. V. Miller (New York: Oxford University Press, 1977), 132.

21. Deuteronomy 34:7.

22. See Xenophon *Apology* 6–9.

23. *The Pre-Socratic Philosophers*, 2d ed., ed. G. S. Kirk, J. E. Raven, and M. Schofield (Cambridge: Cambridge University Press, 1983), 223–24.

24. Xenophon *Memorabilia* 4.8.1.

25. Plato *Gorgias* 464b–482c.

26. Kirk, Raven, and Schofield, *The Pre-Socratic Philosophers*, no. 110, 118.

27. Tripp, *Meridian Handbook*, 449.

28. Gottfried Leibniz, *Discourse on Metaphysics*, #34 in *Philosophical Papers and Letters*, trans. Leroy E. Loemker (Dordrecht: Reidel, 1976), 325–26.

29. Homer *Odyssey* 5.346–75.

30. The Hydra was reputed to have eight of these heads when Heracles did battle with it—a number ($2 \times 2 \times 2$) which corresponds to the three proofs Socrates has unsuccessfully postulated at this point in the dialogue. See Tripp, *Meridian Handbook*, 279–80.

31. Ibid.

32. Plutarch *Life of Theseus* 22.

33. Burger, *The Phaedo*, 29.

34. Plato *Republic* 493a–e comes to mind here.

35. *Greek-English Lexicon*, 9th ed., ed. Henry George Liddell and Robert Scott (Oxford: Clarendon Press, 1992), 244.

36. Ernst Cassirer, *Kant's Life and Thought* (New Haven: Yale University Press, 1981), 251–57.

37. *Greek-English Lexicon*, 244.

38. Homer *Iliad* 2.203–5.

39. Joseph Cropsey, *Plato's World* (Chicago: University of Chicago Press, 1995), 204, points out that readers are reminded as much of Euthyphro as of Job.

40. Kirk, Raven, and Schofield, *The Pre-Socratic Philosophers*, no. 91, 95.

41. Ibid., nos. 477–78, 363–64.

42. Ibid., no. 486, 371.

43. David Hume, *Treatise of Human Nature*, ed. L. A. Selby-Brigge (Oxford: Oxford University Press, 1906), 3.1.1.

44. See Burger, *The Phaedo*, 254 n. 26.

45. Friedrich Nietzsche, *Thus Spake Zarathustra*, 3, "On the Vision and the Riddle," in *The Portable Nietzsche*, trans. Walter Kaufmann (New York: Viking, 1954), 267–72.

46. Tripp, *Meridian Handbook*, 185–87.

47. Plato *First Alcibiades* 121a.

48. Kirk, Raven, and Schofield, *The Pre-Socratic Philosophers*, 222.

49. Tripp, *Meridian Handbook*, 106–7.

50. Diogenes Laertius *Lives of the Philosophers* 2.32.

51. Tripp, *Meridian Handbook*, 181.

52. Euripides, *Hippolytus*, Loeb Classical Library, trans. David Kovacs (Cambridge: Harvard University Press, 1996), 1218–39. Phaethon is mentioned by the chorus shortly after Hippolytus leaves his father's house for the last time (735).

53. Ovid, *Metamorphoses*, Loeb Classical Library, trans. Frank J. Miller, rev. G. P. Goold (Cambridge: Harvard University Press, 1977), 2.127–40.

54. Ibid., emphasis added.
55. Ibid., 2.181–87.
56. Ibid., 2.193–216.
57. Homer *Odyssey* 11.90–151.
58. Homer *Odyssey* 11.601–3.

Chapter 4. Symposium I

1. For the Greek text of the *Symposium* I have used the Loeb Classical Library edition, trans. W. R. M. Lamb (Cambridge: Harvard University Press, 1929). For English translations I have relied heavily on R. E. Allen's excellent translation and commentary (New Haven: Yale University Press, 1991). My study—particularly influenced my interpretation of Aristophanes' speech—has been tremendously influenced by Stanley Rosen, *Plato's Symposium*, 2d ed. (New Haven: Yale University Press, 1987).
2. Xenophon *Symposium* 5.
3. Ibid., 3.10.
4. See Plato *Cratylus* 398c.
5. Plutarch *Life of Alcibiades* 18.
6. For an account that is hardly unsympathetic toward Aristophanes, see Leo Strauss, *The Rebirth of Classical Political Rationalism*, ed. Thomas L. Pangle (Chicago: University of Chicago Press, 1989), 103–26.
7. Homer *Iliad* 14.153–351.
8. We have seen Socrates identify himself with Odysseus in the *Protagoras*, and in the *Lesser Hippias* he champions the claims of Odysseus against Achilles. For an extended account of the Odyssean subtext in the *Republic*, see Jacob Howland, *The Republic: The Odyssey of Philosophy* (New York: Twayne, 1993).
9. Martha Nussbaum, *The Fragility of Goodness* (New York: Cambridge University Press, 1986), 169–70.
10. See Xenophon *Hellenica* 2.
11. Pindar in *Greek Lyric Poetry*, trans. Richmond Lattimore, 2d ed. (Chicago: University of Chicago Press, 1960), 61.
12. Allan Bloom, *Love and Friendship* (New York: Simon & Schuster, 1993), 446–47.
13. Nussbaum, *Fragility of Goodness*, 169.
14. See book 2 of Xenophon's *Hellenica* for details of how the Thirty conducted themselves after the fall of Athens.
15. Aristophanes *The Frogs* 1425.
16. See Xenophon *Hellenica* 2.1.25–26.
17. See Douglas Anderson, *The Masks of Dionysos* (New York: State University of New York Press, 1993), 10–15.
18. Plato *Parmenides* 126a–b.
19. There is considerable difference of opinion over the dramatic date of the *Republic*. Estimates range from 411 (Bloom) to 421 (Nussbaum).

20. *Republic* 494b–495b.

21. See, e.g., Rosen, *Plato's Symposium*, 7–8. Nietzsche conflates the two events in a cryptic utterance; see "The Greek State," in *On The Genealogy of Morality*, ed. Keith Ansell-Pearson, Cambridge Texts in the History of Political Thought (Cambridge: Cambridge University Press, 1994), 185.

22. Rosen, *Plato's Symposium*, 24–25.

23. Ibid., 8.

24. Xenophon *Symposium* 4.19–20.

25. Robert Lloyd Mitchell, *The Hymn to Eros* (Lanham, Md.: University Press of America, 1993), 9–11. The episode referred to is Homer *Iliad* 17.587.

26. See Homer *Odyssey* 4.

27. It is noteworthy that our narrator, Apollodorus, was also termed limp (*malakos*) although his interrogator points out that he is hard on everyone but Socrates (173d). It seems that both he and Aristodemus, although limp spearmen according to the norms of efficient causality, are quite reliable in the slippery realm of formal causality.

28. Homer *Odyssey* 22.1–3.

29. See Jenny Strauss Clay, *The Wrath of Athena* (Princeton: Princeton University Press, 1983).

30. Homer *Iliad* 10.224–47.

31. Ibid., 11.463.

32. Ibid., 5.330–51, 846–87.

33. Ibid., 10.476–569.

34. Ibid., 2.408.

35. Homer *Odyssey* 4.351–570.

36. Mitchell, *Hymn to Eros*, 6.

37. Homer *Odyssey* 4.456–59.

38. Strauss, *Rebirth*, 125.

39. Perhaps the implication is that like Simmias in the *Phaedo*, who made Socrates produce four spurious speeches about the soul's immortality, Phaedrus has inspired many sophistical orations. The first five speeches in the *Symposium* and the first two in the *Phaedrus* come to mind.

40. See *Lesser Hippias*.

41. Mitchell, *Hymn to Eros*, 32–33.

42. Galen (*On the Physical Faculties* 2.9) speaks of his "hairsplitting attention to terms."

43. Hesiod *Works and Days* 12.

44. See Plato *Protagoras* 315d.

45. Xenophon *Memorabilia* 2.1.21–33.

46. Rosen, *Plato's Symposium*, 88.

47. *The Pre-Socratic philosophers*, 2d ed., ed. G. S. Kirk, J. E. Raven, and M. Schofield (Cambridge: Cambridge University Press, 1983), no. 349, 289–90.

48. Ibid., no. 341, 284.

49. Homer *Iliad* 3.17.

50. Aristotle *History of Animals* 9.1.

51. Mitchell, *Hymn to Eros*, 66–67.

52. Kenneth Dover, *Aristophanic Comedy* (Berkeley: University of California Press, 1972), 13.

53. Rosen, *Plato's Symposium*, 120.

54. Hesiod *Theogony* 629–731.

55. Orphic Hymn 37.4. See Hesiod, *Theogony, Works and Days, Shield*, trans. Apostolos Athanassakis (Baltimore: Johns Hopkins University Press, 1983), 50–51.

56. Hesiod *Theogony* 881–85.

57. It is instructive to read the misogynistic accounts given by Hesiod in *Works and Days* 60–106 and *Theogony* 570–616.

58. Hesiod *Works and Days* 91–92.

59. Rosen, *Plato's Symposium*, 120.

60. Isolated in the company of sophistic homosexuals, Aristophanes is speaking as deceptively as Socrates was when he described the education of the young "philosopher-puppies." *The Clouds* provides a much more accurate indication of his feelings about homosexuality: In the debate between just and unjust speech (1085–1104), the unjust forces the just to concede that all advocates, tragedians, and demagogues are, in Dover's memorable phrase (*Aristophanic Comedy*, 115), "wide-arsed."

61. Homer *Odyssey* 8.267–359.

62. Bloom understands this well; see *Love and Friendship*, 435–44.

63. See Hannah Arendt, *The Human Condition* (Chicago: University of Chicago Press, 1958), 22–78.

64. Ibid., 175–245.

65. Homer *Odyssey* 19.393ff.

66. See *Oxford Classical Dictionary*, 3d ed., s.v. "Agathon."

67. See Strauss, *Rebirth*, 116.

68. Aristophanes *Thesmophoriasuzae* 245 ff.

69. Bloom, *Love and Friendship*, 485.

70. Nietzsche, *The Birth of Tragedy*, sec. 11–15, in *Basic Writings of Nietzsche*, trans. Walter Kaufmann (New York: Modern Library, 1967), 76–98, laments this decline but blames Euripides and Socrates for it.

71. For information on Gorgias, see *The Older Sophists*, ed. Rosamond Kent Sprague (Columbia: University of South Carolina Press, 1972), 30–67.

72. Aristotle *Rhetoric* 1419b3.

73. Sprague, *The Older Sophists*, 42.

74. See Nietzsche, "The Greek State," 176–86.

75. Sprague, *The Older Sophists*, 46.

76. Kirk, Raven, and Schofield, *The Pre-Socratic Philosophers*, no. 348, 287.

77. Ibid., no. 214, 195. See also *Cratylus* 440c.

78. Thucydides *Peloponnesian War* 6.15–18.

79. Sprague, *The Older Sophists*, 54.

80. *Meridian Handbook of Classical Mythology*, ed. Edward Tripp (New York: Meridian, 1970), 574–75.

81. See Nietzsche's *Birth of Tragedy*, and "Homer on Competition," in *On the Genealogy of Morality*, 187–94.

82. Kirk, Raven, and Schofield, *The Pre-Socratic Philosophers*, no. 299, 252.

Chapter 5. Symposium II

1. Homer *Odyssey* 11.635.

2. *Meridian Handbook of Classical Mythology*, ed. Edward Tripp (New York: Meridian, 1970), 465–66.

3. Plato *Phaedrus* 255d.

4. Plato *First Alcibiades*, 132d–133c.

5. Aristotle *Metaphysics* 1072b19.

6. Martha Nussbaum, *The Fragility of Goodness* (New York: Cambridge University Press, 1986), 177.

7. Plutarch *Life of Alcibiades* 39.

8. Donald Kagan, *The Peace of Nicias and the Sicilian Expedition* (Ithaca: Cornell University Press, 1981), 71–138.

9. See Nussbaum, *Fragility*, 168–69.

10. *A Midsummer Night's Dream* 4.1.

11. Xenophon *Banquet* 3.10.

12. See Albert Camus, *The Myth of Sisyphus and Other Essays*, trans. Justin O'Brien (New York: Vintage, 1959), 88–91.

13. G. W. F. Hegel, *Phenomenology of Spirit*, trans. A. V. Miller (New York: Oxford University Press, 1981), 404.

14. Homer *Odyssey* 4.242–64.

15. Ibid., 4.266–89.

16. See Euripides *Trojan Women*.

17. See Plutarch *Life of Alcibiades* 23.

18. Robert Lloyd Mitchell, *The Hymn to Eros* (Lanham, Md.: University Press of America, 1993), 180.

19. Homer *Odyssey* 7.159–64.

20. Camus, *Myth of Sisyphus*, 134–38.

21. Homer *Odyssey* 4.176–79.

22. Ibid., 4.561–70.

23. Tripp, *Meridian Handbook*, 264.

24. See *Oxford Classical Dictionary*, 2d ed., s.v. "Helen."

25. See Euripides *Bacchae*.

26. Plutarch *Life of Alcibiades* 9.

27. Homer *Iliad* 17.8.

28. Tripp, *Meridian Handbook*, 524. Siren, when pronounced with the celebrated Alcibiadean lisp, sounds very much like Silenus.

29. Homer *Iliad* 17.32.

30. Tripp, *Meridian Handbook*, 377–78.

31. Plutarch *Life of Alcibiades* 16.

32. Homer *Odyssey* 23.184–204.

33. Friedrich Nietzsche, *Thus Spake Zarathustra*, 2, "Upon the Blessed Isles," in *The Portable Nietzsche*, trans. Walter Kaufmann (New York: Viking, 1954), 198.

34. Plutarch *Life of Alcibiades* 2.

35. Plutarch *Life of Coriolanus* 15.

36. Tripp, *Meridian Handbook*, 357–58.

37. See *Oxford Classical Dictionary*, 3d ed., s.v. "Music."

38. Tripp, *Meridian Handbook*, 357.

39. See Ernst Cassirer, *Kant's Life and Thought* (New Haven: Yale University Press, 1981), 46.

40. Homer *Odyssey* 12.184–90.

41. Plutarch *Life of Alcibiades* 16.

42. Tripp, *Meridian Handbook*, 378.

43. Matthew 14:28–31.

44. Homer *Odyssey* 10.277–306.

45. Thucydides *History of the Peloponnesian War* 6.15; Plutarch *Life of Alcibiades* 17.

46. Plutarch *Life of Alcibiades* 17.

47. Xenophon *Hellenica* 2.1.25–26.

48. See Donald Kagan, *The Fall of the Athenian Empire* (Ithaca: Cornell University Press, 1987), 354–75.

49. Homer *Odyssey* 6.160–69.

50. I am obliged to Robert E. Wood for drawing my attention to this point.

Index

Platonic dialogues are alphabetized; Classical plays are listed under their authors.